When
They Severed
Earth from Sky

Frontispiece: Prometheus bound, his liver pecked by an eagle, observed by Atlas(?). Laconian black-figure cup by Arcesilas Painter, ca. 550 B.C.; Caere.

Elizabeth Wayland Barber
and Paul T. Barber

When
They Severed
Earth from Sky

How the Human Mind
Shapes Myth

PRINCETON UNIVERSITY PRESS

PRINCETON AND OXFORD

Copyright © 2004 by Princeton University Press
Published by Princeton University Press,
41 William Street, Princeton, New Jersey 08540
In the United Kingdom: Princeton University Press,
3 Market Place, Woodstock, Oxfordshire OX20 1SY
All Rights Reserved

ISBN: 0-691-09986-3

Library of Congress Cataloging-in-Publication Data

Barber, E.J.W., 1940–
When they severed earth from sky: how the human mind shapes
myth / Elizabeth Wayland Barber and Paul T. Barber
  p.   cm.
Includes bibliographical references (p.) and index.
ISBN 0-691-09986-3 (alk. paper)
1. Myth.   2. Mythology.   I. Barber, Paul, 1941–   II. Title.

BL312.B37 2005
201′.3—dc22   2004046640

British Library Cataloging-in-Publication Data is available

This book has been composed in Adobe Caslon
Printed on acid-free paper. ∞
www.pup.princeton.edu
Printed in the United States of America
1   3   5   7   9   10   8   6   4   2

To Cassandra

and to Scotty
for his encouragement

Nor can we, in this age of Dictionaries, and other technical aids to memory, judge, what [History's] use and powers were, at a time, when all a man could know, was what he could remember. To which we may add, that, in a rude and unlettered state of society the memory is loaded with nothing that is either useless or unintelligible; whereas modern education employs us chiefly in getting by heart, while we are young, what we forget before we are old.
—Robert Wood, *Essay on the Original Genius of Homer*, 1767 [Parry 1971, xiii]

CONTENTS

List of Illustrations   xi

Acknowledgments   xvii

1   Time Capsules   1

2   The Memory Crunch: How Long a Pipeline?   5

3   The Silence Principle: Of Lethe and the Golden Calf   17

4   More Silence: Movie Reels from Snapshots   26

5   Analogy: Our Brain's Best Talent   34

6   Willfulness: The Atom or Thou   41

7   Multiple Aspects: The More the Merrier   53

8   Multiple Viewpoints: Ear, Trunk, or Tail   71

9   Views through Biased Lenses   89

10   Metaphoric Reality: Magic and Dreams   96

11   Compression: Methuselah and the Eponymous Heroes   113

12   Post Hocus Ergo Pocus: Space Aliens Mutilate Cows!   129

13   Restructuring: New Patterns for Old   139

14   Mnemonics: Behind the Silliness   153

15   The Spirit World: A Realm Reversed   162

16   Of Sky and Time   176

17   Prometheus   218

18   Fire-Breathing Dragons   231

Appendix: Index of Myth Principles   245

Bibliography   253

Index   265

ILLUSTRATIONS

The astronomical diagrams were designed by E. Barber and executed by Bob Turring of Caltech and Dimitri Karetnikov of Princeton University Press. All photos and drawings, unless otherwise noted, are the authors' own.

Frontispiece: Prometheus bound, his liver pecked by an eagle, observed by Atlas(?). Laconian black-figure cup by Arcesilas Painter, ca. 550 B.C.; Caere. [Museo gregoriano Etrusco 16529; photo Vatican Museums.]   ii

1. Crater Lake, Oregon.   8

2. Egyptian sky goddess represented as a cow. Tomb of Seti I, Thebes, ca. 1280 B.C. [After Frankfort 1948, fig. 9.]   21

3. Dead body spontaneously sitting up in its coffin during the wake. Old central European woodcut. [After Barber 1990, 76.]   32

4. Sculpture showing Atlas bringing the Apples of the Hesperides to Herakles. Metope from Temple of Zeus, Olympia, Greece, ca. 460 B.C.   47

5. View from the Athenian Akropolis of the Saronic Gulf.   51

6. Celestial eyes. (a) The moon depicted as an eye. [After Lanzone 1881/1974, 91 and pl. xxxix.] (b) The sun as an eye, worshipped by a baboon at dawn; from Twenty-first Dynasty papyrus of Hent-Taui [British Museum; after Grimal 1963/73, 38].   55

7. Odin's eight-legged horse, Sleipnir. Viking period memorial stone; Alskog, Tjangvide, Gotland. [After Davidson 1969, 45.]   57

8. Archaic European fertility motifs. (a) Simargl on ritual bracelet from Staryj Rjazan'; 11th century. [After Darkevich and Mongait 1967, 213 fig. 2.] (b) Simargls and hops vine on ritual bracelet from Tver'; 12th century. [After Rybakov 1968, fig. 14.] (c) Lozenge-shaped motifs in east European

folk art. (d) Neolithic clay figurines with "sown field" motif, Cucuteni/Tripolye culture (Ukraine and Romania), ca. 4000 B.C. [After Rybakov 1981, 51; Gimbutas 1982, fig. 204.] (e) Albanian "string skirt" from Mirdite area. [From authors' collection.] (f) Palaeolithic "Venus" figure wearing "string skirt"; Lespugue, France, ca. 20,000 B.C. [After photo, Musée de l'Homme.]   68

9. Thera, Greece: inside the blown-out crater.   81

10. Minoan stone stairway shattered by explosion of Thera ca. 1625 B.C.; Room Δ15, Akrotiri, Thera.   82

11. Lava bomb from Thera that flattened a Minoan house ca. 1625 B.C. Akrotiri, Thera.   83

12. Sia (Magical Understanding) and Hū (Authoritative Utterance) accompanying the sun in his boat through the underworld at night. Tomb of Seti I, Thebes, ca. 1280 B.C. [After Aldred 1984, 101 fig. 64.]   99

13. Hittite sword god. Relief cut into live rock, Yazılıkaya, Turkey, ca. 1250 B.C.   101

14. One of twin lava lakes during nighttime eruption of Mauna Ulu, Hawaii, 1972.   109

15. Gorgons in Greek art. (a) Early representation of Medusa's sisters with snake-surrounded cauldrons as heads, from Proto-Attic neck-amphora; Eleusis, ca. 660 B.C. [After Henle 1973, fig. 44.] (b) Typical later representation of Medusa with her snaky locks, from west pediment of temple of Artemis, Corfu; early 6th century B.C. [After Charbonneaux et al., 1971, fig. 24.]   111

16. Shiva the Destroyer. Traditional sculpture, South India. [Collection of T. Battaglia.]   122

17. Mycenae, Greece: "Cyclopean" masonry (2nd millennium B.C.).   147

18. Early Greeks depicted two types of centaurs: (a) those with two human and two equine legs [Proto-Corinthian aryballos, ca. 680 B.C.; Boston Museum of Fine Arts 9512: after Cook 1960, pl. 9B, and Snodgrass 1998, fig. 30], and (b) those with four equine and no human legs, but human head and torso. [Attic neck-amphora by Nettos Painter, ca.

620 B.C.; Athens National Museum 1002; after Arias and Hirmer 1962, fig. 19.] 148

19. Constellations of dark interstellar dust seen in Southern Hemisphere, as named in the Andes. [Compiled from Chartrand 1991, 74, 87, 98, 141; Sullivan 1996, figs. 2.7, 2.9a.] 160

20. Reversals. (a) Curse written with backwards letters on lead "curse tablet", Kerameikos cemetery, Athens; late 5th century B.C. [After Peek 1941, pl. 22.4.] (b) Late Greco-Roman tomb figurines, with some body parts backwards. [Left, from Kephalonia (British Museum); right, from Athens (#7877, National Museum, Athens); after Perdrizet 1899, 194.] 171

21. Soul-bird emerging from dying warrior (Prokris); Attic amphora, early 5th century B.C. [British Museum E477; Weicker 1902, fig. 86.] 173

22. Seasonal shifts. (a) What really happens. The axis on which Earth spins daily is tipped 23.5° with respect to the plane of its annual orbit around the sun (the *ecliptic* plane), causing the seasons. (b) What we *see* in the northern hemisphere. Because Earth is tipped, the sun rises in different places during the year. 181

23. Landscape of mountains and two rivers (and bear eating honey?), engraved on silver vase from Maikop, just north of the Caucasus range, ca. 2500 B.C. [After Rice 1965, 15 fig. 4.] 181

24. The Zodiac originally named a band of twelve constellations occurring along the apparent path of sun, moon, and planets (*ecliptic*), "marking" the band. 184

25. The great "river" of stars "flowing around" Earth. 186

26. Solar eclipse, June 30, 1973, showing sun's corona. [Courtesy of High-Altitude Observatory, National Center for Atmospheric Research, Boulder, CO, sponsored by the National Science Foundation.] 186

27. Ancient representations of celestial bodies as deities. (a) Moon (Sin), Venus (Ishtar), and Sun (Shamash) on Mesopotamian boundary stone of Meli-Shipak II; 16th

century B.C., Kassite era. [Louvre; after Caubet and
Pouyssegur 1998, 176.] (b) Moon, Sun, and Venus on 7th
century B.C. stele of Asarhaddon. [Staatliche Museen zu
Berlin-Preussicher Kulturbesitz, Berlin; after Margueron
1965, fig. 124.] (c) Egyptian divine winged sun-disk, from
relief of Seti I at Abydos, ca. 1280 B.C. [After Aldred 1984,
fig. 17.] (d) Syrian winged sun-disk on stele of god El,
Ugarit, ca. 13th century B.C. [After Weiss 1985, fig. 151.]
(e) Cuneiform sign originating as AN, "star, sky", that came
to signify DINGIR, "deity". (f) "Scorpion Man" inlaid on
Sumerian harp from Ur, ca. 2600 B.C. [After Groenwegen-
Frankfort and Ashmole 1977, fig. 112.]   187

28. Johannes Kepler's Great Trigon (from preface to his
    Mysterium Cosmographicum [1606]).   189

29. Rare massing of the five visible planets in early 1953 B.C.:
    shown at 7 A.M., Feb. 25, from position of Athens. [After
    Starry Night Pro.]   191

30. Current rotation from June to September (viewed about
    10 P.M. from the latitude of Greece or California) of the
    Dippers and Cassiopeia around Polaris.   192

31. In Hindu and Buddhist mythology, gods and demons churn
    the Ocean of Milk. [Watercolor and gold on paper: India,
    Panjab Hills, Kangra; ca. A.D. 1785; Edwin Binney 3rd
    Collection, San Diego Museum of Art.]   193

32. Equator and ecliptic. (a) Polaris (North Star) currently sits
    on an extension of the axis or pole around which Earth
    spins. (b) Because of Earth's 23.5° tilt, the sun never
    appears directly overhead beyond the zone lying 23.5°
    to either side of the equator, the zone of the "Tropics".   195

33. Crosses made by joining the observable points on the horizon
    where the sun rises and sets at the solstices.   196

34. Crosses generated as cultural symbols of equinox and/or
    solstice: (a) On 4th century A.D. Slavic calendrical bowl
    from Lepesovka. [After Rybakov 1987, 167 fig. 31.]
    (b) On twelfth-century Russian ritual bracelets. [From Kiev;
    after Rybakov 1968, figs. 7–8.] (c) As Minoan "double axe"
    figure. (d) Cautes, of the Mithraic cult, standing with legs
    forming the equinoctial cross; on relief from Nersae, A.D.

172. [#650/1: Museo Nazionale della Terme, Rome; after
Merkelbach 1984, fig. 73, and Vermaseren 1982, pl. xx.]   197

35. Northshift. (a) The slow circuit of the extension of Earth's
rotational pole through the stars, known as *precession of the
equinoxes*. (b) The precessional shift of the North Celestial
Pole through the northern stars as it appears from Earth.   198

36. The mythological "pillars of the world".   201

37. "Double axe" signs and stars carved on pillars in cult room
in Minoan palace at Mallia, Crete; mid-2nd millennium B.C.   202

38. Typical Mithraic cult relief. [From Esquiline Hill, Rome,
#368; late 2nd century A.D.; after Vermaseren 1982,
pl. XXII.]   206

39. Zodiac wheel showing position of solstices and equinoxes
in earlier World Ages.   209

40. Mount St. Helens erupting, March 1847. [Oil painting by
Paul Kane; with permission of the Royal Ontario Museum,
© ROM.]   220

41. Field of five ancient barrows (burial mounds), near Jelling,
Jutland, Denmark.   235

42. Decapitated enemies lying with their heads placed between
their feet, on the victory palette of Narmer, ca. 3100 B.C.
[Egyptian Museum, Cairo.]   237

43. Rock drawing at Ramsund, Sweden, of Sigurd slaying the
gold-guarding dragon Fafnir; early Viking era. [After
anonymous photographs.]   239

44. Saint George slaying the Dragon. Woodcut, ca. 1515, from
English edition of B. Spagnuoli's life of St. George. [STC
22922.1, Trinity College Library, Cambridge; courtesy of
the Master and Fellows of Trinity College Cambridge.]   243

ACKNOWLEDGMENTS

We wish to thank Ann Peters, Adrienne Mayor, Joshua Katz, Michael Corballis, and C. Scott Littleton for their kind and patient help reviewing the whole manuscript at some stage and for providing numerous helpful references; likewise Floyd McCoy and Stuart Elliott for reviewing some of the geology and astronomy, respectively; Alan Ferg for other interesting references; John Pohl for electronically stitching together two photos for figure 13 (the rock crevice is too narrow to photograph the sword god clearly with one shot); and in particular C. Scott Littleton for hounding us for over twenty years to keep working on this project, and for "field-testing" part of the book in his class. We of course take full responsibility for our opinions and any errors of fact.

We also wish to thank the University of California Press for permission to reprint the story of Crater Lake from Ella Clark's *Indian Legends of the Pacific Northwest* [1953] in chapter 2; the University of Toronto Press for permission to quote Denton Fox and Hermann Pálsson's translation of a long tale from *Grettir's Saga* [1974] in chapter 18; the Vatican Museums, High-Altitude Observatory at the National Center for Atmospheric Research (Boulder, CO), San Diego Museum of Art, Royal Ontario Museum, and Trinity College Cambridge for permission to print their photographs of artifacts and events (frontispiece and figures 26, 31, 40, and 44); and Tony Battaglia for letting us photograph his "Shiva". Many thanks to the Louis and Hermione Brown Humanities Support Fund for underwriting the cost of producing the astronomical diagrams. All translations, unless otherwise noted, are our own.

When
They Severed
Earth from Sky

1

Time Capsules

The son of Danaë . . . slew the Gorgon, and, bearing her
head adorned with locks of serpents, came to the islanders
bringing them stony death. But, to me, no marvel, if the
gods bring it about, ever seems beyond belief.
      —Pindar, *Pythian Ode* 10 (trans. Race 1997, 363)

Evidence shows that people have had brains like ours for at least 100,000 years. By that time, as the excavated bones show, our vocal tract had developed for speech as we know it [Lieberman 1975, 1991]; and language could not have come into being without both an efficient vocal mechanism and the complexly structured brain necessary for language.

But if people were so smart—just like us—100,000 years ago, why do the myths they passed down often seem so preposterous to us? And not just to *us*. Even ancients like the Greek poet Pindar, who made his living telling such stories ca. 500 B.C., sometimes felt constrained to a disclaimer: "Don't blame me for this tale!" The narrators present these myths as "histories". Yet how can we seriously believe that Perseus turned people to stone by showing them the snaky-locked head of a monster, or that a man named Herakles (or Hercules) held up the sky for a while, slew a nine-headed water monster, moved rivers around, and carried a three-headed dog up from the land of the dead? Or that a man named Methuselah lived for almost a millennium? That an eagle pecked for years at the liver of a god tied to a mountain, or that mortal men—Beowulf, St. George, Siegfried, and Perseus included—actually fought dragons? And how can one view people like the Greeks or the Egyptians, who each believed simultaneously in three or four sun gods, as having intelligence? Didn't they *notice* a contradiction there? Why did people in so many cultures spend so much time and attention on these collections of quaint stories that we know of as "myths"?

The problem lies not in differing intelligence but in differing resources for the storage and transmission of data. Quite simply, before writing, myths had to serve as transmission systems for information deemed important; but because we—now that we have writing—have forgotten how nonliterate people stored and transmitted information and why it was done that way, we have lost track of how to decode the information often densely compressed into these stories, and they appear to us as mostly gibberish. And so we often dismiss them as silly or try to reinterpret them with psychobabble. As folklorist Adrienne Mayor points out, classicists in particular "tend to read myth as fictional literature, not as natural history" [Mayor 2000b, 192]—not least because humanists typically don't study sciences like geology, palaeontology, and astronomy, and so don't recognize the data.

In order to understand how and why myths were constructed to encode real and important data, we must come to understand the possibilities—and hazards—for the collection, processing, and transmission of information in nonliterate societies. Just how much can you keep in your head? Simply put, writing allows people to stockpile data in masses that are not possible when one must rely on memory alone, and it allows people to transmit as much as they want—without much compression—to future generations. Conversely, without writing, people had both to winnow out the key information, presumably according to perceived importance, and to compress it by any means possible until it fit into the available channel: human memory. We have come to term this overarching problem the Memory Crunch.

During two dozen years of empirical research on myths from all over the world, we found that many of these stories could be understood through a series of simple observable principles. These principles show how particular types of myths developed out of actual events: how people crunched down the information into the limited channel available for transmission, enhanced its memorability, then shot these little time capsules of knowledge down the pipeline to the listeners of the future.

Not all myths are of this type, of course, but many more of them turn out to stem from actual events and real observations of the world than twentieth-century scholars have commonly believed, and possibly all types of myths can be understood better through understanding the close relationships between myth, language, and cognition. At any rate, myths encoding verifiable facts proved the easiest place to begin recognizing the cognitive processes involved.

Working initially from a few myths whose historical or archaeological origins are independently known and verifiable, we first noticed a dozen or so rather specific principles. (One of us works principally in Old World archaeology and linguistics, the other in comparative literature and folklore.) This empirical list increased slowly to about forty principles, over the next fifteen years, as we happened on more and more usable data. Then, abruptly one day, they all collapsed down into four overarching principles, *each of which has clear correlates in linguistic process*. Why were we so surprised? After all, myth is transmitted through language, and it is the same human brain with its peculiar design features that must handle both language and the data it encodes *into* language. These myth principles start to make the inner workings of myth rationally intelligible on many levels.

Discussion of the four fundamental "mytho-linguistic" principles— Silence, Analogy, Compression, and Restructuring—forms the greater part of this book. For each, we present the more specific principles we discovered that fall under its sway, together with parallel insights about language and a multitude of examples from world mythology. If Indo-European myths (especially Greco-Roman, Germanic, Slavic) and those of the Pacific Northwest preponderate, that is where the combined knowledge and interests of the present authors are strongest.

What this book is not about is archetypes, the stuff of C. G. Jung and Joseph Campbell. Those aspects of myth that appear "universal" are, in our opinion, the result of pitting human cognition against the small-channel problem just described—common responses to common problems.

Why would one want thus to "strip the veil of mystery" from mythology? Some people won't want to; they don't have to read this book. But for students of cognition, the practical structure of myth gives interesting new insights into the language-oriented brain that spawned myth. And for archaeologists, the decoding of myth provides the possibility of restoring a certain amount of actual history to the "prehistoric" world, the world before writing. Writing was invented a mere 5,200 years ago, but we have been speaking and presumably mythmaking for 100,000 or more. That's a lot of history lost.

To recover what is left of these precious time capsules, we begin with some of the most transparent mythologies available and build our way, principle by principle, toward the knottier stuff.[1]

---

[1] For the reader's convenience, the Myth Principles from the entire book are reprinted together in the Appendix (pp. 245–51), in the order discussed, with hierarchical indentation.

The Memory Crunch: How Long a Pipeline?

MEMORY CRUNCH

When all accumulated wisdom must be stored in the brain and transmitted orally (as in a nonliterate society), people reserve the formal oral tradition for transmitting the information they consider most important, often for survival.

A long time ago, so long you cannot count it, . . . the spirits of the earth and the sky, the spirits of the sea and the mountains often came and talked with my people.

Sometimes the Chief of the Below World came up from his home inside the earth and stood on top of the mountain—the high mountain that used to be. . . . One time when the Chief of the Below World was on the earth, he saw Loha, the daughter of the tribal chief. Loha was a beautiful maiden, tall and straight as the arrowwood. Her eyes were dark and piercing; her hair was long and black and glossy. . . .

The Chief of the Below World saw her and fell in love with her. He told her of his love and asked her to return with him to his lodge inside the mountain. There, he said, she would live forever and forever. But Loha refused to go with him.

Then the Chief of the Below World sent one of his warriors to a feast of the tribe, to plead for him and to arrange for a marriage with Loha. . . .

But again the maiden refused. And the wise men of the council would not command her to go. . . . When the messenger returned to the middle of the mountain and reported the maiden's answer, the Chief of the Below World was very angry. In a voice like thunder, he swore he would have revenge on the people of Loha, that he would destroy them with the Curse of Fire. Raging and thundering, he rushed up through the opening and stood upon the top of his mountain.

Then he saw the face of the Chief of the Above World shining among the stars that surrounded his home. Slowly the mighty form of that chief descended from the sky and stood on the top of Mount Shasta. From their mountaintops the two spirit chiefs began a furious battle. In a short time all the spirits of earth and sky took part in the battle.

Mountains shook and crumbled. Red-hot rocks as large as the hills hurtled through the skies. Burning ashes fell like rain. The Chief of the Below World spewed fire from his mouth. Like an ocean of flame it devoured the forests on the mountains and in the valleys. On and on the Curse of Fire swept until it reached the homes of the people. Fleeing in terror before it, the people found refuge in the waters of Klamath Lake.

[After a discussion,] . . . two medicine men, the oldest and most revered of the Klamath people, rose from the water, lighted their pine torches, and started toward the mountain of the Chief of the Below World. From the waters of Klamath Lake, the people watched the flare of the torches move up the long ridge on the east side of the mountain . . . to the top of the cliff which hung over the entrance to the Below World. . . . There the medicine men paused for a moment, watching the flames and smoke coming up through the opening. Then they lifted their burning torches high above their heads and jumped into the fiery pit [as sacrifice].

. . . The Chief of the Above World, standing on Mount Shasta, saw the brave deed of the medicine men. He saw that it was good. Once more the mountains shook. Once more the earth trembled on its foundations. This time the Chief of the Below World was driven into his home, and the top of the mountain fell upon him. When the morning sun rose, the high mountain was gone. The mountain which the Chief of the Below World had called his own no longer towered near Mount Shasta.

Then rain fell. For many years, rain fell in torrents and filled the great hole that was made when the mountain fell upon the Chief of the Below World. The Curse of Fire was lifted. Peace and quiet covered the earth. Never again did the Chief of the Below World come up from his home. Never again did his voice frighten the people.

Now you understand why my people never visit the lake. Down through the ages we have heard this story. From father to son has come the warning, "Look not upon the place. Look not upon the place, for it means death or everlasting sorrow." —Klamath story, recorded 1865 [Clark 1953, 53–55]

Who can doubt that we have here a volcanic eruption, with its river of fire, quakes, ash-fall, and lava bombs? Certainly no one who has followed the recent eruptions of Etna, Pinatubo, and Shasta's neighbor Mount St. Helens.

Active volcanos outside of Hawaii generally erupt rather seldom, in human terms: maybe once every few centuries or millennia. Yet when they do, they wreak havoc, and it is just as well not to be living in the path that the lava and other lethal flows will take. So one can understand that people who had experienced devastation from a fiery mountain would view it as a life-and-death matter to warn their descendants of the danger. But the message might have to traverse hundreds or even thousands of years to do its job.

Is transmission of oral information across centuries even possible? We read in the newspaper about how unreliable the witnesses to accidents and crimes can be a month later. What hope is there that verbal information could survive so long intact?

The Klamath story quoted above refers specifically to the place we know as Crater Lake—in fact, the story was related as answer to a young soldier at Fort Klamath when he inquired why the native people never went to that breathtakingly beautiful spot (figure 1). Geologists have reconstructed that a volcano dubbed Mount Mazama formerly towered

Figure 1. Crater Lake, Oregon, the enormous bowl formed by the cataclysmic eruption of a volcano, Mount Mazama, nearly 7,700 years ago. Later extrusions built up the
small cone-shaped island.

14,000 feet high between Mounts Shasta and St. Helens. It certainly once
qualified as "high", just as the story says; and, equally correctly, the giant is
no longer there. After emptying its magma chamber of lava in a catastrophic eruption, Mazama collapsed to form a crater 4,000 feet deep
which, as the narrative relates, never erupted violently again and gradually
filled with water to form today's magnificent Crater Lake. That eruption,
so accurately described and vehemently warned against in the tale, has been
ice-dated to 7,675 years ago [Zdanowicz, Zielinski, and Germani, 1999].

So yes, real information can reach us intact across more than seven
millennia of retelling. Even if we might not agree with their explanation of *why* these things occurred, the Klamath tribe in the 1860s still
knew in considerable detail of events observed *millennia* earlier.[1]

---

[1] Adrienne Mayor points out to us that Vine Deloria Jr. came to the same conclusion
about the Klamath myth of Crater Lake in his book *Red Earth, White Lies* [1995, 194–98].
We find Deloria also interprets much the way we do the Bridge of the Gods (The Dalles),
the disappearance of Spokane Lake, and various other Pacific Northwest myths—all as
recording specific geologically reconstructible events. And he too has collected massive evidence for the extreme longevity of these myths. Both we and Deloria are also indebted to
Dorothy Vitaliano's book *Legends of the Earth* [1973], which appeared not long before we
began collecting our Myth Principles.

Nor is this longevity of information an anomaly. Investigating another part of the world, Bruce Masse reports his surprise at

> the realization that the majority of Hawaiian myths were firmly attached to Hawaiian chiefly genealogies, . . . [which] purported to go back in unbroken lineage for more than 95 generations before Kamehameha I, . . . [including] several Pele myths in which the volcano goddess had battles during the reigns of named genealogical chiefs . . . , battles that resulted in the production of discrete named lava flows whose locations were known historically.
>
> Much to my surprise, the radiocarbon dates for these lava flows matched not only the relative order of the named chiefs in the genealogical record, but closely matched absolute dates as well if a 22-year period were used for the length of each chiefly generation. [Masse 1998, 55]

Evidence abounds from several continents, in fact, that properly encoded information has passed unscathed through the oral pipeline for one to ten thousand years and more—for example, in Australia [Dixon 1984, 153–55, 295]. But the conditions must be right for this to happen.

First of all, the information must be viewed as important, as in the Klamath warning about innocent-looking Crater Lake, which, for all they knew, might explode again next week. (Similar taboos against entering the heartland of a former vast catastrophe came to exist among Evenki shamans and herders after the 1908 Tunguska "cosmic event", which was thought locally to have resulted from two shamans battling [Menges 1983, 4–6].) After all, you can remember only a limited (even if fairly large) number of stories to pass down, so anything added to the corpus of stories to retell had better deserve its place—it is ousting something else. This being so, we can state as another working hypothesis the Relevance Corollary, that *formal oral mythologies are neither unimportant and "off the wall" nor random in their content.*[2]

Second, the information must continue to correspond to something still visible to the hearers, such as Crater Lake to the Klamath. If tellers of volcano myths migrate away from all volcanos, the original meaning of those myths is sure to become clouded or lost.

The third condition for intact transmission is that it be encoded in a

---

[2] Linguists may compare Grice's "Maxim of Relation" in conversational rules [1989, 27]. "Off the wall" is taken as referring to things that seem unexpectedly irrelevant and goofy.

highly memorable way. If Uncle Nestor, so boring he puts everyone to sleep, is elected clan storykeeper, the stories aren't going to survive. Best would be to elect Uncle Mitty, who can turn the dullest incident into a cliff-hanger. But even Uncle Benji, the village idiot, incapable of really understanding any of the stories, can do the job if he can remember and repeat them just as he heard them.

An unbroken chain of good memories is part of the condition. But that chain is more likely to stay intact if the information is either embedded vividly (so as to be more memorable) or encoded into the story multiple times (so there is a back-up). The two methods are not unrelated.

The latter strategy is called *redundancy*. Communication theorists like Claude Shannon have studied the properties of redundancy in information systems since the 1940s. Language itself is about 70 percent redundant, under normal circumstances, just to ensure that our messages get through all the noise—literal and figurative—in the system.

To convince yourself of this high redundancy, consider telegraphs. Telegraphs were billed by the number of words, so people used to cut costs by paring out as many redundant words as they could locate, leading to what is still known as *telegraphic speech* (e.g., "Reached Paris; send money"—trimmed to half the usual words). Evelyn Waugh once reduced his discovery of the untruth of a story (that an American nurse was killed when an Abyssinian hospital was destroyed) to the two-word cable: "Nurse unupblown" [Stannard 1986, 409]. A professor of cuneiform studies at Yale used to tear columns of the *New York Times* in half lengthwise, then make us reconstruct the text from just one half—to get us in practice for deciphering broken clay tablets from the Bronze Age. Early in the column, you're in doubt about how to fill many of the blanks, but by the time you get partway down, key words have occurred in your half often enough that you can go back and fill them in, thanks to redundancy in the message structure. In the story of Crater Lake, we heard about the anger of the Chief of the Below World, but also about his Curse of Fire, about the battle waged, about all the hot rocks and ashes flying around, about the river of fire coming down, and so forth: two or three of these could disappear without the central events and message getting lost.

Sheer redundancy in the text helps. But the more vivid each event or image in the story is, the less likely it is to drop out. The image of two elderly medicine men hesitating with their torches on the rim of the caldera, then jumping straight into the lava, will stick in most people's brains for quite a while. Why do some things stick so? Cognitive scientists have learned that recall is greatly enhanced when an image is encoded into several brain systems at once, rather than into just one—another type of redundancy [see, for example, Schacter 2001, 102–3, or Luria 1968]. The story as told invites one to imagine the fiery torches and lava in the night (stark visual images) and the men hesitating before jumping to their deaths (powerful emotional stimuli), as well as providing a stream of words which the linguistic sectors of the brain perceive, store, and decode. So the brain may have stored it in not just one but three or more places. These observations give us another step forward:

REDUNDANCY STRATEGY
Because of the importance attached, particular information will tend to be encoded with a high degree of redundancy and/or vividness, except *where the piece of knowledge is believed to be universal.*

The last clause, the exception, is a troublesome problem, paralleled in linguistics, that we refer to as the Silence Principle. It will be explored in chapters of its own when we are ready for it.

Note that what is old tends to be viewed as rather dull: a restaurant you've already been to generally doesn't excite your senses as much as a brand-new one. And have you noticed (as Thomas Mann did in *The Magic Mountain*) how much longer it seems to take to drive to a place you've never been than it does to get home later? All your senses are furiously busy registering all that new data on the outbound; it's much duller on the way home. So a "good" storyteller will pepper a narrative with the new and vivid. Now: when important cultural information is being transmitted, one is not allowed to tamper with the key information; therefore the vividness must come in the noncentral details. Note how the Klamath teller makes the girl come alive with details about her eyes, hair, and stature—all of which have nothing to do with the core message, but which help us remember that her beauty was perceived as the cause of the whole misfortune. The elderly chief who told the story was an effective keeper of the tradition even as he embellished it.[3]

---

[3] Such embellishments, and even the overall narrative forms of these tales, seem to follow the storytelling "scripts" developed within that culture. See Roger Schank's work on narrative scripts, summarized in Schank 1995, 7–9.

In fact, for truly bizarre and un-understandable events, such as a huge comet appearing in the sky or even the constellations themselves, novel associations may be the best route to memorability. Thus it's much easier to remember the location of the Pole Star if someone tells you it's on the end of a big spoon-shaped group of stars and is pointed to by two stars in an even bigger and more obvious spoon nearby called the Big Dipper. Spoons, not to mention cattle and dogs and scorpions, are odd things to find in the sky, but their weirdness is just what makes the images associated with the chaotic panorama of stars memorable, even to children:

The Cow jumped over the Moon;
The Little Dog laughed to see such sport,
And the Dish ran away with the Spoon.

Each patch of sky becomes a gigantic Rorschach blot, the more picturesque the better: centaurs, lions, and flying horses populate our northern sky, while llamas, jaguars, and *yutu*-birds pass above the Andes [Zuidema 1982].

Studies show, in fact, that human memory works far better precisely when the random data-points can be shaped into interactive stories [e.g., Bourne, Dominowski, and Loftus 1979, 65]. Jeremy Campbell, the science journalist, describes a famous experiment as follows:

Hermann Ebbinghaus, the nineteenth-century founder of scientific memory research, who used nonsense syllables in his memory tests to insure that the pure act of recall was not tainted by meaning, found that people forget up to 80 percent of what they learn within twenty-four hours. After that the loss is less rapid. This swift loss of information from the conscious mind became known as "the curve of forgetting." Yet the Ebbinghaus curve is not a universal law. It does not apply when . . . the information to be remembered takes the form of stories rather than nonsense syllables carefully drained of context. The . . . inexperienced, naïve person is [sometimes] intrigued by the nonsense syllables and tries to make sense of them, attaches images to them, notices interesting properties of the list as a whole. Because he enriches them in this way, extending their artificially cramped context, he is able to remember as many as 75 percent of them a day later, throwing the Ebbinghaus curve into reverse. [Campbell 1982, 223]

And so it is with memorizing constellations for such useful purposes as navigation and time-telling. Thus the "off-the-wall" quality of so much inherited lore may be a sign not of the simplicity but of the cleverness of the encoders.

But there is another problem. If our theories of volcanism hold up better against the attacks of skeptics than ancient theories do, it's not because we're smarter but because we have enough more information now, thanks to writing, to deduce real cause and effect. Some 2,500 years after the first Greek attempts at science, we've amassed far more data about, for example, geology: surveying the earth's surface and probing its innards so that we know largely what underground forces cause volcanos to erupt. We even know the difference between basaltic volcanos like Kilauea that flow like water—where scientists rush *toward* an eruption rather than away—and dangerously explosive volcanos like Pinatubo, Krakatoa, Vesuvius, Etna, Thera, and the Lassen-Shasta-Mazama-Hood-St. Helens-Rainier-Baker chain up the west coast of North America. And we know that major differences in the chemical composition, and hence viscosity, of the magma cause these differences in behavior.

Determining the causes of even slightly complex effects requires a lot of data, usually more than one head can hold and more than one individual can observe. Preliterate people were often *cut off* from the opportunity—and tools needed—to "figure things out".

Brain scientists, on the other hand, have found that our minds seem to insist on forming explanations no matter what. Those who study memory have learned that people are heavily predisposed to "come up with after-the-fact explanations that specify a deterministic cause of the outcome" [Schacter 2001, 146]. That is, our brains will if possible latch onto a plausible reason why an event should have come out the way it did (whether or not that was the actual cause) and this explanation will then become an inextricable part of memory. Thus, studies show that jurors apparently *cannot* mentally set aside evidence they've heard but are then told is inadmissible [Schacter 2001, 147]. This phenomenon is known as *hindsight bias*.

Those who study hemispheric functions adduce evidence that in particular the "analytic" side of our brain, the language-processing hemisphere, is programmed to produce explanations for everything. This act is presumably part of its toolbox for crunching the masses of disparate incoming data down to manageable amounts, and for minimizing the Pushme-Pullyou dilemma by integrating the perceived world. Various experiments suggest that it jumps to conclusions, concocts what it wants, and forces behavior accordingly on the whole organism, even when other parts of the same brain have data that flatly contradict this "explanation".

Researchers have observed such brain-fights most starkly among so-called split-brain patients, victims of a type of epilepsy not controllable by drugs, who have therefore undergone surgery separating the two hemispheres of the brain. With the corpus callosum cut, there are no pathways for most types of information to pass from one side of the brain to the other: one side remains ignorant of what is taught or shown to the other side alone (through hands or eyes). (For everyone, the left hemisphere controls the right hand and the right hemisphere the left hand. But in 95 percent of the population, language and one's abilities for analytic and sequential reasoning reside principally in the left hemisphere.) In one particularly graphic case, caught on videotape, Dr. Michael Gazzaniga of Dartmouth flashed the word "orange" to the patient's right hemisphere and a picture of a bird to the left hemisphere, then told the patient to draw what he had seen. The left hand came forward, chose an orange pen, drew a circle and embellished it with a stem and some speckles: a very nice orange.

"Whaddaya got?" Gazzaniga inquires. The patient shakes his head, staring at his own drawing. "What did you see?" prompts Gazzaniga.

"Orange," he says slowly.

"That's the color. What did you see in the picture?" (This question directs the young man's attention to what he saw with the language-side of his brain, which was the only side to have seen an actual picture.)

"Bird. I think I started on it, but I can't do a bird too well." He smiles a bit sheepishly.

"You can't do a bird too well?" Gazzaniga echoes.

The patient shakes his head slowly, while his left hand picks up a pen, approaches the drawing, wavers, then throws the pen down with a frustrated motion. "I can't do it."

"Try it with your right hand."

The right hand quickly picks up a pen and adds beak, wings, feet and tail to the circle.

"Whaddaya got?" says Gazzaniga.

"A bird. A sick-looking bird—but I can't do birds either," the young man explains with a rueful smile.

"You're not good on birds?"

"No, I don't do animals."

Commenting on the scene later, Gazzaniga says, "And then you say, 'Why did you do that?' and he fumbles for a minute and he says, 'Baltimore oriole? I dunno—I just picked up orange.' So you have here the separate activities represented in the drawing: the right hemisphere picks the right color pen, draws a picture of an orange, does more than you ask, and then the right hand—from the left hemisphere—comes in and turns it into a bird, and then gives you an explanation as to why you have an orange-colored bird. This left-brain interpreter *insists* on interpreting action. It will not let things go—it *demands* an explanation."[4]

One might add: whether it knows what it's talking about or not. In fact, the language-side of the brain brooks no counterevidence. What it "knows" explains all by definition. Or, put another way, what the language side chooses to encode into language becomes The Explanation.

In the face of such a strong biological demand for explanation at all costs, what surprise is it, then, that people cut off from working out principles of cause and effect will turn to other means of putting together some sort of explanation? *Where permanent record-keeping is unavailable, so that there is not enough memory-space to accumulate the data needed to demonstrate cause and effect for complex phenomena, other types of "explanation" may be proffered or sought.* Data show clearly that the most prominent of these other types of explanation has been analogy.

That is, if we can't say that X is that way because Y *caused* it, we can still plausibly say it's that way because it *resembles* (works like) Q. The stars move across the sky because they are *like* a river flowing past. The sun moves across the sky because it is *like* a boat moving along a river, or a chariot moving past us on a road. Just as we live inside a house or lodge, so the Chief of the Below World must live inside something, apparently a big mountain. And that "explains" why he could come out of the mountain when he felt like it, just as we can come out of our houses when we want. Analogy is so central a part of the principles by which myths evolve (and still today, one might add, of "modeling" in modern

---

[4] Walter 1988, transcribed from video by E. Barber. This case is of course extreme, but it by no means stands alone; see Schacter 2001, 157–59; Gazzaniga, Ivry, and Mangun 2002, 672–75.

science) that no fewer than thirteen of the roughly fifty principles we observed empirically turned out to fall under this category; they will be treated presently.

But before we are ready to explore the varieties of analogy with real insight, we must understand the devil that will get in our way at every turn, clouding our eyesight and destroying our data. We referred to it once before: the Silence Principle.

3

The Silence Principle: Of Lethe and the Golden Calf

SILENCE PRINCIPLE
What everyone is expected to know already is not explained in so many words.

Feedback is the mechanism by which we control the flow of information in a conversation. Every six seconds or so we provide it, with such automaticity that we hardly know we've done it. Station yourself near a telephone conversation when the guy on the other end is doing most of the talking. What you hear at this end is: "Yeah . . . Unh-hunh . . . Sure . . . Yeah . . ." Time it: every three to six seconds the listener checks in. When the speakers can see each other, some of this feedback may be done visually, but on the phone there's no second channel [Joos 1967; Turner and Pöppel 1983].

And what are we feeding back? We're letting the other person know whether we comprehend the messages, and whether the rate of information-flow is about right (as in the example above)—or too fast ("What's that?" "Did what?" "Who?")—or too slow ("Yeah, yeah"; "I know."). We detest being told things again that we already know well; we want to move on to the new and juicy stuff. So if our conversational partner is covering too much old territory, we get more and more impatient, not to say ruder and ruder, as we try to hurry things along.

If "not stating the already known" is a mandate in simple conversations [cf. Grice 1989, 26–27], how much more so is it in social dealings! When we get into an elevator, we all turn and face the door and look up at the numbers of the passing floors because we all know that in American society you aren't supposed to stare (that is, look for more than the briefest moment) at strangers within eight feet of you [Hall 1969]. But the elevator is so small that you're within eight feet of everyone, so you have to put your eyes somewhere safe: up or down. We never discuss the matter with strangers in the elevator ("Keep your eyes to yourself!"—not allowed). Only the little kid who doesn't know the drill yet gets told off: "Freddie! Don't stare at the woman—it's rude!" A quick, sheepish smile to the woman; a sharp thumb in Freddie's neck to swivel him toward safer vistas.

In short, the only time such things that "everyone knows" ever get said is when we are trying to socialize children.

This rule carries over in the telling of myth. Why waste time saying what everyone knows? Get on with the informational parts of the story.

But what a disaster those omissions can lead to for the study of myth—for *we*, many cultures and centuries removed, may *not* know what the people whose mythology it is all knew so well and hence did not say. In short:

LETHE EFFECT
What is never said may eventually be forgotten entirely.

The most famous examples of the Lethe Effect[1] have to do with the names of divine spirits. Among the ancient Hebrews, for example, the name of their god was considered so sacred that it became impious to say the name aloud—although it was written down in what we know as the Old Testament. But the Hebrew script, like the Arabic, transcribed only consonants, leaving the reader to supply the appropriate vowels. Because this particular name stopped being said, eventually no one knew any more what the correct vowels were, so now no one *could* say it. All that remained was the skeleton: YHWH. The Silence Principle had wiped out the data.[2]

Another example of this phenomenon is what linguists dubbed Circumpolar Dropout when they noticed that languages all around the Arctic Circle regularly lose their words for the major game-animals hunted by people there. The cause was traced to a prevalent belief that each type of animal was protected by a spirit—a Bear Spirit, a Fox Spirit, and so forth. If the Bear Spirit heard you plotting to kill bears, the reasoning went, it might hide all the bears safely away and you would starve for lack of meat. To circumvent this, you would refer to bears by a euphemism as you plotted the kill: "the brown one" (whence English *bear*, *bruin*), "the honey-eater" (Russian *medved'*), and so on [Meillet 1958, 282–85]. Thus the Indo-European word for a bear, reconstructed as *$h_2\acute{r}ktos$ [Mallory and Adams 1997, 55] and retained by the more southerly languages like Latin and Greek (with *ursus* and *árktos*, respectively), was lost up north through Silence.

Note how hard it would be to spot the losses, the victims of the River of Forgetfulness, if we did not have either written text or closely related languages to tip us off. Indeed, noticing what is *not* there is one of the most difficult tasks of all. Linguists clearly have an advantage here, with their arsenal of related languages, and we will often turn to the linguists for help. For in order to interpret the results of Silence, we

---

[1] Lethe, Greek for "forgetfulness", was one of the five rivers of the Underworld in Greek mythology. Its waters were thought to cause dead souls to forget their past lives.

[2] Almost. Translators into languages whose scripts require vowels have had to invent vowels to add, the most famous articulation being *Jehovah* (*j* and *v* alternated as spellings for *y* and *w* respectively in various European languages). But Biblical scholars use *Yahweh*, the vocalization of which came down through the line of highest priests and was verified recently by a Hellenistic inscription [Robert Littman, personal communication 2003].

need *some* sort of outside information to bridge the gap, whether linguistic or physical.

Observe also that the context of both these examples, though linguistic, is religious belief—a central realm of mythology. Although they are harder to spot and to interpret, nonlinguistic examples of the Lethe Effect also abound. Let us start with a myth where the writer kindly gives us a nudge.

The Icelander Snorri Sturluson (1179–1241) relates how the gods punished Loki for causing the death of Baldr. They bound him to stones in a cavern, then

> took a poisonous snake and fastened it up over him so that the venom from it should drop on to his face. His wife Sigyn, however, sits by him holding a basin under the poison drops. When the basin becomes full she goes away to empty it, but in the meantime the venom drips onto his face and then he shudders. [Sturluson 1971, 85–86]

At this point, Snorri clearly felt that his Christian audience (for whose education he wrote his *Edda*) would not have learned the background necessary to interpret this story properly, so he steps out of the narration a moment, deliberately breaking the usual "silence" to instruct us, and adds: "—you call that an earthquake." We'll get more help from Snorri later.

Now consider the Golden Calf. Moses comes down from the mountain at dawn with his tablets and finds the Children of Israel worshipping a Golden Calf. What's that all about? Why a calf? Why not a goat or a dog or a manna bush? If we form the hypothesis that we are not told *because originally everyone knew*, we can make some headway.

Where had the Children of Israel been living? In Egypt, of course—the country from which they were escaping after centuries of servitude. One can reasonably conjecture that in all that time they had absorbed something of their captors' culture. In fact, Moses seems particularly incensed because in his absence they have somehow *reverted* to the religious practices of others.

So what do we know about Egyptian religion? Even fifth-graders today can tell you the Egyptians worshipped primarily the sun—something that the Egyptians' neighbors in the Levant were well aware of (considering how often they borrowed the Egyptian winged sun-disk in their art). What is less widely known, but which could well have been known by folk who had lived in ancient Egypt for centuries, was that

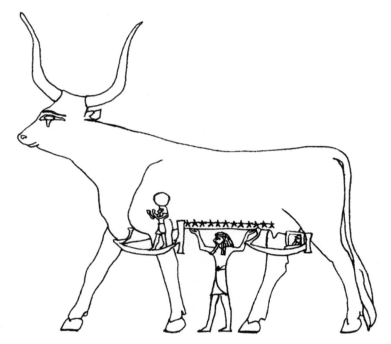

Figure 2. Egyptian sky goddess represented as a cow standing above the earth, supported by a helper, with the stars on her belly. Boats carry sun and moon. Tomb of Seti I, Thebes, ca. 1280 B.C.

the Egyptians viewed the sky (among other things) as a giant cow-goddess "standing four square over the earth" [Frankfort 1949, 27] (figure 2). And each morning she gave birth to . . .

A golden Calf.

There it is, suddenly sitting like molten gold on the horizon.

In worshipping a Golden Calf at dawn, the Children of Israel would simply be reverting to Egyptian sun-worship: they were probably relieved that the sun finally came up, after all that thundering during the night. And why would the storyteller need to explain something so obvious?

Note that whenever the Lethe Effect kicks in, we run the risk of losing precious data altogether, to the point that the myths it affects may eventually become un-understandable. Some of this loss is caused actively. Religious taboos often trigger destruction of the information, as in the case of how to vocalize YHWH. (Social taboos have quite the reverse consequences: almost every American kid soon knows *all* the words you aren't supposed to say that pertain to body functions and parts, and many of these terms have etymologies that go back thousands of years. Not only has it always been fun to fool Mama and Papa, it's even more fun to flout them—whereas offending an omniscient and probably omnipotent spirit is another matter.) But other losses occur quite unintentionally, as when we omit saying what we think everyone knows. As long as the culture remains essentially unchanged, as long as children grow up socialized into the same knowledge-base as before, Lethe is held at bay. But as soon as major migrations or technological revolutions occur, so that the circumstances to which the myths refer live on only in the minds of those who knew Life Before the Change, then the trouble begins.

The meaning and references of the Klamath tale were quite clear to the eighty-year-old Chief Lalek, who related it. From where he sat he could still look up at the remains of the dangerous mountain. Although technology was beginning to change with the coming of the White Man, the locale at least was still the same, so his interested young listener could see the evidence and understand it too.

But what happens when the new generations can no longer perceive what is referred to—either because the group moves away from the relevant data or a new cultural group with totally different values moves in or takes over? We, for example, are likely to view the following passage from a Modoc story (from Northern California) as fairly quaint and arbitrary at first glance:

> Late one spring, while the Sky Spirit and his family were sitting round the fire, the Wind Spirit sent a big storm that shook the top of the mountain [they lived in]. It blew and blew, and roared and roared. Smoke blown back into the lodge hurt their eyes. At last the Sky Spirit said to his youngest daughter, "Go up to the smoke hole and ask the Wind Spirit to blow more gently. Tell him I am afraid he will blow the mountain over."
>
> His little daughter was glad to go. . . . She put her head out of the hole and looked toward the west. The Wind Spirit caught her long hair, pulled her out of the mountain, and blew her down over the snow and ice. She landed among the scrubby fir trees at the edge of the timber and snow line, her long red hair trailing over the snow. [Clark 1953, 10]

But there is real information in there. Focus on the long red strands trailing down a mountain inside which is a smoking fire. This story in fact concerns Mount Shasta, another very active volcano that is so high (14,400 feet) that permanent glaciers cloak it. Apparently the tale records a relatively minor eruption that included a lava flow coming part way down the western flank. (We'll find hair as an image for lava repeatedly as we proceed.)

In fact, the volcano myths told by native peoples of the Pacific Northwest, odd though they may seem at first, are still fairly reconstructable to us, because we are the first *new* people to come into the area since the events occurred, and we know how to ferret out the geologic data to verify them. But imagine how muddy the waters would be if the original observers had passed their stories on to new people who simply took them at face value and then repeated what they could recall of the seemingly random details, finally passing a garbled version on to yet another group who knew even less about the subject, and so forth. We face this situation in Greece, for instance, where Minoan stories passed to the incoming Greeks who gave them to the Etruscans and Romans next door and thence to us millennia and several technological revolutions later (not to mention continents away).

Under such circumstances, any key point or assumption passed over in silence in the original version will likely cause a vortex of confusion to grow and grow around it.

But nonliterate cultures are not alone in generating difficulties through what they do not say. We, too, pass over key assumptions of our own in silence, failing to recognize and cope with what we do not articulate. And this aspect of the Silence Principle can be as devastating to the study of myth as the side we have just explored.

Imagine, for example, two people having a conversation using words which they both "know" but for which they have different definitions. Decades ago, as an unwary native of the West Coast, one of us went into a café in Boston, looked at the menu, and said, "I'll have a chocolate milkshake." A few minutes later a glass of slightly frothy chocolate milk arrived. "But I ordered a milkshake," said I. "There it is," said the waiter. "But where's the ice cream?" I queried. "Milkshakes don't have ice cream," came the reply. "If you wanted ice cream in it you should have ordered a frappe."

Now imagine the conversation when the participants have *really* different assumptions:

"Well, then, who's playin' first?"

"Yes."

"I mean the fellow's name on first base."

"Who."

"The fellow's name on first base for St. Louis."

"Who."

"The guy on first base."

"Who is on first base."

"Well, what are you askin' me for?"

"I'm not asking you, I'm telling you. Who is on first."

". . . Well, all I'm tryin' to find out is what's the guy's name on first base."

"Oh, no, no. What is on *second* base."

"I'm not askin' you who's on second."

"Who's on first."

"That's what I'm tryin' to find out."

"Well, don't change the players around." [Costello 1981, 36–37]

(This famous Abbott and Costello skit, of which only an eighth is quoted, twanged such sympathetic strings in the audience that it flung its authors into stardom overnight.)

When Bronislaw Malinowski was living among and studying the Trobriand Islanders early in the twentieth century, he awoke one morning to hear

> loud and, it seemed to me, quarrelsome vociferation from the other side of the village, and, being always on the alert for some sociological "document," I inquired from the natives in my hut what it was. They replied that Gumguya'u—a respectable and quiet man—was talking to the *baloma* [spirits]. I hurried to the spot, but, arriving too late, found the man exhausted on his bed, apparently asleep. The incident did not arouse any excitement, because, as they said, it was his habit to talk to the *baloma*. [Malinowski 1948, 140]

Malinowski never thought to ask his hut-mates what their assumptions about spirits were, so they didn't explain; nor did they think to ask him his assumptions about sleep and dreaming. Why should they? His assumptions, indeed, were so far from theirs that it did not occur to him that they called conversing with the spirits what he would call talking in one's sleep—even though some twenty pages later he remarks that "at times, the *baloma* appear to men in dreams" [Malinowski 1948, 159].

In fact, later research has shown that Malinowski made quite a few mistakes stemming from the Silence Principle—but this is not to fault Malinowski unduly. As with the frappe, if you don't even know there's a difference in assumptions, you don't know to ask for it to be explained until a misunderstanding has both occurred *and been recognized* as such. The problems engendered by Silence are truly diabolical. (Similarly Charles Allen, in *Tales from the Dark Continent* [1980, 137] remarks on "an almost continual battle between African servants and their employers. It wasn't from lack of sympathy on either side. The real problem was each side had entirely different basic assumptions.") Later researchers were able to go back and patch up mistakes made in understanding the Trobriand Islanders, but with myths of several millennia ago, there may be no going back. We will have lost some keys forever.

Apparently, however, there is at least one type of myth which can bring some of the unmentioned social assumptions of a culture to light: namely, myths of so-called Trickster figures (see chapter 6). The trickster is a plastic character who constantly plays tricks on others and predictably is not what he presents himself as: he lies, cheats, masquerades, and so on. Inasmuch as he regularly *breaks* the "proper" rules and taboos, with comical and/or disastrous effects, he tells us much about what the assumed rules are. As William Hynes puts it, "In belief systems where entertainment is not separated from education, trickster myths can be a powerful teaching device utilizing deeply humorous negative examples. . . . Breaching less visible but deeply held societal values serves not only to reveal these values but to reaffirm them" [Hynes and Doty 1993, 207]. If such stories have survived, we then have a working method we could call the Socialization Antidote: *Information on the basic and otherwise unstated assumptions of a culture may be teased out of those statements and stories by which adults socialize children.*

4

More Silence: Movie Reels from Snapshots

RATIONALIZATION SYNDROME
What is not known but only surmised may nonetheless be perceived and stated as known, in explanation of things observed.

In the story of Crater Lake, we saw a rather clear description of a volcanic eruption, complete with incandescent river, fiery boulders flying about, and ash-fall. These were mixed together with equally direct statements about the life habits of spirits thought to cause such eruptions.

We moderns tend to assume that the events and details in a story are all of equal "value" in the world—that the narrative contains either *all* "truth" or *no* "truth". And if we don't happen to believe that volcanos are to be explained as a mountain that a spirit is using as his home (fireplace and all), we throw the whole thing out as nonsense, instead of carefully distinguishing two quite different parts of the story: observation and explanation. And so we come up with the Baby-with-the-Bathwater Reflex: *Heavily literate cultures tend to disregard the truth of the earlier events reported in myths and legends, because they can't brook the explanations—that is, they ignore the phenomena described because they reject the mechanisms indicated.*

Because our language faculty is designed to tamp the world into coherent patterns or rules (explanations) for itself, whether or not it has the data to do so "correctly", human narratives generally contain explanations—whether or not they truly explain the observed data. The brain can supply such things quite glibly: remember the bird and the orange. But it is often oblivious—hence silent—as to what it really knows versus what it has invented as rationalization. And it can be quite subtle about intertwining the two. (See Schacter [2001, 88–137], for analysis of types of false memories.)

The obfuscation is not necessarily deliberate. It appears that the conscious part of the brain is unaware of *most* of the cognitive chatter that goes on inside our heads, receiving only a final opinion or "answer" from this or that great network of neurons, without being privy to either the data or the probabilistic processes that gave rise to that answer. Jeremy Campbell, who gives a very readable summary of how the "neural network" or "connectionist" approach to cognitive structure accounts for this problem, points out that, since the nonconscious networks routinely "fill in the missing parts of information that is incomplete, the version of the world that is tossed up to consciousness may be largely fictitious. And since only the product, not the processes, of a decision by a network's behind-closed-doors parliament is open to inspection, the conscious mind may have no way of knowing which part is fact and which part is fiction" [Campbell

1989, 203].[1] So how do we learn to distinguish observation from explanation? Let's start with an example.

The accounts of outbreaks of vampirism recorded by officials of the Austro-Hungarian Empire tell us repeatedly that those whom people dug out of their graves and proclaimed vampires had not decomposed, being often plumper than when buried, with fresh-looking blood at their mouths [Barber 1988]. The villagers then took steps to kill these blood-sucking vampires by as many means as possible (staking, decapitation, cremation, and so forth) to ensure that they didn't come back to hurt the living any more.

The medical doctors sent by the government to keep an eye on things described one such scene thus:

> [the villagers] found that [the exhumed dead man] was quite complete and undecayed, and that fresh blood had flowed from his eyes, nose, mouth, and ears; . . . that the old nails on his hands and feet, along with the skin, had fallen off, and that new ones had grown; and since they saw from this that he was a true vampire, they drove a stake through his heart, according to their custom, whereby he gave an audible groan and bled copiously. [Barber 1988, 16]

Grew new skin and nails? Bled copiously? *Groaned?* Can't be: dead men don't talk, nor do they grow fat in the grave. Throw the old wives' tales out!

But not so fast. Each of the *observations* here happens to be clinically verifiable down at the coroner's office. Dead bodies often do get plumper—from the gases formed by decomposition. Furthermore, pressure from the gas (not to mention from a pounded stake) can force the person's own blood out at the orifices. (Blood typically coagulates soon after death but often reliquifies later.) The tendency of the nails to fall off, exposing the smooth pink nail-bed (not, in fact, new nails—but who's going to get close enough to scrutinize?), was so well known to the ancient Egyptians that they tied the nails on with little metal toe- and finger-caps. The peeling of the outer layer of skin, exposing a fresh-looking layer beneath, is well known to forensic pathologists as "skin slippage". And shoving a stake into the chest can push air out of the

---

[1] The active human propensity to "rationalize" the bare facts of a story was studied at length by Sir Frederic Bartlett [1932], whose discussion (especially 84–89) mentions what we call the Silence Principle, Rationalization Syndrome, and (below) Stripping Procedure and Movie Construct.

lungs past a still-intact glottis or voice-box, producing a groaning sound—though not articulated speech—exactly as in life.

So it's all true—except for the *explanation* that he was plumper because he was sucking blood from the living and that all of these things occurred because the dead man's spirit had not yet vacated the body: in short, that he was still somehow alive.

But we are free to examine and accept the observations without embracing the explanation. That leads us to the Stripping Procedure: *In order to understand the true original events, we have to see clearly what the events are. In order to do that, we must strip the explanations from the story.*

As a countercheck, note that if one temporarily accepts the explanation, then the actions that follow seem rather logical. If you truly believed that the vampire was alive, then rekilling its body would seem the natural next step. And if the original means of death had not been sufficient to separate the animating principle from the flesh, it would behoove you to try everything in your arsenal this time around.

Once again we see that people weren't so silly, they just didn't have enough facts at their disposal to come up with theories more to our taste. Note, too, that not only are their observations given to us tangled with their explanations, but their explanations are a function of their belief system, which in turn has suffered from the Silence Principle during transmission.

Similarly, in the Crater Lake story, when we remove the explanations we find a geologically verifiable description of the eruption and collapse of Mount Mazama. (We get the added information that the Klamath tribe fled into the lake while two of its elder members jumped into the inferno shortly before the final collapse. Although we cannot verify *these* details, we no longer have cause to reject them.) Now turn to the explanation that we peeled away. If you truly believed that something as extreme as the river of fire chasing you from your home had been sent in revenge by the Chief of the Below World, then it would make sense to resort to something as extreme as human (self-)sacrifice as a countermeasure.

Thus another very efficient principle for analysing myth is the Logic Cross-check: *Investigating the logic of the actions of the participants serves as a useful cross-check that we have suitably separated their explanations from their observations.*

The ways the brain has of filling in the gaps in its knowledge, much as it fills in the eye's blindspot, are numerous. For example, linguistic research shows that if people are asked to repeat a sentence that is too long and complex for them to remember verbatim, they will reword it in such a way as to get the general sense across. Or if given short ones, they will combine them to capture the sense. Jeremy Campbell summarizes another well-known memory experiment, in this case conducted by John Bransford and Jeffrey Franks, who constructed lists of sentences as follows:

> At the highest level of complexity was a sentence like:
>
> > The rock which rolled down the mountain crushed the tiny hut at the edge of the woods.
>
> This same idea was broken down into parts and represented by four shorter and simpler sentences:
>
> > The rock rolled down the mountain.
> > The rock crushed the hut.
> > The hut was tiny.
> > The hut was at the edge of the woods.
>
> Students who took the test were given only some of these shorter fragments. They were not given any of the long sentences which expressed the complete set of ideas, so that they were exposed to no more than bits and pieces of the full meaning of the complex sentences. Nor were the students allowed to spend time thinking about the material. . . . At the end of this stage of the test, the complete list of sentences was read out, and the students were asked to say how familiar each sentence sounded to them. . . . In general a top rating was given to the sentences which combined all the ideas, even though the students had never heard these sentences before. . . . Actual familiarity turned out to have almost nothing to do with how the students responded. All that mattered was that a sentence was or was not compatible with the complete, most complex idea which the students had abstracted from the short fragments. [Campbell 1982, 224–25]

In other words, as Campbell puts it, "Out of disconnected elements, a complete meaning is constructed, and that is what a person remembers." Frederic Bartlett, in his classic experiments about remembering stories [1932], came to similar conclusions.

Over the years, we have repeatedly encountered a similar phenomenon in the oral retelling of myths and stories:

MOVIE CONSTRUCT

Explanations that were derived from seeing only the result of an event (as in a single snapshot) tend to be presented as an integral part of a story that moves through time (as in a movie reel).

That is, the story we receive has often been put together or "reconstituted" from single events or observations, on the basis of an explanation treated as given rather than as deduced. There is no overt indicator that this is the case, of course, since the narrators assumed that their hearers would make the same unstated assumptions as they did. Take, for example, the following account of an Austrian exhumation from 1893:

> To the horror of the authorities it was discovered that not only had [the pregnant woman] been buried alive in a trance-like or cataleptic condition but she had put up the most incredible struggle within the coffin. During the course of this she had given birth to a child. Both had suffocated to death. [Masters 1972, 79]

Everything here is explanation/rationalization. But what had people actually *seen*? They could only have seen (1) the dead bodies of mother and baby (where they expected the body of a pregnant woman), and (2) evidence of violent movement within the coffin (where they expected "dead quiet"). Now, forensic pathologists will tell you that it often happens that the pressure of those decomposition gases we mentioned typically forces an unborn foetus out of a dead mother—so-called "coffin-birth"—and causes many other sorts of movements in dead bodies, even sitting upright (figure 3).[2] (One reason we get the dead out of sight as fast as possible is that we don't care to watch such manifestations, especially in a loved one. But that means that most of us know al-

---

[2] Accounts of the dead sitting up occur more than once in European accounts of vampirism [Barber 1988]. A homicide officer recently told us that he and his partner were once asked to identify at the local morgue the body of a biker they had seen killed in a shoot-out the day before. Just as they walked into the cold-room, the body on the slab sat bolt upright.

"We never drew our guns so fast in our lives," he admitted sheepishly, "—even though we had seen him die. Then we put them down. You just don't expect that."

Figure 3. Dead body spontaneously sitting up in its coffin during the wake. Old central European woodcut.

most nothing about these processes.) In other words, all the end results can be accounted for by simple decomposition.

The writer of this account, however, ignorant of modern forensic pathology, has deduced that the mother had (a) not been dead when buried, (b) been in a trance instead, (c) awakened, (d) struggled, (e) given birth to a live baby, and finally (f) suffocated in the coffin with her newborn. A complete newsreel. And no mention is made of the actual state of affairs that the gravediggers observed (1 and 2, above), everything being couched in terms of what are silently *assumed* to be the causes or explanations of these final results.

What is particularly comical (or scary) is that half of this newsreel was invented by a modern author, Anthony Masters [1972], on the basis of his own assumptions. The much simpler 1896 report from which he got the case [Hartmann 1896, 5–6] says that three days after death the woman was buried, and a few days later, on suspicion of poisoning, exhumed:

It was then found that she had but very recently died, and the appearance of her body indicated that she had undergone a terrible struggle. Moreover, she had given birth to a child in her coffin. The physician who had signed her certificate of death was sentenced to a few weeks' imprisonment as a punishment for his carelessness.

No mention of trance, awakening, giving *live* birth, or suffocation! Movie Constructs are still alive and well.

Jeremy Campbell has a further remark of interest here. He points out that when "information is recollected, the elaborations added by the brain may behave like a memory, so that people have the mistaken impression that the extra information is part of the original message. Once placed in memory, the two kinds of information are not easily disentangled. The students in the test were *certain* that they had heard the full, most complex sentences expressing the complete idea, when in reality they had constructed them out of fragments" [Campbell 1989, 225; see also Schacter 2001, 88–137, on sources of false memories]. Similarly, in myth, as in many eyewitness statements in court and numerous memory experiments [e.g., Bartlett 1932, 84–89], the observations and constructed explanations come at us in a tangle.

So when we are confronted with fantastic myths like that of Prometheus having his liver pecked out by an eagle as he lies chained to a mountain, or Loki having snake venom drip on him as he lies chained to rocks, we can do better than throwing them out, or even than merely guessing the two tales are somehow related. But to understand them, we must understand the cornerstone of how our brains handle data: analogical patterning.

5

Analogy:
Our Brain's Best Talent

ANALOGY PRINCIPLE
If any entities or phenomena bear **some** *resemblance,
in any aspect, they must be related.*

A nalogy sits at the very core of language itself. As children we hear *book, books* and *cat, cats* and figure out for ourselves—by analogy—that the plural of *cup* will be *cups*. That this and not imitation alone is the underlying process becomes quite clear from the child who, equally cleverly, comes up with *foot, foots*. We know that no such form was used in his or her presence, therefore the child made it up by extracting and reapplying analogically a pattern or rule based on other forms heard.

That means that ever since we set our feet (or foots, as the case may be) on the road to language, our brains have been selected for adeptness at doing analogies—in fact, rewarded for it, since the child who demands that Mama put shoes on his *foots* will get them just as surely as if he had said *feet*. The message (the whole point of language) gets through even though the form is unusual, because an adult can make the same unconventional analogy in a flash.

We often initiate some unconventional stuff ourselves, as adults, especially when we encounter new and unfamiliar forms. Thus when a French word for a small green legume came into English long ago, as in the ditty "Pease porridge hot, pease porridge cold", we thought, well, there are a lot of little green balls inside the pease pod, so just one of them would be a *pea*. That is, so many speakers of English noticed the resemblance of the consonant sound on the end of *peas(e)* to the common English plural suffix that they assumed an *s*-less form must be the singular and the form with the -*s* the plural, by analogy to practically every other noun in the language. We assume that if two entities bear a resemblance, they must be related. Linguists call this particular form of analogical change *back-formation*; the process that formed *foots* is *extension* or *generalization*. There are other types of linguistic analogy too, and we have been doing all of them for millennia. All we need is to perceive a pattern or resemblance and, like a bridleless horse, we're off and running.

And so we find it in mythology, the child of language. If any entities or phenomena bear a resemblance, in any aspect, people assume they must be related—where points of resemblance include form, behavior, cause, significance, or whatever.

As with language, analogy of form is the easiest to spot, and we have seen examples already. If the mountain smokes like a chimney, then it plausibly *is* the chimney of a supernatural creature's home; and just as we gather with our family around the fireplace, so, by analogy, this creature will gather with his family around his gigantic fireplace—and likewise send his kid off on an errand.

Sometimes the analogy must have begun as a way of describing the indescribable to those who weren't there. Thus if a gigantic tidal wave rushes onto land, roaring and shaking the earth and destroying everything in its path, it may be likened to a bull on the rampage—in Aegean mythology, the Bull from the Sea. A woman who witnessed the great Alaska quake of 1968 from her house on a hillside reported that the ground opening up in multiple furrows looked like something being raked open by an invisible giant's claw. Before written records, it only takes a touch of the Silence Principle (dropping the word "like") to change this into an actual giant raking the ground open.

In this simple way, analogy can often provide a very satisfying explanation for How Things Are. It can also provide a guide for how to act. For instance, one of the most famous analogical acts of the ancient Near East was the ritual "sacred marriage", in which the king mated with the high priestess in imitation of the desired mating of the divine male and female principles of nature. The purpose, of course, was to promote fertility by analogical means.

Or take another example. If I am very angry, I might well be mollified by an expensive gift that says, "I'm sorry." So if the Chief of the Below World is enraged, those experiencing his Curse of Fire might succeed in placating him with a gift, a sacrifice. If the Nile does not rise at the proper time with its life-giving floodwaters, then perhaps the river is angry at something and needs a bribe or two.

We tend to take the moral high ground today in our view of things, because we strive to discover cause and effect, the logical or "scientific" explanation. The cause of the Nile's mysterious late-summer flood in Egypt is perfectly ordinary: most of it comes from spring monsoons in Ethiopia and some from spring meltwaters around Lake Victoria, both of which lie so far south of Egypt that the floodwaters reach the mouth of the Nile only months later. Less rain and/or delayed melting in these distant areas are what retard the Nile flood. But because the Nile is over four thousand miles long with a vast area of formerly impassable swampland in its midregion, nobody got the data together to figure out the exact sources of the Nile until the late nineteenth century. In the meanwhile, those whom the flood affected strove to provide an analogical or "mythical" explanation by observing shared similarities. The Nile, *like* a responsible citizen, rose because it chose to do its part, and failed to rise because, *like* a balky one, it refused to. Fortunately, two can play that game: if the Nile is (like) a citizen, treat it accordingly. To keep life on course, the pharaoh "made gifts to the Nile every year about the time when it was due to rise. To these sacrifices, which were thrown into the river, a document was added. It stated, in the form of either an order or a contract, the Nile's obligations" [Frankfort and Frankfort 1949, 24].

Analogy is so plastic that we will consider its application to mythology in nearly a dozen specific forms. Much of our reasoning, however, while involving very apt analogies, simultaneously falls into a rather slippery logical fallacy. Over the millennia we have become very good at analogical reasoning, but we have done little to wire up our brains for pure logic, especially deductive logic. As a result, most people's minds simply duck out for a siesta when "if P" and "then Q" come into the conversation.

In fact, the more that cognitive scientists try to construct artificial intelligence, the more they find our brains to be *unlike* computers based on serial logic. Instead, our brains have grown up to access masses of related data simultaneously, sifting for the best overall pattern-match to known experience, so as to turn up practical solutions to such things as evading the lion's jaws as fast as possible. This inbuilt preference for navigating from ready experience rather than airtight logic turns up repeatedly in mythic thinking.

But in so navigating, we often slither into what logicians call the Fallacy of Affirming the Consequent: *I know that "if P, then Q" is true; I have Q (not P); so I assume that P must be true.* Let's put that into (our preferred) concrete terms. I know that (P:) if Sam is driving in, then (Q:) it's time for dinner; so I conclude that since it's now time for dinner, Sam must be driving in.

In practice, 99 percent of the time I'm right—as the clock strikes 6:30, Sam turns into the driveway. But despite the high percentage of *success* of this gambit, it is not a deduction that follows the laws of *logic*, as we can see if we change the values of P and Q.

I know that (P:) if I have a rattlesnake, then (Q:) I have a snake with a poisonous bite. But that does not mean that if I have a snake with a poisonous bite it is a rattler. It could be a cobra or a copperhead, for instance. The problem is that I have Q, not P; and it was P that entailed Q, not the other way around. Yet we behave much of the time as though an implication and its reverse were equivalent. This is because, since we prefer practical situations over abstract ones, we tend to rely on what we know *usually* happens rather than on a tight logical analysis.[1]

The Fallacy of Affirming the Consequent leads in all sorts of interesting directions. Let's take a simple one. We keep dishes in the cupboard, and whenever we need dishes we go get them from the cupboard, because that's where they reside. Analogously, we keep clothes inside the closet and go fetch them from there when needed. Likewise, whenever we need fire, we go and get it from matches—or, in previous ages, from flint. Therefore fire resides inside matches and/or flint:

P	Q
If dishes reside in cupboards,	we can get dishes from cupboards.
If clothes reside in closets,	we can get clothes from closets.
If X resides in Y,	we can get X from Y.
	We can get fire from flint,
Therefore fire resides in flint.	

Many cultures do, in fact, have myths that fire made its home in flint or in certain kinds of wood. The next question, of course, is how it got there; and the answers are variously that the flint (or tree) must have eaten Fire, or hidden Fire from an enemy at some time in the past. Either way, it now has Fire inside it. And so, courtesy of the Fallacy of Affirming the Consequent, we have the Container Corollary: *A source container and a resident "thing contained" may be assumed where scientists consider cause and effect the appropriate relation.*

Take, as illustration, the following myth, told by a variety of tribes living from northern Washington to northern California. It tells of Coyote's attempt to steal fire for mortals from three old skookums (evil spirits) who night and day guarded the only fire, up on top of a mountain. Coyote stationed the fastest animals at intervals up the mountain, and when he finally succeeded in stealing a firebrand, he ran as fast as he could, with the skookums hot on his heels. Exhausted, he passed the brand to the nearest animal he had stationed, which ran to the second, and so on in relays down the mountain:

> All hoped the skookums would soon be tired out. At last, when only a coal was left, it was given to squatty little Frog. Squatty little Frog swallowed the hot coal and hopped away as fast as he could hop. The youngest skookum,

---

[1] We are indebted to discussions with our colleague William Neblett and to his book *Sherlock's Logic* [1985] for coming to understand this aspect of the phenomenon.

though she was very tired, was sure she could catch Frog. She seized his tail, and held tight. But Frog did not stop. He made the biggest jump he had ever made. And he left his tail behind him in the skookum's claws. Ever since, frogs have had no tails.

Still Frog did not stop. He made a long, deep dive into a river and came up on the other side. But the skookum leaped across. A second time she caught up with Frog. He was too tired to jump again. To save the fire, he spat it out of his mouth on Wood, and Wood swallowed it. The other two skookums joined their sister. All three stood by, helpless, not knowing how to take the fire away from Wood. Slowly they went back to their lodge on top of the mountain.

Then Coyote came to the place where the fire was, and the people came close, too. Coyote was very wise. He knew how to bring fire out of Wood. He showed people how to rub two dry sticks together until sparks came. He showed them how to use sparks to make chips and pine needles burn. [Clark 1953, 189]

And so, to this day, Wood contains Fire, and Fire resides in Wood.

Possibly as an extension of this idea of the resident in the container, or possibly from sheer analogy of form, carved or graphic images are often treated as containing or providing residences for supernatural spirits associated with those forms (see chapter 15). By setting up such an image, one could hope to entice the deity to come into residence to hear one's prayers. The renowned Egyptologist John Wilson provided the following discussion of this subject in an essay on the nature of the Egyptian worldview:

A god represented something important in the universe: the sky, a district of Egypt, or kingship. In terms of his function[,] that god had extensiveness and intangibility. But he might have a localization in our world, in a place where he might feel at home; that is, a shrine might be specified for him. In that shrine he might have a place of manifestation in an image. This image was not the god; it was merely a mechanism of stone or wood or metal to permit him to make an appearance. This is stated by the Egyptians in one of the creation accounts. The creator-god acted for the other gods, and "he made their bodies like that with which their hearts were satisfied. So the gods entered into their bodies of every (kind of) wood, of every (kind of) stone, or every (kind of) clay . . . in which they had taken form." [Memphite Theology] These images were provided for them so that they might have places in which to take visible form. Thus the god Amon might be at home in a stone statue of human form, in a specially selected ram, or in a specially selected gander. He remained himself and did not become identical with this form of appearance, and he had a different form of appearance for a different purpose, just as humans might maintain different homes or might have different garments. [Wilson 1949, 72–73]

The parallelism of these religious images to containers for residents is apparent. But the god may also be postulated to have a particular *form* because his or her *behavior* resembles something visible. (We are now analogizing from behavior to form.) Thus the Egyptians likened the round sun rolling across the sky each day to another ball that they frequently saw propelled great distances: the dung ball pushed by the industrious dung beetle, or scarab. Hence scarabs made in precious materials were often used to represent the sun deity.

Since a deity, then, can take up various "residences", we must quell our surprise at the variety of manifestations. Thus Zeus/Jupiter may appear equally in a planet, a lightning storm, or an oak.

Another, more opaque case of "containment" occurs in the Egyptian myth of Isis and Osiris. Seth jealously kills his brother Osiris, then puts the body into a chest, which he throws into the Nile so it will be carried away. When Isis learns of the murder, she searches far and wide for her husband's body. Eventually she finds it, but not in Egypt. At Byblos, far up the east coast of the Mediterranean, she locates the body and coffin "inside" a tree being used as a pillar in the king's palace [Walle 1963/73, 36]. Reworded: there is a special tree that exists only up in the Levant that contains Osiris, Lord of the Dead. We know from numerous documents that the Egyptians could obtain only from the Levant certain tree-resins they needed for the "proper" embalming of the dead, and when widespread warfare cut them off from this trade, the Egyptians lamented bitterly their inability to tend the dead properly. Here, with these resins, we have Osiris-in-a-tree. That this (lucrative) tree formed the "pillar" of the local kings' palaces may have been true monetarily as well as literally: analogy on another level.

But to understand better the many forms that analogy takes in myth, we need to turn to the most pivotal of all the myth principles, a joint offspring of the Analogy Principle and the Fallacy of Affirming the Consequent.

6

Willfulness:
The Atom or Thou

If the wind blows, somebody is blowing it; if the earth quakes, somebody is shaking it.

—C. Bagley [1930/91, 62]

WILLFULNESS PRINCIPLE
Humans will things to happen, then set about to make them happen. Therefore if something happens, it must have been willed.

Suppose a tree suddenly falls over in the forest. If others account for this by saying that somebody invisible pushed it, the explanation probably seems implausible. But consider *our* explanation: that an unimaginably large number of unimaginably small and invisible particles, working in concert but without any cognitive capacities to coordinate their activities, *pulled* the tree down. Is that really easier to believe?—especially for someone who knows nothing of the complex theory of gravitational pull by atomic particles?

Without thousands of years of recorded data fed through the geniuses who led to modern physics, the simplest explanation is that the tree fell either because it chose to or because someone willed it to do so—an analogy of cause, if you like, to daily life.

But if we can't *see* anyone or anything making many of the observable things happen, then we must conclude that some possessors of wills are invisible.

Enter the deities and spirits: invisible possessors of will, who can make things happen out of nowhere. They push trees over in the forest, bang things in the night, cure you of illnesses they gave you in the first place, make the rivers rise and the sun, moon, and stars cross the sky. The question is now not "*What* made the tree fall?" but "*Who* made it fall?" and to answer the latter, one's entire attention and data-collecting capacities are focused in a different direction.

The Frankforts, in their groundbreaking essay "Myth and Reality", refer to this as the "I/Thou" principle: "The fundamental difference between the attitudes of modern and ancient man as regards the surrounding world is this: for modern, scientific man the phenomenal world is primarily an 'It'; for ancient—and also for primitive—man it is a 'Thou'" [Frankfort and Frankfort 1949, 12].[1] They continue:

An object, an "It", can always be scientifically related to other objects and appear as part of a group or a series. . . . [H]ence, science is able to comprehend objects and events as ruled by universal laws which make their behaviour under given circumstances predictable. "Thou", on the other hand, is unique. "Thou" has the unprecedented, unparalleled, and unpredictable character of an individual, a presence known only in so far as it reveals itself. [Frankfort and Frankfort 1949, 13]

[1] Their essay, which we first read in 1976, was the original inspiration for much of this work. The other essays in the same book, by Egyptologist John Wilson and Sumerologist Thorkild Jacobsen, have provided much additional data.

Thus, for example, we moderns view the properties of flint in terms of its chemical structure, which we have deduced from a great backlog of laboratory analysis. But the Sumerologist Thorkild Jacobsen describes the ancient Near Easterner's knowledge of flint by saying that

> a particular lump of flint had a clearly recognizable personality and will. Dark, heavy, and hard, it would show a curious willingness to flake under the craftsman's tool though that tool was only of horn softer than the stone against which it was pressed. Now, this characteristic personality which confronts one here, in this particular lump of flint, may meet one also over there, in another lump of flint. . . . Wherever one met it, its name was "Flint", and it would suffer itself to flake easily. That was because it had once fought the god Ninurta, and Ninurta had imposed flaking on it as a punishment. [Jacobsen 1949, 143–44]

To the person who experiences the world as "Thou", the behavior of flint reveals submissiveness that must have resulted from punishment for wrongdoing, not silica with a structure leading to conchoidal fracturing. As the Frankforts put it, "'Thou' is not contemplated with intellectual detachment; it is experienced as life confronting life" [Frankfort and Frankfort 1949, 14].

Consider again the first myth we encountered, that of Crater Lake. From widespread studies we have come to view volcanos as vents for liquid rock melted by tectonic forces inside the earth. On the macroscale, one volcano is pretty much like another. But those who suffered from the explosion of Mount Mazama had only gotten as far as noting that some mountains had fire inside them. On the microscale, when that fire came forth it had "the unprecedented, unparalleled, and unpredictable character of an individual". By the Willfulness Principle, a clearly malevolent Will was revealing itself in pouring forth the river of fire—nay, the Curse of Fire.

Indeed, each of the volcanos up the coast was regarded as involving a quite different Will, as revealed by their different behaviors. Mount Shasta was the abode of a beneficent spirit (variously, the Chief of the Above World, or the Sky Spirit); Mounts Hood and Adams were said to be two warrior-sons of the Great Spirit who fought as rivals for the love of Sleeping Beauty Mountain [Clark 1953, 1]; another myth posits (our) Mount Rainier as the estranged wife of "a very tall and handsome young man" (our Mount Baker), both of whom keep stretching higher and higher to try to see each other [Clark 1953, 39–42].

Note the analogies on every level: two mountains that are getting higher are like two people stretching to see better. Two nearby mountains that erupt are like people fighting over something. In fact, two mountains that look similar must be members of the same clan or family, just as among humans the members of a family often look very much alike. Thus we arrive at the

KINSHIP PRINCIPLE
If two (willful) phenomena are perceived as alike, they must be kinsfolk. (Scientists say, like effects imply like causes; but myths say, like effects imply kinship between the willful beings.)

All over the world, the Winds are described as siblings [e.g., Bagley 1930, 62–63], and the Sun and Moon as brother and sister, although which gender belongs to which depends on the culture. In the Greco-Roman tradition, the moon goddess Artemis/Diana was twin sister to the sun god Apollo, but for the Norse the sun was a goddess and the moon her brother. Likewise for the Japanese: the creator's daughter Amaterasu received sovereignty over the sun and her brother Tsukiyomi over the moon.

Sometimes analogies of parent/child seem more apt, as in an episode in another myth of the Pacific Northwest:

Fair Maiden kept on standing there [at the coast], and the winds kept on blowing round her. At last the Changer came to her and said, "Why don't you lie down? If you stand, the winds will blow, and the whirlpools will keep on sucking in the people. Soon there will be none left."

So Fair Maiden lay down, and the Changer transformed her into Spieden Island. When her child was born, it was a small island of the same shape as Spieden and lying beside it. Today it is called Sentinel Island. [Clark 1953, 41]

Or note the names in this discussion of the big and little volcanos lying along a rift at Rabaul Harbor in New Guinea:

Folklore has it that the active volcano "Father" or "Ulawun" to the southwest, with two other hills known as "South Son" and "North Son," alternate in "smoking" with the Rabaul volcanoes known as "Mother" and her two offspring "North Daughter" and "South Daughter." [Jaggar 1945, 36]

Likenesses run in families. Indeed, because they are alike in their superior powers, the gods must all be related to each other. Working out
their family trees, however, may take eons.

To us, in the era of science, resemblance may stem from natural laws
or causes, historical relatedness (through either inheritance or borrowing), or pure accident. Linguists find it so, when tracing similar-sounding
words of similar meaning in different languages. Thus the word for
"mother" in many languages sounds something like English *mama* for
two "natural" reasons: first, consonant-plus-vowel syllables, repeated,
constitute the first attempts at vocal production in all children (our
brains just happen to be built that way), and second, pressing the lips
together is not only one of the simplest ways of cutting off the air-
stream (*ah* is what we sound like with our mouths wide open), but it is
the articulation most visible to infants watching adults speak and one
well under control from nursing. On the other hand, the resemblance
among English *stood* and Latin *status*, Greek *statós*, Sanskrit *stitáḥ*,
Russian *stal* (all meaning "stood") results from historical relationship:
all five languages are changed later forms of a common ancestor-
language we call proto-Indo-European, and this word was inherited
by each from that language. We could have chosen any number of inherited words for our example: English *new* corresponds to Latin
novus, Greek *né(w)os*, Sanskrit *návaḥ*, Russian *novyj*. We could also
choose similar words with a quite different historical relation: French
sandwich and Russian *sanvich* resemble English *sandwich* because the
first two languages borrowed it from English (after the fourth Earl of
Sandwich made the concept popular in the late eighteenth century).
But—case 3—English *bad* and Persian *bad*, which mean the same, or
German *hab-* "have" and Latin *hab-* "have" are the result of purest
accident (Latin *cap-* "capture" being the true cognate of Germanic *hab-/
have*.)

Natural laws, historical relatedness, accident: filing accurately into
these three categories requires masses of information.[2] Nonliterate cultures do the best they can, filing data according to shared resemblances,

---

[2] Anthropologists typically divide this same idea slightly differently, to the same purpose,
speaking in terms of (1) independent invention or "convergence" (a common response—
whether innate or merely practical, or even accidental—to a common stimulus), (2) borrowing or "diffusion" from one culture to another, and (3) common inheritance from the same
mother culture. Robert Blust has applied the paradigm, with interesting successes, to disen-
tangling the origins of several myths across the world [especially Blust 1999, 491, for discussion of method].

that is, by the "sharing of essentials" (as the Frankforts like to put it) on some level—any level.

By analogy to our own behavior, these spirits or unseen willers will probably act much like us. Thus, in the story of the Sky Spirit's daughter getting blown down the mountain, the Sky Spirit was presented as living with his family in a high-roofed lodge with a smoke-hole above the fire, exactly as the local people lived. Gods may live like us; they may also get angry or hungry, go to war or on a mission, fall in love or into a trap.

Just as people make choices in their behavior, so presumably do the gods and spirits; and we can try to influence those choices as we would each other's. When the Nile is refusing to rise, we can probably influence its behavior by offering a gift or a bribe, or presenting a contract: "if you do this for us, we'll do that for you", or even, "we've done this for you, so you owe us that". Covenants and binding agreements with the gods have been quite common through the ages, and much religious art has been produced to record such covenants, so that both the humans and the gods would remember what they were bound to do. The votive statue (or cloth, or candle) sitting patiently by the altar may fall into this category, just as surely as the painting representing a crucial mythic or religious event. The woolen *peplos* that the Athenian women made each year and gave to Athena to clothe her wooden statue depicted the battle of the gods and giants, a horrific contest which Athena helped the gods win. The dress thanked the goddess for saving her people— while reminding her please not to let those giants ever get loose again [Mansfield 1985; Barber 1992]. And just as mortals make visible reminders of their covenants, so may gods—as in the rainbow promising that a Great Flood will never again wipe out mankind.

Marcel Camus taps deep into our instant understanding of such matters in his film *Black Orpheus* (1959). The main character, a musician, tells the two young boys dogging his heels that he plays his guitar on the hillside early each morning to make the sun come up. One night he is murdered. In a panic the boys search out his guitar and scramble up the hill, trying desperately to play it in his stead—until the sun finally appears.

Covenants are one thing. But we can also try to trick the gods to get our way, as we might trick each other. By throwing sacrifices into the Nile *before* it rose, the pharaoh could trick the river into being the one behind on obligations: "I've already paid my half; now it's your turn."

Figure 4. Sculpture showing Atlas (right) bringing the Apples of the Hesperides to Herakles, who, with a cushion and a little help from Athena, holds up the sky. Metope from Temple of Zeus, Olympia, Greece, ca. 460 B.C.

When Atlas returned with the Apples of the Hesperides to where Herakles had temporarily shouldered the weight of the sky for him (figure 4), Atlas told Herakles he was glad to be rid of the burden and that Herakles could keep the job forever. "Uh, sure," says Herakles, thinking fast. "But would you just take it back for a moment while I adjust the pad on my shoulders?" As soon as Atlas had the sky back, Herakles picked up the prize apples and walked off.

Mortals tricking the gods gets really dicey, since gods clearly have powers we don't. But there was ample evidence that the gods tricked each other. Coyote tricked not only the skookums, but also his own sisters, in the story of how he obtained fire. At first he couldn't think of a plan to get the fire:

> So he decided to ask his three sisters who lived in his stomach in the form of huckleberries. They were very wise. They could tell him what to do.
>
> But at first his sisters in the form of huckleberries would not help him. "If we tell you," they said to Coyote, "you will say that you knew that yourself."
>
> Coyote remembered that his sisters did not like hail. So he looked up into the sky and called out, "Hail! Hail! Fall down from the sky."
>
> His sisters were afraid and cried, "Stop! Stop! Don't bring the hail. Don't bring the hail. We will tell you whatever you need to know."
>
> Then his three sisters told him how he could get a brand of fire from the three skookums and how he could bring it down the mountain to the people.
>
> When they had finished talking, Coyote said, "Yes, my sisters. That is what I thought. That was my plan all the time." [Clark 1953, 187–88]

In fact, Coyote is a classic example of what anthropologists call a trickster figure.

Tricksters occur in the mythologies of many cultures—for example, Maui in Hawaii, Hermes in Greece, and the prototype of Brer Rabbit in Africa.[3] Possibly the most renowned trickster from European culture was the Germanic Loki, a highly ambiguous figure treated as sometimes doing great good and sometimes great evil. Although a member of the race of giants (inherently evil), he hung out most of the time with the race of gods (inherently good, just as in Greece). The gods frequently begged him to defeat their enemies with his tricks; but he was constantly playing pranks on the gods too, for which they punished him. He cut off the grain goddess Sif's golden hair and even caused the death of Baldr, a favorite among the gods. For his transgressions he was chained to a mountain and tortured. This ambivalent deity will become less opaque as we go.

[3] For Tricksters see chapter 3 and Hynes and Doty 1993; for Coyote specifically, see Bright 1993.

Meanwhile, as we consider myths about willful beings, we must beware. Since *anything* that "happens" may be perceived as Willed, we mustn't assume that everything presented as having a will and a name is a living "person" in our sense. This holds not just for the Nile and the Chief of the Below World but, as we shall see, for Loki and Sif, Prometheus, Herakles, and so on.

If divine manifestations that resemble each other are kin, then opposites must hate each other:

ADVERSARY PRINCIPLE:
If two phenomena are perceived as the opposite of each other, they must be bitter enemies.

In Christian tradition, God and Lucifer are archenemies, one the principle of all that is good, the other of all that is evil. Interestingly, in the Bible this story is presented initially starting from the other end, much as in the Movie Construct. Lucifer (literally "bringer of light") was once high in Heaven, we learn. But when Lucifer set himself up as rival to God's power, he was thrown out of heaven like a meteor to become God's opposite, both in nature and in location:

> *How you are fallen from heaven, O Lucifer, son of Dawn!*
> *How you are cut down to the ground . . . !*
> *You said in your heart, "I will ascend to heaven,*
> *above the stars of God I will set my throne on high;*
> *I will sit on the mount of assembly in the far north;*
> *I will ascend above the heights of the clouds,*
> *I will make myself like the Most High."*
> *But you are brought down to Sheol, to the depths of the Pit.*[4] [Isaiah 14:12–15]

---

[4] Descriptions from other cultures collected by Masse [1998, 71 and passim] make "Lucifer" sound awfully like a supernova, especially one that apparently exploded in the Big Dipper (northern sky!) around 2700 B.C. Such explosions can shine brightly during the day for weeks before diminishing to the size of other stars. Masse [1998, 71] quotes a Mayan myth in which the sun complains: "It is not true that he is the sun, this Seven Macaw [Big Dipper], yet he magnifies himself, his wings. . . . But the scope of his face lies right around his own perch; his face does not reach everywhere beneath the sky" (as the sun's rays do). See chapter 16 for other myths encoding astronomy.

Another interesting pair of opposites, though not so starkly black and white, is Athena and Poseidon. They are constantly at loggerheads with each other, contesting for possession of Athens and fighting each other for the life and homecoming of Athena's devotee, crafty Odysseus. To see this opposition clearly, we must investigate what each is in charge of. Translators call Athena the goddess of wisdom; but that's not quite accurate (even if it might be, later, for her approximate Roman counterpart, Minerva). We see Athena revered as the protectress of her city of Athens, in charge of the fertility of its inhabitants, flocks, and crops, as well as goddess of warfare, shipbuilding, spinning, and weaving. That covers a lot. But it all falls into place if we take seriously her epithet as goddess of *tékhnē* (whence our word *technology*), which designates all that human craft can accomplish (including agriculture and warfare). Poseidon, for his part, was associated with the sea, but in Homer his chief epithet is "Earth-Shaker"—he is the bringer of earthquakes. How are quakes and ocean connected? Myths repeatedly associate him with quake-born, ocean-borne killer tsunamis (the roaring, pounding "bull from the sea"), such as that which he sent to fulfill Theseus's curse on his son Hippolytos, drowning the lad as he drove his horses along the shore. Poseidon is, in short, lord of all that is wildest and most untamable in nature—just the opposite of Athena's purview.[5]

This opposition shows up immediately in their contest for rule of Athens. Poseidon, seismic to the core, struck a rock and produced a salt spring, while Athena created the first olive tree—the most important and versatile domestic plant in the Aegean. Finding the salt spring remarkably less useful than the olive, the citizens voted Athena as winner. Poseidon revealed his displeasure by sending a tidal wave—what else?—in revenge, but Athena saved her people by stopping it at the foot of the Acropolis.

(Yes, it's entirely possible that an actual tidal wave, such as that from the eruption of Thera in 1625 B.C., could build up enough height in funneling up the Saronic Gulf to reach the Acropolis, more than three miles—five kilometers—inland [figure 5]. We'll meet similar waves in chapter 8. Note too that we are again told the explanation as part and parcel of the observation. Observation: a tidal wave came, stopping at the Acropolis. Explanation: since Athens was saved, it must have been Athena who saved it, by turning the tide in the nick of time; and it must have been Poseidon who sent it, since he was in charge of such waves.)

[5] This happens to parallel Claude Lévi-Strauss's well-known dichotomy encapsulated in his book title, *The Raw and the Cooked.*

Figure 5. View from the Athenian Akropolis of the Saronic Gulf, five kilometers away. Poseidon is reputed to have sent a tidal wave this distance—possibly the tsunami from Thera.

The method by which we fine-tuned our understanding of Athena's nature, by comparing it to that of her chief adversary, is widely useful enough to state as an analysing principle, the Adversary Method: *To help determine the domain of a deity, investigate the nature of his or her enemies.* Hilda Davidson, struggling to understand the often hazy remnants of Norse mythology, also came upon this method. Discussing Thor (who repeatedly battles evil giants and particularly the World Serpent, to save both men and gods from destruction), she remarks that despite all the distortions and losses "much may still be learned of the nature of a god by the adversaries whom he encounters" [Davidson 1981, 89].

Of all the adversary relations one might imagine, perhaps the most global is that encompassed by the Mesopotamian worldview. As Jacobsen explains, every type of event and thing in the entire world was perceived as possessing a Will, but the Mesopotamian person's experience of Nature

was not nearly so safe and reassuring as it was to the Egyptian. Through and under it he sensed a multitude of powerful individual wills, potentially divergent, potentially conflicting, fraught with a possibility of anarchy. He confronted in Nature gigantic and wilful [sic] individual powers.

To the Mesopotamian, accordingly, cosmic *order* did not appear as something given; rather it became something achieved—achieved through a continual integration of the many individual cosmic wills, each so powerful, so frightening. [Jacobsen 1949, 139]

Thus the universe was seen as run by an entire parliament of divine Willers who argued things out on high. Helpless humans, by contrast, served as their insignificant slaves, mere pawns of the mighty.

7

Multiple Aspects:
The More the Merrier

MULTIPLE-ASPECTS PRINCIPLE
A phenomenon may be explained mythically as many times as it has "significantly" different aspects.

Our modern desire to capture a single picture is photographic and static, whereas the ancient Egyptian's picture was cinematic and fluid. For example, we should want to know in our picture whether the sky was supported on posts or was held up by a god; the Egyptian would answer: "Yes, it is supported by posts or held up by a god—or it rests on walls, or it is a cow, or it is a goddess whose arms and feet touch the earth." Any one of these pictures would be satisfactory to him, according to his approach, and in a single picture he might show two different supports for the sky: the goddess whose arms and feet reach the earth, and the god who holds up the sky-goddess.
[Wilson 1949, 53–54]

Our science teachers train us to collect evidence for phenomena, in the hope that we may eventually compress the data into predictive rules or "scientific laws". If I perceive that the toast always falls jam-side down when I drop it, I want to formulate a law, on the premise that like effects have like causes, and then figure out why the law works that way. If I find an exception, I want to figure out what rule governs the exception.

But if the world consists of willful beings who make things happen by personal choice—beings who make my toast land on its sticky side out of spite or amusement—then one is not led to search for impersonal rules, but rather to ask "Who caused that?" and "Why me?" *Any* avenue of approach related to the situation might lead to the key; *any* resemblance to or point of contact with something else may prove useful to the problem of the moment. The circumstances under which I upended my toast today differed from yesterday's debacle. To know what Willer(s) to appease, it behooves me to collect as many analogies as possible to the situation to be explained. A phenomenon may be explained in this way as many times as it has significantly different aspects.

Each manifestation of the situation has its analogies. Like the Egyptians, the Greeks had several "sun gods", but each represented a different aspect of the sun and its activities. Helios was at base the light-giving disk, whereas Hyperion (literally "going over") fastened on the sun in its aspect of crossing the sky each day, and rosy-fingered Eos ("dawn") represented the phenomenon of sunlight reappearing each morning. Each of these aspects of the sun contributes in important (willful) ways to the total picture. But then what's left for Phoibos ("bright") Apollo—that handsome and vibrant young man who gave oracles and at least in classical and late Greek times, as sun god paralleled his twin sister, Artemis, as moon goddess? His attributes give him away: he appears to represent all that the sun causes by shedding its warming rays on us—vibrant life, hence youth and beauty. And oracles? To understand this, we need to know that most ancient Mediterranean peoples believed vision occurred through light coming *out* of the eye (cf. Plato, *Timaeus* 45; you've seen evidence—animal eyes shining back at you and your lantern/flashlight/headlights at night). By analogy, the great producer of light in the sky must be an eye (cf. figure 6). But its light shines on everything in the world, so it sees—hence knows—everything.[1] Who better to ask for information, then, than the owner of that all-seeing eye?

[1] This notion that seeing is knowing is so old within Indo-European languages and cultures that one of the principal Indo-European verbs of knowing is simply the archaic perfect

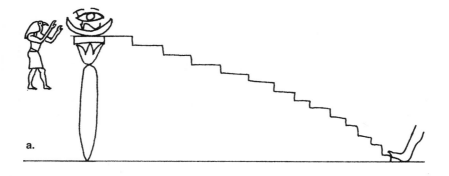

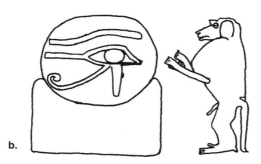

Figure 6. Celestial eyes. **(a)** The moon depicted as an eye, identified by its crescent and by the ibis-shaped moon god Thoth, sitting atop fourteen steps symbolizing the fourteen days it waxes from new to full moon. **(b)** The sun as an eye, in a disk sitting on the hieroglyph for "horizon", being worshipped by a baboon at dawn; from Twenty-first Dynasty papyrus of Hent-Taui.

Each analogy has its uses. Thus in Egypt, the sky as cow is useful for explaining the birth of the sun each day, while the cow/goddess arched over the earth helps explain where the stars and other celestial bodies are affixed. The four posts of the sky conveniently uphold the four cardinal directions, or the four points where the sun rises and sets at the solstices (chapter 16). If those celestially appointed pillars were to fall, life as we know it would stop.

Many analogies carry emotional baggage. In Norse mythology, gods

of the verb for "see"—as in Greek *(w)oîda* "I know, I have seen", from *(w)eídō* "I see" (cognate with Latin *video* "I see", and English *wit, wisdom*). For celestial lights as eyes, compare, for instance, Hawaiian myth [Masse 1995, 471 and passim]. Odin, whose one eye represents wisdom, should also fit here.

basically do good deeds, whereas giants do evil ones. The gods bring fertility and life, whereas the giants—many of whom are "frost giants"
(quite understandable in the Far North)—bring harm and devastation
to both gods and men. This differentiation can get quite specific. Thus
Thor is the valiant storm god who brings the life-giving rainstorms
while his lightning smites your enemies (evildoers all) and destroys their
crops. On the other hand, Thiassi is the evil storm giant who blasts *you*
with lightning and destroys *your* crops with his floods. In short, Thor
and Thiassi here represent the positive and negative aspects of the same
phenomenon. The Greeks made the same distinction between beneficent gods living on Olympus and evil giants chained underground for
their transgressions. Interestingly, the gods in the frigid North emerge as
much gloomier and more aware of their own potential doom than the
cheerful gods of the South, while the Northern giants cause mayhem on
a far more frequent schedule than those of the sunny South.

Each analogy has its frame of reference, its viewpoint. The Frankforts remark that the myth-user "wants to find a cause as specific and
individual as the event which it must explain. . . . Since he does not isolate an event from its attending circumstances, he does not look for one
single explanation which must hold good under all conditions. Death,
considered with some detachment as a state of being, is viewed as a substance inherent in all who are dead or about to die. But death considered emotionally is the act of hostile will" [Frankfort and Frankfort
1949, 25]. Thus the traditional vampires of Europe revealed their presence by willfully causing the deaths of their fellow villagers: if everyone
was getting sick and dying, a vampire must have a grudge against the
village. But at the same time death was viewed as something one could
"catch" from others, simply by getting too close. Old women had to
wash and dress the dead; if they caught death, too bad—society would
still survive [Barber 1988].

Because a phenomenon may have so many aspects, modern scholars
of myth in particular and of ancient cultures in general do well to cultivate as a working method the knack of dollying their mental "camera"
around to as many different viewpoints as possible. Until we see what
the mythmakers are looking at on this particular occasion—from their
point of view or "camera angle"—it may be impossible to understand
what they are talking about. We'll refer to this powerful method as
solving the Camera-Angle Problem: *To understand what a story is talking about, we may have to observe the situation from a very particular
viewpoint.*

Linguists studying language acquisition in children often report this phenomenon. Until you see what Baby is looking at, you can't understand what Baby is trying to communicate. To interpret a toddler's declaration, "Mommy sock!", you need to know whether the child is looking at its own feet or at Mommy's feet, or diving in the laundry basket [Bloom 1970, 9–10, 47–48]. The child's gaze silently provides all that context for interpretation that adults learn to encode into the utterance itself.

In mythology, to understand what (let's say) the Egyptians talk about, you have to see what the Egyptians saw. We had to get into our viewfinder the Egyptian sources of their all-important mortuary supplies to see how Isis might find Osiris inside a tree at Byblos. To understand why Ptah's creation of the universe takes place on a primeval mound of mud that differentiates itself from the waters of chaos, we have to focus on what Egyptians saw when the all-covering Nile floodwaters began to recede each year: the tip of a mound of mud here, then one there, growing in size until the whole land of Egypt gradually reappeared, completely refertilized and ready to bear new life-giving crops. Life, to the Egyptian, began each year with and on those mounds. Some have suggested that the shape of the pyramids constitutes a geometric analog of the Primeval Mound of Mud [Wilson 1949, 60].

Hilda Davidson posits a camera-angle solution to the origin of Odin's eight-legged horse, Sleipnir (figure 7). Odin included among his duties the receiving of the dead. So Davidson places her camera to watch

Figure 7. Odin's eight-legged horse, Sleipnir, that carries off the souls of the dead. Viking period memorial stone; Alskog, Tjangvide, Gotland.

the bier on which a dead man is carried in the funeral procession by four
bearers; borne along thus, he may be described as riding on a steed with
eight legs. Confirmation of this is found in a funeral dirge recorded by Ver-
rier Elwin among the Gonds in India. It contains references to Bagri Maro,
the horse with eight legs, and it is clear from the song that this is the dead
man's bier. . . . One verse of it runs:

> *What horse is this?*
> *It is the horse Bagri Maro.*
> *What should we say of its legs?*
> *This horse has eight legs.*
> *What should we say of its heads?*
> *This horse has four heads. . . .*
> *Catch the bridle and mount the horse.*

The representation of Odin's eight-legged steed could arise naturally out of
such an image, and this is in accordance with the picture of Sleipnir as a
horse that could bear its rider to the land of the dead. [Davidson 1981,
142–43]

(Noting the pairs of horses sometimes found in the entryways of Mycenaean Greek tombs, one may wonder if this conception of the eight-
legged steed carrying the dead goes back to earlier, Indo-European
times.)

Mott Greene, too, in his perceptive book *Natural Knowledge in
Preclassical Antiquity*, notices the effects of Camera Angle—for example in his essay on Egyptian fractions. He points out that whereas
our mathematical efforts move toward finding the most *general* solutions to the use of numbers, the Egyptians had "no concept of number in abstraction from things numbered" [Greene 1992, 35]. Instead, both numbering and fractions constituted direct ways of
dealing with material goods, such as divvying the available loaves of
bread and jugs of beer among the workmen or quarrying appropriate
blocks of stone for a job—a purely "practical measurement of quanti-
ties, areas, and volumes" [Greene 1992, 34]. To understand why the
Egyptians never moved beyond their seemingly cumbersome system
of "unit fractions", Greene demonstrates, we need to see what problems they were looking at. We need to see the world from their camera angle.

In fact, after tackling several more problems that have baffled scholars because they had inappropriate camera angles (see chapter 8), Greene concludes, "there is a wisdom in assuming that the people whose works one studies [such as myths and other literature] are fully capable of describing their world", and that one is obliged to make that assumption at the very least "until one knows enough about that world to assay what they said about it" [Greene 1992, 87]. In other words, the onus is on *us* to find the appropriate position from which to assess their reports, rather than simply dismissing the reports as empty—like a deaf man dismissing the phenomenon of sound as an old wives' tale. If we have become deaf, we must strive to build a sound spectrograph, just as we have built devices to show the presence of light waves beyond our range of vision.

The Principle of Multiple Aspects creates some curious eddies around it. Because a phenomenon may be broken up into as many pieces as it has significantly different aspects, and because different cultures have different camera angles, we may find that pieces do not match well from one culture to the next. We see this effect all the time in cross-linguistic studies—as in the famous example of the rainbow.

To speakers of English this spectrum clearly consists of six colors: red, orange, yellow, green, blue, and violet. Except, of course, for folks who insist on a seventh color, indigo, between blue and violet. So which is it, six colors or seven? Neither, and both . . . and anything else you please. Physicists assure us that the visible spectrum, the rainbow, consists of an *even gradation* of electromagnetic wavelengths from the longest (red) to the shortest (violet) that we can see. So any divisions we make are all in our heads. If we already find cultural variation within English, the variations beyond it proliferate almost limitlessly. (We perceive color via cones in the back of the eye that react at peak to different wavelengths; physiologists find that our brains, too, peak in their reactions to certain sectors of visible light. These findings of how our heads work explain some of the cross-cultural correlations that we find, but still do not entirely explain a rainbow cut into, say, six pieces as in English. Much remains culturally arbitrary. [Compare Pinker 1995, 59–64.])

The classical Greeks, for instance, saw the spectrum of colors in five basic units, not six, and not spread linearly across the wavelengths but largely split between light and dark, as in many languages.[2] One could lay out their terms graphically as follows (with the red end of the spectrum at left and the violet end at right):

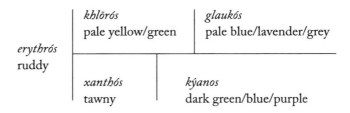

	khlōrós pale yellow/green	*glaukós* pale blue/lavender/grey
erythrós ruddy	*xanthós* tawny	*kýanos* dark green/blue/purple

Thus *erythrós* (cognate with English *red* and from which we borrowed *erythro-cyte* "red blood cell") denotes colors at the red end of the spectrum. As in Balkan folk dress, it seems to lump what we would call bright orange and deep pink together with red. From there on, pale is distinguished from dark or intense. Thus *khlōrós* (whence Eng. *chlorophyl*) refers to all those pale yellow-to-green colors you see in the grass when you lift a brick lying on it for days, whereas *glaukós* (borrowed in Eng. *glauc-oma*) encompasses the remaining pale colors, seen in sky and mist: light blue and lavender shading off into grey. (So there is no need to translate Homer's epithet *glaukôpis Athénē* as "grey-eyed Athena"— she could perfectly well be blue-eyed.) The dark side, on the other hand, breaks the spectrum not between our green and blue, as the light side does, but between green and yellow. Thus *xanthós* covers the tawny yellows (plus light brown), while *kýanos* (whence Eng. *cyan-ide*) refers to dark green, dark blue, and purple. And suddenly our camera attains the proper angle to see why Homer can refer to the "wine-dark sea": the dark blue-green of the ocean (as we see things) falls into the same color-box for the Greeks as dark purply-red wine.

Such nonmatching divisions weigh heavily for the argument that traditional literature, like poetry and like the prose of great stylists, simply cannot be translated into another language without major loss of content. You can explain till you're purple, but the instant *recognition* of deep-seated relationships and structure cannot be re-achieved. Robert

---

[2] Some languages, such as Jalé and others of Highland New Guinea, have basic color terms only for "bright" versus "dark". More languages distinguish red but *otherwise* categorize colors only as light and dark: for instance, many tongues of the Niger-Congo family, but also Pomo (California), Toda (southern India), and Arawak (South America) [Berlin and Kay 1969, 23–25, 52–63, and passim].

Frost encapsulated it by saying, "Poetry is what gets lost in translation" [Winokur 1986, 63], while Joshua Katz has pointed out to us an interesting discussion of this problem by Stephanie Jamison that he dubs the *Goldilocks Principle*:

> The word "porridge" is a fairly rare one for American English speakers, and for most of us—however long removed from childhood—it has one strong semantic association. This single word, no matter what context we hear it in, can instantly evoke the whole narrative complex of Goldilocks and the Three Bears, the bowls of steaming porridge, the messy beds. The word "oatmeal" on the other hand does not. Alertness to the different associational ranges of two apparent synonyms can give a window on the cultural knowledge of the speakers who have these unconscious distinctions. But marginal vocabulary is not the only source of this knowledge. The same instant access to the same narrative is given by the perfectly well-formed, syntactically uninteresting English sentence, "Who's been sleeping in my bed?" Formulaic language of this sort binds a speech community with invisible semantic fetters. [Jamison 1996, 11]

But the next language will not have the same bindings.

Phenomena such as these have led us to call the incommensurateness in how people divide and label things the

RAINBOW COROLLARY
Different peoples divide up the same world differently, as they fasten onto different aspects within the multiplicity.

Consider water. We view it simply as H_2O. But the Hawaiians distinguish *wai* "sweet water" from *kai* "salt water", and *kai*, the shallow ocean near shore, from *moana* "deep sea" (the line between turquoise *kai* and lapis *moana* being sharply evident to the eye). The Mesopotamians, for their part, divided water into the sweet waters that spring from the earth (*Apsu*), the salty sea (*Ti'amat*), storm waters that pelt us from above (*Enlil*), and water as a generative agent (*Enki*) [Jacobsen 1949, 153–61, 184–86]. The early Indo-Europeans, living as they did in the vast, landlocked expanses of western Eurasia, seem to have centered their notions of water on storms and great rivers (both of which abound in that area), without much regard for the ocean. Or so we gather from the comparative reconstructions of both their vocabulary and their myths. Thus the daughter cultures typically have as one of their top deities a lightning-wielding god of storm clouds (such as Roman Jupiter, Greek Zeus,[3] Indic Indra, Germanic Thor, or Slavic Perun), and another, often his brother, who presides over bodies of water (e.g., Roman Neptune, Greek Poseidon [a hybrid character, as we have seen], Indic Apām Nápāt, and probably Irish Nechtan [Littleton 1973]). The Egyptians, however, experienced all water as coming from the Nile (rain did not fall in Egypt), so those foreign countries not watered directly by the Nile simply had their Nile above them—a view of rain that most of us would not recognize readily. A hymn to Aten states: "Thou makest that whereon all distant countries live. Thou hast put (another) Nile in the sky, so that it may come down for them . . . in order to moisten their fields" [Wilson 1949, 46]. These Niles, in turn, flowed from Nun, the "primordial waters out of which life first issued", which continued both to flow under the (platter-shaped) earth and to encircle it as the sea [Wilson 1949, 54–55].

The sheer multiplicity of divine principles available to be worshipped often leads to a further perturbation of the picture. If two cultures become closely familiar with each other's religions, thanks to invasion or intense trade, people begin to see yet more aspects of the world than before, aspects which their new acquaintances view as willful and hence potentially dangerous if slighted. Prudence suggests that one adopt these new divinities. We wouldn't want to offend a deity, now, would we? As Pindar says, "It is proper for men to speak only good about the gods—for there is less blame that way" [*Olympian Ode* 1:35].

HEDGING YOUR BETS

If someone else is worshipping a different (Willful) aspect than you, add or graft it onto your pantheon to be safe.

The Romans, for example, adopted the Egyptian cult of Isis, and the people of late classical Crete borrowed the Egyptian cult of Nofert (which presently got Christianized as St. Onouphrios or Onofre).

Examples of hedging abound among people barely converted to Christianity. Russian ethnographers working in remote parts of Siberia in the twentieth century often commented on seeing Christian icons inside a nomad's tent set up right beside non-Christian idols or shamanistic equipment [Diószegi 1960/68, 125]. But a millennium earlier,

---

[3] Zeus and Jupiter (or Jove) are also related etymologically—seen more easily in the form of Zeus's name used for prayers and invocations: *Zeû páter* "Zeus the Father", equalling *Jupiter* "Jove the Father".

the missionaries and priests trying to convert the Slavs to Christianity complained of the identical thing in Russian huts. The Russians even coined a term for it: *dvoeverie* "double belief".

Evidence for double belief permeates the mythologies of Europe. Long before Christianity, the Indo-Europeans had perfectly good water gods, within a pantheon representing life as they knew it on the steppes. But when that branch we know as the Greeks arrived in Greece and settled among the local Aegean populace—who had their own full pantheon mirroring life as they knew it in the Aegean—the Greeks clearly discovered that their deities did not cover quite everything. One important omission was tsunamis. Earthquakes they already knew: giants chained to the earth caused quakes—age-old giants like Prometheus, who has a good Indo-European name [Watkins 1995, 256n]. But killer tidal waves were new. So they grafted what was apparently a local god (Poseidon) in charge of both quakes and giant ocean-waves into their pantheon where our comparisons would lead us to expect the linguistic and functional equivalent of Neptune/Apā́ṃ Nápāt, Lord of Waters.

Athena was also grafted in: her name is non-Indo-European and her functions superfluous. She wields the lightning? Zeus already does that. In charge of war? The Greeks already had a perfectly good war god, and a culturally more appropriate male at that: Ares, whose name probably connects etymologically with the Iranian word for an elite warrior band, *Aryā-* "Aryan", center of early Indo-European society, and with the Greek word "best", *áristos* (whence our word *aristo-cracy*, borrowed straight from Greek).[4] Men dominated Indo-European society from top to bottom.

So why this uppity goddess? Evidence shows clearly that many early Aegean groups organized themselves matrilineally, with all inheritance, including kingship, coming down through the female line (see chapter 13). We even have one matrilineal law code, preserved from early classical Crete: a Minoan holdover [Willetts 1967]. If infiltrating Greeks wished to live in Athens, the city that traditionally *belonged* to Athena, they had better find some way to graft her into their pantheon, and a politic way at that. Fine: make her Zeus's favorite daughter, born straight from his head without a mother, sharing his magisterial traits as a precocious and indulged offspring. From just the right camera angle, Athena makes sense.

---

[4] Warren Cowgill, personal communication 1965.

Note that any time we find two deities in a single culture who seem to have the same purview, we do well to suspect grafting from elsewhere. Take Prometheus, whose name is Indo-European. He was a giant (evil) who, like Loki, hung around with the gods (good), and did humankind the signal service of bringing them fire and teaching them all manner of crafts, such as the fiery forging of metals. As such he became the divine overseer of crafts and metalworking. The gods did not take kindly to the stealing of Fire, of course, reasoning (Movie Construct:) that it made humans more nearly like gods, so they punished Prometheus by fastening him to a mountain and setting an eagle to peck at him (see chapter 17). But the Greeks had a second god of crafts and smithing, Hephaistos, whose forge lay inside Mount Etna—you could see the smoke and sparks when he was at work. Everything points to Hephaistos as a late graft into Greek lore from another—clearly Mediterranean—culture. Even his name has no Greek etymology.

As so often, a strongly parallel phenomenon exists in language, and this method of investigating doublets has proved tremendously fruitful in archaeolinguistics. To see how this works, consider the masses of double vocabulary in English that resulted from three centuries of French-speaking overlords in England after the Norman Conquest of A.D. 1066. The Anglo-Saxon underling *lived* in a *room* and *sweated* as he *ate*, after feeding the *cows*, *sheep*, and *swine*; whereas the nobleman *inhabited* a *chamber* and *perspired* as he *dined* on *beef*, *mutton*, and *pork*. The peasant's words—and the grammar—come straight from proto-Indo-European (through five thousand years of sound changes), or at least from proto-Germanic (two thousand years back), whereas milord's terms (still mostly with upper-class connotations even today) got grafted into English from French, just the way Hephaistos and Athena got grafted into the Greek pantheon.

Now take a prehistoric example. Ancient Greek textile vocabulary overflows with pairs of words for the same or nearly the same things, one term having an Indo-European etymology and the other not. The Indo-European terms prove sufficient only for the equipment of a simple band-loom, whereas the additional words necessary for operating the large warp-weighted loom are all borrowed, and we find two words each (one Indo-European, one not) for most of the tools and operations necessary for simple band-weaving (warp, weft, weave, beat in) and thread preparation (spin, spindle, thread, sew, needle, et cetera). This matches the archaeological record. The warp-weighted loom and its use developed into a sophisticated craft in a specific area of south-*central*

Europe in the early Neolithic, long before the Indo-Europeans broke apart, and this loom never spread east of the Dniepr River. So we must conclude that the Greeks moved into this textile-rich culture from the east and borrowed the more sophisticated craft, words and all, just as they borrowed Athena, goddess of weaving [Barber 1991, 260–82].

The trick is to spot the telltale signs of such mergings and turn them to account in reconstructing the past, using the Doublet Clue: *Double terminology or doublets within a belief system (especially en masse) indicate that one culture has absorbed another culture and/or changed its environment or technology. The doublets can be milked accordingly for information about the former natures of these cultures and the changes that occurred.*

Syncretism, a form of "doubling", happens all the time, all over the world. The ancient Slavs clearly took over deities like Simargl (figure 8a–b) from the Iranians, bolstering their own panoply of fertility spirits [Rybakov 1968], while the early Norse tribes apparently doubled their pantheon by adding the somewhat hazy Vanir (fertility gods, perhaps of earlier farmers in the area?) to the sharply defined Aesir—a second race of gods that included Thor, Odin, and other Indo-European types. According to the myths, the Aesir vanquished and absorbed the Vanir after much fighting. Hilda Davidson, in her careful summary of Norse mythology, puzzles that "we have the strange double of Odin, the god Od (*Óðr*), who is said to have been Freyja's husband, for whom she wept after he left her" [Davidson 1981, 154]. Now, Odin and his wife Frigg belong to the Aesir, whereas Od (apparently a "dying god" so common in fertility cults) and Freyja belong to the Vanir [Davidson 1981, 111–12]. Freyja and Frigg, like Od and Odin, are also doublets, both goddesses having to do with procreation and childbirth. (The clear etymological connections in both pairs of names suggest that those "earlier farmers" were fellow Germanic-speakers, of a different—lost?—dialect group.)

Deleting deities from the pantheon, on the other hand, causes far more trouble than adding or grafting, although for the same reason: fear of offending divine powers. Thus when Socrates appeared to advocate the position that there was one divine principle instead of a bunch of silly "gods" seducing each other, stealing, and having other undignified adventures, he was sentenced to death as too dangerous to the community. Similarly, Christians advocating the Trinity have repeatedly branded as heretics those Christians who maintain the unity of God. Before that, the Romans persecuted the monotheistic Christians for failing to pay homage to the vast Roman pantheon. Long before any of these, the Egyptian New Kingdom pharaoh Akhenaten declared that the Aten (sun-disk) was the sole god of the universe, thereby ousting the traditional throng of Egyptian deities. Upon his death, the priests of Amon-Ra reinstated the old religion, systematically destroyed Akhenaten's monuments, and expunged the heretic-king's name from the records, thereby attempting to destroy the immortality due a pharaoh, and perhaps to placate the gods he had demoted.

HERETIC SYNDROME

Treat as heretics those who wish to **reduce** *the pantheon: it threatens your security.*

Even taking away part of God's perceived domain can raise the alarm, as Galileo found to his distress when he showed evidence that Earth was not the center of the universe.

Another little eddy spawned by Hedging one's Bets involves what William Sullivan aptly terms *guerrilla syncretism*. This occurs when one culture is forced to swallow the religion of another and resorts to subterfuge. Sullivan elaborates:

> Because [Spanish] churchmen meted out severe punishment, up to and including death, for unrepentant adherence to the old ways, the Andean peoples quickly learned to take on the appearance of piety while continuing, to the extent possible, exactly as they had done before.
>
> One such example transpired on the Eve of All Souls' Day (Halloween). In Inca times the ancestors were thought to return annually to earth, and this festival was celebrated at the December solstice. The custom was to provide food and drink, thus maintaining the correct relationship with the ancestors. The peasantry, recognizing the pagan roots of a Christian custom, had taken to propitiating the ancestors on the day allotted to the ancestors in the Christian liturgical calendar. To this day, in Mexico and Peru, native peoples bring a picnic dinner to the cemetery on All Hallows' Eve, waiting for the dawn, and the return of the dead. [Sullivan 1996, 34]

It is known as *Día de los Muertos*, the Day of the Dead. Ironically, even the people of Rome had been loath to give up their ancient household protectors, the Lares and the Penates, when first Christianized, and they syncretized them into a system of patron saints still extant today.

East Slavs acted similarly. Instead of giving up their old belief system, they merely renamed their divinities with seemingly Christian names and kept on as before. Thus the storm god Perun stepped into the persona of the biblical prophet Elijah (Rus. *Ilja*), associated with whirlwinds, while the midsummer festival that involved jumping into lakes for a midnight swim (plus a lot else during the night) became the festival of John the Baptist ("John the Bather": *Ivan Kupala*). Even in the twentieth century, rural farmers in such places as Bulgaria and Ukraine who considered themselves Christians continued to carry out flatly pagan fertility rituals, such as the winter, spring, and summer Rusalii, adjusted slightly to fit the calendar of the church [Barber 1997]. As recently as 1993, in the newly reopened cathedral in Kiev, we saw ritual towels embroidered with symbols of fertility and protection—symbols traceable directly back to the Neolithic—freshly tied to the brass rails around the saints' coffins. For centuries such non-Christian towels decorated the Christian icons in the icon-corner of the farmhouse; and at a wedding, the groom and his bride sat, appropriately, under the icons of the Savior and the Mother of God—for protection and, yes, fertility: a case of Guerrilla Syncretism with archaic pagan images of male and female [see, e.g., Ivashneva and Razumovskaja 1981, 36–37]. The faces and names changed, but the purposes lived on.

For such crucial projects as fertility and protection, however, the multiplicity of aspects that simple agrarian societies have found to revel in has yet another purpose than simply hedging one's bets. The more aspects one can appeal to, the stronger the magic will be. Thus, among the East and South Slavs, the bride was seated successively or simultaneously on the kneading trough, on furs (borrowed if necessary), with someone's baby boy on her knee, under the icon of the Mother of God, and so on, while she was ritually pelted with hops, coins, grain (cf. our rice-throwing), and, in recent times, candy; and the marriage bed was made on top of sheaves of wheat and rye, and often in the barn among the fertile animals. All this was intended analogically to saturate her with hoped-for wealth and fertility—the more symbols and aspects of them the better.

The Principle of Multiple Aspects spills over bounteously into ritual and magic. Individual objects used for ritual purposes presumably carried more efficacy if loaded with multiple symbols of such qualities as fertility. Thus if a ritual towel or wedding bracelet has an ornamental design resembling at once a cloning hops vine and a woman in labor and perhaps a frog (which in shape resembles a pregnant woman squatting with her legs spread for parturition: figure 8b), so much the better:

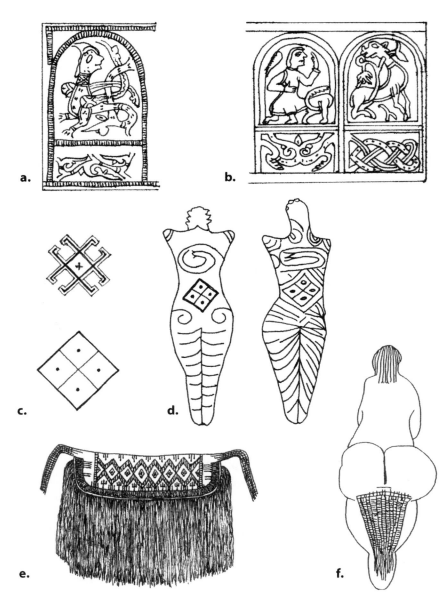

Figure 8. Archaic European fertility motifs. **(a)** Simargl, a four-footed "sprouting" vegetation deity (with "sown field" motif on collar), on ritual bracelet from Staryj Rjazan'; 11th century. **(b)** Simargls (above) and hops vine resembling frog and birthing woman (below left), on ritual bracelet from Tver'; 12th century. **(c)** Lozenge-shaped motifs: simple version of "hooked lozenge" (vulva) above; "sown field" below. **(d)** Neolithic clay figurines with "sown field" motif: furrows incised, dots impressed by grains of wheat; Cucuteni/Tripolye culture (Ukraine and Romania), ca. 4000 B.C. **(e)** Albanian "string skirt" from Mirdite area, worn by women of childbearing age, decorated with fertility lozenges. **(f)** Palaeolithic "Venus" figure wearing "string skirt"; Lespugue, France, ca. 20,000 B.C.

the fertility magic will be the stronger for it. Hops recommend themselves as symbols of fertility by the masses of cone-shaped fruits they produce, by their adventitiousness (spreading quickly by underground runners as well as by seed), and by the speed with which the vinetips grow in the spring—clocked at sometimes six inches per day [Rybakov 1968; Barber 1997].

Rural dress in East Europe, particularly that of brides, is similarly saturated with multiple symbols of fertility and protection encoded into color, design, placement, material, number, and anything else that can be drafted for the task. Thus, for example, red (life-affirming) ornaments typically appear at the openings to the clothing, to ward off the (Willful) sickness demons that might otherwise climb in. Protective roses adorn the sleeves and fronts of both men's and women's shirts, while the women's carry in addition rows of lozenges for fertility. Lozenges come in two chief varieties (figure 8c): one with rays or hooks around it, representing the vulva, and the other with an X inside that divides it into four small lozenges, each with a dot inside. The latter is known as the "sown field" motif and is supposed to represent a field with plowed furrows (the interior lines) sown with seeds (the dots).

Is "sown field" a late interpretation, cobbled up by or for anthropologists?

No. The motif can be traced in East European art back through the centuries all the way to the Neolithic cultivators of East Europe, ca. 4000 B.C., when the Tripolye farmers (in today's Ukraine and Romania) made clay figurines of naked women, some of which have this design incised on the belly or buttocks (figure 8d). The dots in these cases were made by impressing actual grains of wheat into the clay: truly a sown field, about to produce new life. Beliefs and their symbols, just like volcano myths, can survive 6000 years.

And longer. Until recently, women of childbearing age in this area wore a garment called a back-apron. Prepubescent girls were not entitled to wear it: donning it showed the community the girl had reached physical maturity and could be courted for marriage [Barber 1999 including figs. 2.1–2.4]. Traditionally it was woven in a squared pattern (first depicted on female figurines in the Late Neolithic and Bronze Ages) and often embellished for extra potency with the "sown field" motif and/or the hooked lozenge. It also carried little pompoms or fringes, remnants of a yet older tradition still in use from the Urals to the Adriatic, in the form of an apron nicknamed a *string skirt* (figure 8e–f). Like the squared back-apron, the string skirt marked its wearer as a woman who had reached childbearing age, and it was still in use quite recently among the (non-Indo-European) Mordvins east of Moscow and among diverse groups in the Balkans—Slavs, Romanians, Greeks, Vlachs, Albanians.[5] We can trace the string skirt back through the Iron Age (depicted in Archaic and Hellenistic art, and mentioned by Homer), the Bronze and Neolithic Ages (preserved in graves and depicted on numerous figurines), all the way to the Gravettian "Venus figures" of 20,000 B.C., some of whom wear such skirts over obviously mature female anatomy (figure 8f). If a belief system and its specific symbols can survive so staunchly for over 20,000 years, why not a myth?

[5] We own a string skirt worn daily by a woman in northern Albania as recently as 1998 (figure 8e). The woman expected to wear such garments (she had others) the rest of her life "because we always have". It still serves as the badge of honor of matured women and is decorated with a narrow band of hooked lozenges. In many regions, the sacred fringes were gradually displaced to shoulders, head, or sleeves, or to the edges of a woven apron in the local ethnic dress; but they were seldom lost altogether in the area Christianized by the relatively tolerant Eastern Orthodox Church [Barber 1999].

8

Multiple Viewpoints: Ear, Trunk, or Tail

MISMATCH EFFECT

The same real event reported by two different sources may be reported in wildly different forms, which may therefore seem unrelated at first glance.

Another serious eddy generated by the multiplicity of possible views is that the same noteworthy event experienced by two different people or cultures may go down in history (oral or otherwise) in almost unrecognizably different forms, as the tellers fasten onto different aspects to report. The famous Sufi story of five blind men encountering different parts of the same elephant—trunk, ear, leg, and so forth—encapsulates this problem.

Bearing the elephant-feelers in mind, imagine the 1980 eruption of Mount St. Helens, a well-documented natural event, as described by people (A) on the mountainside, (B) in the Toutle River valley, (C) in Portland, and (D) in eastern Washington and Idaho.

Group D, farthest away, did not see the actual eruption (at 8:32 A.M.) but experienced it soon afterwards as a choking blizzard of ash that blotted out the sun all day, covering everything inches deep in gritty, grey-white, lung-destroying powder and making "life as usual" quite impossible for a while. In Yakima, Washington, 85 miles due east, *National Geographic* reported that

> midnight gloom arrived at 9:30 in the morning and streetlamps burned all day. In memory it has become Black Sunday. . . . It was more than blackness—it was blackness that hid the unknown. No headlights could cut it, to reveal the stalled car ahead. Largely composed of fine volcanic glass particles, the cloud was itself a mass of cutting edges. For insects, the edges quickly abraded wax coatings and allowed vital body fluids to escape—dehydration and death. Some small creatures quickly choked. . . . Larger creatures avoided suffocation but seemed disoriented. . . .
>
> Like their neighbors, the Zirkles have grim memories of Black Sunday. "The darkness came so fast there was no time to think about trying to run, even if we'd wanted to," Bill said. His wife, Pat, and three children fled indoors, expecting the most horrendous thunderstorm of their lives. They were right, but it heralded ash instead of rain.
>
> "And it was close," Bill said, "so close that you saw lightning and heard thunder almost at the same time. One bolt hit between me and a neighbor—jarred the ground." [Findley 1981, 50, 53, 61]

(Volcanic ash-clouds typically carry supercharged static electricity.) Two days after the eruption, the *San Francisco Chronicle* reported:

> In parts of Eastern Washington, Idaho and Montana—where as much as six inches of ash covered the ground in some places—the fallout forced the

closing of schools, businesses, train stations, airports and highways. . . . In many areas, emergency shelters were set up to aid residents who had difficulty breathing, and stranded motorists whose cars stalled with clogged air filters. . . .

"The wind's blowin' out of the trees like a blizzard," [a police lieutenant] said. "The only things open are medical facilities, food stores and emergency operations. You can't even drive on it—it's worse than driving on ice."

The lieutenant said merchants . . . who attempted to hose the ash off their sidewalks only managed to produce "a gooey mud that's really slick."

A man in Spokane said that it looked like "the contents of a vacuum cleaner bag" had been dumped on the city.

A Morton, Wash., resident said going out of doors was "like sticking your head in the fireplace and stirring up the ashes." [Jennings 1980, 1, 4]

Group C had a ringside view of the eruption—relatives telephoned us and described the towering pillar of smoke overshadowing their house that Sunday morning. A magnitude 5.0 earthquake and huge soundwave generated at the moment of explosion announced the proceedings. (Even 200 miles away, the blast "sounded like artillery", said a Washington resident: "Our house was just shaking" [Petit 1980, 1].) A geological report described the pillar thus:

In the air, boiling into the sky to an altitude of 65,000–80,000 feet (20,000–25,000 meters), the volcano's vertical plume of gas, ash, steam, and dust trailed off to the northeast. Inside that tall plume could be seen strong convective upwelling currents, while stratus clouds were entrained or "drawn in" at several levels within the vertical column. At the same time, violent flashes of lightning were seen throughout the height of the column, and as the mushroom cap formed, it began expanding outward at an altitude of about 50,000 feet (15,000 meters). [Rosenfeld and Cooke 1982, 16]

But Portland, Oregon, lay well beyond the path of the hot pyroclastics and blessedly upwind of the ash-cloud that engulfed much of Washington (Group D).

Group B scrambled for their lives as a wall of thick, muddy, ninety-degree water, laden with half-cooked trout and thousands of trees snapped off by the initial blasts, raced down the valley toward the sea. "I could hear it crackling from my house. . . . It was wall-to-wall logs", said a man living near the bottom of the mountain [*San Francisco Chronicle* May 19, 1980, 1].

Most of Group A didn't live to tell what they saw, but the few who did struggled to describe things so extraordinary and horrific that sometimes only similes sufficed:

[A member] of a tree-planting crew, at work on the foot of the mountain itself, only three miles from the summit on the south side . . . remembers the instant of stunned disbelief when the eruption began: "There was no sound to it, not a sound—it was like a silent movie, and we were all in it. First the ash cloud shot out to the east, then to the west, then some lighter stuff started shooting straight up. At the same time the ash curtain started coming right down the south slope toward us. I could see boulders—they must have been huge—being hurled out of the leading edge. . . ."

Northwest of the peak, some 14 miles away, a four-man tree-thinning crew was caught by the blast. They tried to walk out, their scorched clothing sticking to burned skin. . . .

At Cougar, 12 miles southwest of St. Helens, Mort and Sandy Mortensen . . . stared at the ash cloud devouring the sky. "It just kept spilling over and turning darker," Sandy said, "until all the daylight you could see was a long way off and looked like it was coming through a curtain." [Findley 1981, 43, 45]

A geological report adds another scene:

On the ground during the blast, too, a group of fishermen, trapped on the Green River, 16 miles (26 kilometers) northeast of the peak, found themselves near the periphery of the devastated area. They were badly burned, and survived only by jumping into the river when they first became aware of the explosion. They suffered burns, however, when they came up for air, and when they left the protection of the water. The heat, they said, came in waves, over a period lasting perhaps 10 or 15 minutes. [Rosenfeld and Cooke 1982, 12]

Now place all these viewpoints into separate mythic traditions. Group D tells of the sun hiding its face for a long time in thick, palpable darkness, whereas Group B recounts a flood of unparalleled proportions drowning their world, and Group A speaks of unimaginable heat blasting from a mountain. Group C, for its part, talks in measured terms of a gigantic pillar of smoke, riddled with lightning, rising to the sky. Would we recognize these stories as the same event? Only, at best, after much careful piecing.

Note that the clearest picture comes from the closest witnesses who did not suffer truly major damage (especially Group C). Those at ground zero are much too busy to analyse the big picture, while those too far away simply can't see much.[1]

Scholars who have worked on reconstructing the explosion of Thera, now dated by the geologists to about 1625 B.C., may recognize the parallels to the above zone-by-zone descriptions of the eruption of Mount St. Helens. The two events are geologically similar, since both volcanos contain very viscous lava that builds up to high-pressure explosions known as Peléan eruptions (after Mount Pelée in Martinique). But the eruptions differed greatly in size (see table 1). For all the havoc of the Washington eruption, Thera blew out of itself many times as much debris, then abruptly collapsed into its own emptiness, like Mount Mazama. And because Thera is an island, the collapse allowed the surrounding waters of the Aegean Sea to rush in, triggering major tsunamis as well [McCoy and Heiken 2000a]. To study the myths generated by Thera, then, we must also arm ourselves with some recent descriptions of sea-girt explosions and tsunamis.

Records of the massive 1883 eruption of Krakatoa, an island volcano in the straits between Java and Sumatra, provide helpful parallels. Several times bigger than Mount St. Helens, though smaller than Thera, its last and largest series of explosions was heard 2,200 miles to the east (3,500 km) in Alice Springs, Australia, and 2,900 miles west (4,650 km) at Rodriguez, an island most of the way to Madagascar [Simkin and Fiske 1983, 146]. That is one loud noise. A captain sailing some 75 miles to the north entered into his ship's log: "So violent are the explosions that the ear-drums of over half my crew have been shattered. My

---

[1] C. Scott Littleton tells us that anthropological fieldwork done in the areas around other catastrophic events also shows that different zones spawn different types of reports and stories—in particular, a zone around the catastrophe center where the perspective is small but very vivid and personal; a second zone slightly farther away where the perspective is much wider and the details rather accurate as to what happened; and a third zone yet farther away in which surmises built on hearsay tend to run rampant. Littleton's students found this sort of zoning after the massive Sylmar quake on Feb. 9, 1971, for example. (Far-away relatives called us to make sure California hadn't fallen into the ocean.) Littleton had seen a similar zonal analysis (which we have been unable to locate) done on accounts of the 1948 Texas City firestorm, and one could clearly do such a study of the attacks of Sept. 11, 2001.

Table 1. Comparative Data for Several Great Eruptions

VOLCANO:	DATE	CUBIC EJECTA/PLUME HEIGHT	DEATH TOLL
MT. MAZAMA (CRATER LAKE), Oregon	5675 b.c.	42 cubic km [F] or more [Z]	
THERA, Greece	1625 b.c.	100 cubic km [M] / Up to 36 km [M] *ash-fall from E. Peloponnese to central Turkey to lower Nile delta [McCoy, p. c. 2003]*	
VESUVIUS, Italy	79 a.d.	3 cubic km [F]	most inhabitants of Pompeii and Herculaneum
TAMBORA, Indonesia	1815	80 cubic km [F]	92,000 [U]
KRAKATOA, Indonesia	1883	18 cubic km [S] / 80 km [L,F] (= 5 cubic mi) (26 km [S]) *ash-fall over 827,000 sq km [J]*	36,400 [S]
PELÉE, Martinique	1902	10.8 cubic km [U]	28,000 [U]
MT. ST. HELENS, Washington	1980	5 cubic km [R] / 60,000 ft [R] (= 1.5 cu mi) within 1 hour *ash-cloud travelled 4000 mi by end of day [R]*	
PINATUBO, Philippines	1991	5 cubic km [USGS] / 18 mi [D]	

(Compiled from: Dumanoski 1981 [D], Findley 1981: 54-55 [F], Jaggar 1945: 40 [J], Luce 1969: 78, 83 [L], McCoy and Dunn 2000 [M], Rosenfeld and Cooke 1982: 4-5 [R], Simkin and Fiske 1983: 235, 96, 15 [S], Ursulet 1997: 179 [U], USGS website for Long Valley Observatory [USGS], Zdanowicz et al. 1999 [Z].)

last thoughts are with my dear wife. I am convinced that the Day of Judgment has come" [Simkin and Fiske 1983, 97].

The ash-cloud from Krakatoa rose so high (variously calculated by captains at 17 to 21 miles [27–34 km], or over 90,000 feet) that it entered the stratosphere, where winds carried its debris around the world, causing cooler weather and gorgeous sunsets [Simkin and Fiske 1983, 96–97, 154–60]. Slowly descending to earth, some of the detritus fell on the Greenland ice sheets, leaving a unique signature in the ice layers—layers that geologists can now count like tree rings. It was from such a signature, in fact, that scientists finally determined when Thera actually exploded [Zielinski et al. 1994]. The thick ash-cloud from

Krakatoa also spread out in the Sunda Straits, so densely that nearby sailors (like the residents of Yakima, Group D) could see neither the sun nor each other. The government mail ship *Loudon*, having just managed to survive a triple tsunami that wiped away the town of Telok Betong before the crew's very eyes, attempted to steam out of the bay that faced Krakatoa from the northwest:

> We hoped soon to be out of the Bay of Lampong. But we would not get away that easily. It became darker and darker, so that already at 10 a.m. there was the most Egyptian darkness. This darkness was complete. Usually even on a dark night one can still distinguish some outlines of, for instance, white objects. However, here a complete absence of light prevailed. The sun climbed higher and higher, but none of her rays reached us. Even on the horizon not the faintest light could be seen. . . . This darkness continued for 18 hours. [Simkin and Fiske 1983, 94]

The young son of the captain of the *W. H. Besse*, a Boston ship just entering the straits from the southwest, recalled that "the air seemed to be filled with dust, so much so that we feared suffocation. It became black, so black you couldn't see your hand before your face. I've never imagined that the atmosphere could be so dense" [Simkin and Fiske 1983, 100]. Flurries of lightning, bouts of St. Elmo's fire on the rigging, and occasional glimpses of fireballs on the volcano provided the only breaks in the blackness.

Tidal waves crashed into the shores on both sides of the strait, killing over 36,000 people and uncounted numbers of animals (Group A): .

> Owing to the darkness and terror, reliable observation of the height of the waves was almost impossible. They are thought to have reached 36 m. [120 ft.] in places. The lighthouse-keepers at Vlakke Hoek, 88 km. away, recorded them at 15 m. [50 ft.] high. Another quite reliable estimate is from Telok Betong where the water washed to within 2 m. of the top of a hill 23 m. [75 ft.] high. It was at this port that the gun-boat *Berouw*, which had been moored in the harbour, was carried nearly 3 km. inland and left at nine metres above sea-level. In general it may be safely reckoned that at distances of between 50 and 80 km. from the volcano the waves averaged 15 m. high, and that they tended to pile up much higher at the head of bays. [Luce 1969, 80]

Under those ships sailing nearby in deep water, as the eruption progressed, the tidal waves passed with less harm (since it is only in the shallows that such a wave gains height), while the sailors noted "a confused sea with heavy squalls from different directions" [Luce 1969, 151] or, as another captain put it, "squalls, storms, and seas as high as the heavens" [Simkin and Fiske 1983, 91]. Ships like the *Loudon* and the *Besse*, however, that were steaming through shallower water had to use all their seamanship to survive, dropping both anchors with all available chain, then steering straight into the oncoming walls of water. On the *Loudon*, the first

> tremendous wave came moving in from the sea, which literally blocked the view and moved with tremendous speed. . . . One moment . . . and the wave had reached us. The ship made a tremendous tumbling. . . . The wave now reached Telok Betong and raced inland. . . . The light tower could be seen to tumble; the houses disappeared; the steamer *Berouw* was lifted and got stuck, . . . and everything had become sea in front of our eyes, where a few minutes ago Telok Betong beach had been. [Simkin and Fiske 1983, 94]

During a brief lull, the *Loudon* attained somewhat deeper water, but at the cost of moving closer to the volcano. Soon its men had to start clearing the decks of hot rocks that fell thick and fast:

> While we were engaged in this struggle, and enveloped in the sheer blackness of a veritable hell, a new and terrible danger came upon us. This was the approach of the tidal wave caused by the final eruption, which occurred about 12:30 to 1 p.m. The wave reached us at 2 p.m. or thereabouts, and made the ship tumble like a see-saw. Sometimes she was almost straight on end, at other times she heaved over almost on her beam ends. We were anchored and steaming up to our anchors as before. . . . [T]he Captain was lashed with three ropes along the engine-room companionway, while I [the second engineer] was lashed down below to work the engines. [Simkin and Fiske 1983, 92]

(The captain was later awarded a governmental gold medal for his heroism and skill in saving the mail ship and its passengers.) Farther away, the *Besse* experienced the tidal waves as "a current beyond anything you can imagine, . . . a current like a millrace running by the ship, to such an extent . . . that we thought that the vessel would either drag its anchors or pull its bow out of the ship" [Simkin and Fiske 1983, 101].

As for what being hit by a tidal wave on land is like, we must extrapolate from reports of little tsunamis, like a mere four-to-five-footer that hit near Hilo, Hawaii, immediately after a nearby 7.2 earthquake in 1975. A young man camping on the beach recounts:

> I saw the wave coming and it hit us and I was in the swirling water. . . . We couldn't even stand up. I've lived in Hawaii all my life but no quake was like this one. We fell to our hands and knees.
>
> There were several tidal waves. The first one came up onto the beach only about 25 yards. We all ran inland. The second wave hit me and dragged me 50 yards.
>
> After it subsided I got up and ran more, until I came to a crevasse about 10 feet deep and 8 feet wide.
>
> I looked back and saw Dr. Mitchel and yelled, "Do you need help?" He had a shocked look on his face. Then the big one came and I was in the swirling water fighting to breathe.
>
> I became unconscious.
>
> The last thing I remember is fighting to get my breath. I'll never forget that sound—the sound of the wave coming. Then it slams into your body and you just fly. [Nelson 1975; order altered for clarity]

These images are echoed by one of the few survivors of Krakatoa's lashing of the Sumatra coast. The Controller at Beneawang wrote of the "terrible noise" of each tidal wave as it rushed in. After the second wave demolished his hilltop home, he says, "I got hold of a few pieces of thin wood and managed to stay afloat until the water returned to the sea and I felt solid ground under my feet. . . . Suddenly the water returned with the same force. . . . The water took hold of me, turned me around and threw me away with a terrible force." When finally beached again, he found all his clothes had been ripped off, and he was so exhausted he could not move for at least an hour, despite the constant rain of lava-mud [Simkin and Fiske 1983, 89].

Now let us return to the eruption of Thera, which occurred in the Middle Bronze Age in the heart of a long-inhabited area. This was such a huge event that it cannot have gone unnoticed by those living around it, nor can it have been deemed unimportant. In fact, quite a number of interesting accounts have survived in the mythologies of surrounding peoples. The Minoans were living on Crete, 70 miles south, and the

Mycenaean Greeks had recently moved in next door, on the Greek mainland to the northwest, setting up major centers at such places as Mycenae and Tiryns and infiltrating long-standing pre-Hellenic settlements like Athens. The Hittites, another partly literate group, had just set up their kingdom in central Anatolia (Turkey) to the east; if literate peoples controlled the Aegean shore of Turkey, we do not have their texts. How we divide these populations into Zones A, B, C, and D to understand their camera angles will depend, of course, on the circumstances of the eruption.

Archaeological evidence shows that Thera came to life with enough serious preliminary grumblings that the residents packed their valuables, stowed their other goods neatly in their basements, and got off the island; for, quite unlike Pompeii and Herculaneum, which lie at the foot of Vesuvius in Italy, Thera and its excavations have produced no bodies (Group A—wipeout). Then the volcano blew its heart out in an immense column of fiery rock and ash; but as the center emptied, the sides began to crack, letting surrounding seawater into the superheated interior—a particular hazard of island volcanos. The mix vaporized so violently that it blew out nearly half the rim and created fierce tsunamis in the lateral directions of these forces [McCoy and Heiken 2000a]. When the pyrotechnics subsided and the ash-cloud cleared away, where once a mountain had stood lay a huge crater that still today drops sheer from the shattered rim—a thousand feet to sea level and another thousand straight down to the sea floor (figure 9).

At the site now called Akrotiri, quakes snapped entire stone staircases (figure 10), and the intense base-surge blasting out from the initial eruption scoured colorful murals off the facing housewalls, while lava bombs smashed down random buildings (figure 11) and the mounting weight of ash broke through the roofs, catching the falling household objects in a thick white cushion before they hit the floor, in a three-dimensional time capsule. It buried the whole under more than a hundred feet of ash (called tephra in its deposited form: figure 9), tossing out many cubic kilometers of pulverized rock (see table 1). We know from the pattern of traceable fallout that winds pushed the ash-cloud largely to the southeast, across central and eastern Crete (Group D), while tsunamis slammed into the surrounding shores (Group B), leaving a bathtub ring of pumice on nearby islands, wrenching aside huge wall-stones at the Minoan harbor of Amnissos on the north shore of Crete, and causing characteristic underwater landslides in a wide swath across the Mediterranean floor [McCoy and Heiken 2000a, 1243–46].

Figure 9. Thera, Greece: inside the blown-out crater, cliffs rise sheer about 1000 feet from water level—and descend another 1000 feet straight to the bottom of the caldera. Note thick white tephra (from the 1625 B.C. explosion) atop layers of red and black lava.

Figure 10. Minoan stone stairway shattered by explosion of Thera ca. 1625 B.C.
Room Δ15, Akrotiri, Thera.

The Greeks and anyone else living in Attica and Euboia, barely north
of the ashfall, would have had the best ringside seat (Group C).

From just that area, shortly after the invention of the Greek alphabet
(and hence just at the end of the oral pipeline), we have a typical Group
C description of a catastrophic event.[2] As you read this epic passage,
from the early Greek poet Hesiod's poem *The Theogony* ("The Birth of
the Gods"), keep in mind the Willfulness and Movie Construct principles. It purports to describe the gods (beneficent spirits) closing in battle with some upstart giants (nasty spirits), in this case the race of Titans, as the culmination of a long feud:

> *Terribly the boundless sea echoed all around,*
> *and the earth roared loudly: wide heaven groaned,*
> *shaking, and great Olympus [throne of the gods] shook from its foundation*
> *under the charge of the deathless ones, and heavy quaking reached*

---

[2] The Greek alphabet was invented about 800 B.C.; Hesiod, who composed the epic
quoted below, lived ca. 700 B.C., just early enough still to be composing orally and late
enough that his poems got written down, thus roughly at the end of the oral pipeline.

Figure 11. Lava bomb from Thera that flattened a Minoan house ca. 1625 B.C., while other houses nearby remain to three stories. Akrotiri, Thera.

gloomy Tartarus [the underworld], and the sharp pounding of feet
in the ineffable rush of their mighty blows.
For thus they hurled at each other their baleful missiles.
And the cry of both sides reached the starry sky
as they bellowed, and they came together with a great battle shout.
Nor did Zeus still hold back his might, but now indeed
suddenly his mind was filled with rage and he showed forth
his whole strength, and all together from the sky and from Olympus
he came, hurling lightning continuously, and the bolts
flew thickly amid thunder and flashing
from his powerful hand, whirling swiftly with sacred flame.
All around, the life-giving earth resounded,
burning, and all around, the great boundless woods crackled with fire.
The entire land seethed, as did the stream of Ocean
and the harvestless sea. The hot blast surrounded
the earthborn Titans, and a boundless flame reached to the bright upper air;
the gleam blinded their eyes, for all that they were strong,
as it flashed with lightning and sparks.

A supernatural heat seized the yawning void; and it seemed, facing it,
seeing with the eyes and hearing the sound with the ears,
just as if Earth and wide Heaven above
collided, for so huge a boom would roll forth
if Earth were being hurled up while Sky were falling down from above:
just such a din arose from the deities colliding in strife.
And the winds brought together quakes and dustclouds
and thunderclaps and lightning and smoking thunderbolts. . . .
And there in the forefront they stirred up the sharp fight:
Kottos and Briareos and Gyges, insatiable in battle—
three hundred rocks from their stalwart hands
in quick succession they launched, and with their missiles overshadowed
the Titans, and under broad-pathed earth
they sent them and bound them in grievous chains,
conquering them with their hands despite their audacity,
so far beneath the earth as sky is above it. [Hesiod, *Theogony* 678–721]

Noise and quakes, missiles, lightning and thunder, fire and terrible heat; then a huge shaft of fire going sky-high, an indescribably loud noise, more flying rocks, and finally everything ending up as far below the surface as it had been above it. That's just about what the geologists reconstruct for Thera. In fact, Mott Greene, recognizing a volcano like Thera as unlike any other in its specific eruption pattern, lines up the precise *sequence* of events in Hesiod and those reconstructed from the geology of Thera, thus demonstrating that this account could refer *only* to Thera, out of the whole Mediterranean volcanic zone. His table of events (starting about fifty lines before the Hesiod passage quoted above) is as follows:

Hesiod	Thera
1. a long war	1. premonitory seismicity
2. both sides gather strength	2. increase[d] activity
3. terrible echoes over sea	3. first phase explosions
4. ground rumbles loudly	4. tectonic earthquakes
5. sky shakes and groans	5. air shock waves
6. Mt. Olympus trembles	6. great earthquakes
7. steady vibrations of ground	7. earthquakes
8. weapons whistle through air	8. pyroclastic ejecta
9. loud battle cries	9. explosive reports
10. Zeus arrives: lightning, thunder, fields, forests burn	10. volcanic lightning, heat of ignimbrites

11. Earth and sea boil	11. magma chamber breach
12. immense flame and heat	12. phreatomagmatic explosion[3]
13. sound of earth/sky collapse	13. sound of above
14. dust, lightning, thunder, wind	14. final ash eruptions
15. Titans buried under missiles	15. collapsed debris

[Greene 1992, 61–62]

Greene also distinguishes this list from the characteristic patterns of the other active Mediterranean volcanos like Vesuvius, Stromboli, and Etna—the last of which finds *its* characteristic signature in the very next battle that Hesiod reports: Zeus *vs.* Typhoeus [Greene 1992, 63–71].

For the heavy involvement of Zeus's lightning in both battles, compare, in addition to passages already quoted, the account by a group rowing a boat on a lake in a pitch-black cloud of ash, trying to escape an eruption of Calbuco, Chile, in 1929:

> We were wrapped in the "fire of Saint Elmo" produced by the high electric tension. From our clothes and flesh we gave off sparks, and our heads seemed to be surrounded with aureoles. Suddenly the lightning flashed, followed immediately by thunder. . . . Simultaneously the discharges from our bodies stopped. [Jaggar 1945, 137]

And as Mount Pelée in Martinique was revving up in 1902, the governor wrote of the electrical charge being "so intense as to render the telephone operators' work almost impossible" [Ursulet 1997, 102].

Returning to Thera, we find a quite plausible Group D (ash-cloud) account in the following passage, from 600 miles to the southeast—just the direction the ash-cloud headed, to judge from the geology:

> And there was a thick darkness in all the land of Egypt three days; they did not see one another, nor did any rise from his place for three days. [Exodus 10:22–3]

---

[3] Greene [1992, 60] explains the term and phenomenon thus: "If the volcano in question is an island, and if the magma chamber is breached while the magma is still being erupted, the violence of the explosion can be many times magnified by the vaporization of inrushing sea-water coming into contact with the incandescent magma, in a so-called *phreatomagmatic* eruption, akin to the explosion of a giant steam boiler." We had developed our zonal analysis of the myths before encountering Greene's sequential analysis. Together they constitute an argument far beyond chance.

This passage (containing the "Egyptian darkness" referred to by the *Loudon* passenger) is followed soon after by the description of Moses' people making their way out of Egypt:

> And the Lord went before them by day in a pillar of cloud to lead them along the way, and by night in a pillar of fire to give them light, that they might travel by day and by night; the pillar of cloud by day and the pillar of fire by night did not depart from before the people. [Exodus 13:21–22]

Anyone who has watched an eruption or big brush fire can tell you that bright sunlight overwhelms the glow of lava and fire when you view it from afar, so it looks dark—what is visually prominent is the great cloud of smoke and ash rising from it. But the moment the sun goes down, you can see the fire with startling clarity from great distances. In short, an eruption typically looks dark in the daytime and glows fiery bright at night. That this scene pertains to a gigantic eruption is underscored by the very next event to happen: the tsunami-like parting of the waters that allows Moses and his flock to pass, then closes over their pursuers. (For people moving north down the Nile valley to where the Delta opens out, an eruption pillar over Thera would indeed be ahead of them. But whether the Exodus as described actually occurred in 1625 B.C. is another matter. We will see in a later chapter that *time* often gets foreshortened in the retelling of myths, with different stories that have some points of resemblance—Analogies—getting conflated into one narrative. Thus Exodus as we have it may contain details from several different time periods—several different trips out of Egypt.)[4]

The Theran tsunami also may well account for the tidal wave, already mentioned, that Poseidon reportedly sent against Athens, the one Athena stopped at the foot of the Acropolis five kilometers inland.

Another Group C description of the ash-pillar from Thera probably lies fossilized in the Hittite myth of Ullikummi. A defeated deity named Kumarbi begets the "rebel" Ullikummi to challenge the storm god Teshub (also Kumarbi's son, who had displaced him as King of Heaven: see chapter 16) and plants the child on the shoulder of the ancient being who supports the world, Ubelluri. The young giant grows up from the sea with tremendous speed, till he is 9,000 leagues tall. Terrified at his sudden appearance, the gods struggle to defeat the bellowing monster, but in vain—in fact, at one point they fear Ullikummi has

---

[4] Jan Assmann [1997], we find, came to the same conclusion by quite different routes.

overpowered the storm god himself. Finally Ea, the god of wisdom, goes to Ubelluri, who complains that he lives in so remote a region that he knows nothing of what happens in the world:

"When they built Heaven and Earth upon me,
I knew nothing.
But when they came and they cut Heaven and Earth apart with a cutter,
this, too, I knew not.
Now, something makes (my) right shoulder hurt,
but I know not who he is, this god!"
When Ea heard those words,
he went around Ubelluri's right shoulder,
and (there) the Basalt [Ullikummi] stood on Ubelluri's right shoulder like a shaft![5]

Then the gods get the bright idea of fetching the ancient cutter (variously described elsewhere as an adamantine blade or sickle) with which Earth and Sky had been sliced apart at the beginning of time, and of using it to sever the burgeoning monster at the feet. Although the text is fragmentary and we have no ending, apparently the "rebel" is vanquished—presumably by this ruse of cutting asunder from Earth what is reaching Sky.

Turkey is far closer to Thera than Egypt, and the enormously tall ash-pillar—standing on the shoulder of the world with its feet in the ocean and bellowing—must have been visible from many high points, just as the column above Mount St. Helens in southern Washington could be seen easily from Mount Rainier near Seattle in the north. Eventually, of course, the ash-pillar that seems rooted to the earth separates *from the bottom*, once no more ejecta are being fed into it, and then it slowly disperses.[6]

Volcanism has disturbed human life since our species came into being—quakes, tsunamis, explosions, lava flows, ash-blankets, and so

---

[5] The translation of Ubelluri's speech is the literal one of Güterbock [1952, 29], slightly transposed out of the Hittite word order to read more easily; that of Ea's action follows Hoffner [1990, 59].

[6] We wonder whether this eventual separation of a volcanic ash-cloud from its source on the ground might lie behind one of the prodigious feats ascribed to Herakles: throttling the giant Antaios ("Inimical"), son of Poseidon the Earth-Shaker, who could only be defeated by being lifted completely off his mother, Earth, from whom the giant got his power.

forth. Except for occasional meteorites and asteroids that hit the earth (such as those that flattened the Tungus forests in 1908,[7] or hit Yucatan and extinguished both the dinosaurs and the Cretaceous era sixty-five million years ago), seismic upheavals are about the strongest forces of nature that humans face. All such catastrophic events will constitute important information for descendants to know about and hence will turn up in mythology in considerable numbers. But most important of all to warn about, precisely because one can pinpoint the exact *source* of trouble, is a volcano.

In California, everyone knows about the San Andreas Fault. But when a quake occurs it is unlocalizable—it just "happens": everything in your house shakes equally. There are, in fact, thousands of smaller faults in all directions, any one of which could be the source of *this* quake, and you need modern technology to find the epicenter, by triangulating from three seismometers—or three radio/television stations. (We've learned that if we can find and tune to a television station *between* us and the source, we have an early-warning system for the long series of aftershocks: the studio reporters yell, we grab a doorpost.) Tsunamis and ash-clouds, too, often come from sufficiently far away that, without technology, the source may be unknown, so that one such event comes to sound much like another.

But witnessing a volcanic eruption directly is different: you know where it comes from, you can see it, and it runs its course with no more than a generic resemblance to other eruptions. It has all the uniqueness of "Thou". So myths generated by volcanos tend to be quite specific and idiosyncratic—and more numerous than most other classes of myth. Furthermore, an eruption leaves layers of debris that are both decipherable and datable, especially for volcanos that erupt only rather seldom, like most of those in the Mediterranean and the Pacific Northwest. Thus geologists and archaeologists have a fighting chance of pinning down the sources and dates of the myths engendered. Even the incessant eruptions of Kilauea are now being correlated to the Hawaiian genealogical chants, which span a millennium [Masse 1998, 55]. Volcano myths can in this way give back a measure of history to the prehistoric.

---

[7] I. M. Suslov [see Menges 1983, 4–6] collected interesting catastrophe-zone myths and stories that this event generated among local Tungus survivors.

9

Views through Biased Lenses

Mirror, mirror on the wall, who is the fairest of them all?
—The Queen, in *Snow White*

"FAIREST OF THEM ALL" EFFECT
People tend to select and pass down the view or version of events that puts themselves in the best light—and enemies in the worst light.

Remembering is always transformation and reconstruction.
—Jan Assmann [1997, 365]

Wen a natural event like an eruption propagates myths among different cultures, the differences of viewpoint are largely geographical. But viewpoints can become quite personal and cultural when the event has been generated by humans—a battle or a migration, for instance. People like to look good, especially to their friends and relations; so the selfsame battle may sound entirely different in the clan histories of the two opposing sides. Thus we find that both the Hittites and the Egyptians claimed victory at the Battle of Kadesh, fought in 1275 B.C. around the Syrian city of Kadesh: each side describes in glowing terms the total discomfiture of the other. Yet outside evidence shows it to have been something of a draw. Readers of ancient Egyptian war reports soon notice, in fact, that Pharaoh seems *always* to win his battles, and we begin to take such reports with a whole spoonful of salt.

A famous recasting of history to one's own glory occurs in the medieval poem *Le Chanson de Roland* (*The Song of Roland*), in which Roland leads Charlemagne's rear guard in a heroic stand against a hundred thousand heathen Saracens. The book-length epic details how Roland and his brave troops fall, down to the last man, to allow their king to escape the treacherous attack, as they cross the Pyrenees back to France after a parley with the wicked Saracens. Other records indicate, however, that in 778 Charlemagne's small rear guard, led by Roland, was wiped out by a local band of Basque sheepherders.

Cognitive scientists studying memory find, in fact, that "self-enhancing biases are pervasive features of attempts to reconstruct the personal past" [Schacter 2001, 149]. Furthermore, cultural memories are invariably distorted by the biases of the cultural group, whether glorifications or other fostered images [cf. Schacter 1997, 16]. At a time when literature was oral and communal, its recitation promoted, among other things, communal solidarity. (Twice in the *Song of Roland* someone says starkly, "Pagans are wrong, Christians are right!"[1] And Aristophanes' main point in *The Frogs* was that Athens no longer had any tragedians who could whip up the necessary public solidarity in the theaters to win the war against Sparta.) Because they are promoted, we are told, the "culturally valued and memorialized activities are more easily retrievable than culturally denigrated, repressed, or stigmatized activities" [Schudson 1997, 359]. And just as experiments have shown that "adults remember from their own lives, not what they experienced

---

[1] *Laisses* 79, 246. Although written down, this epic behaves in most ways like the "oral" epics of Homer and Gilgamesh, and unlike the literary creations of Vergil and Milton.

but what they learn they are conventionally supposed to have experienced", so cultural memories become structured—retained or obliterated—according to the many values of the society [Schudson 1997, 358].

Michael Schudson calls this process *conventionalization* and lists it as one of four typical ways in which cultural memory becomes distorted. Another he calls *narrativization*, which he describes as "an effort not only to report the past but to make it interesting" by getting it "encapsulated into some sort of cultural form", usually a narrative [Schudson 1997, 355]. But, as he puts it, "Narratives simplify." You can't cram absolutely everything that actually happened into a good story or it becomes hopelessly cluttered and tedious. So you pick and choose—according, among other things, to the process of conventionalization—and the rest drops into the River of Forgetfulness.

The third process Schudson calls *instrumentalization*, pointing out that often "memory selects and distorts in the service of present interests", where present interest may be "strategic" (propagandistic) or "semiotic" (in the service simply of trying to understand one's world) [Schudson 1997, 351]. Most of the myths cited so far in this book have been of the latter sort, whereas myths entangled in the Fairest-of-Them-All Effect are generally strategic.[2]

Looking at the evidence from myth, one might add a third source of "present interest": communal emotions [cf. Schacter 1997, 18]. Jan Assmann [1997], for example, gives a very shrewd analysis of the Hebrew memory of the Exodus and the Egyptian memory of the Hyksos as being emotionally (as well as strategically and semiotically) opposing views of the same events. The Egyptians tell how the Hyksos from the Levant invaded Egypt and ruled it for centuries with great cruelty to the natives, until the Egyptians rose up and expelled them at sword-point back to the Levant. The Old Testament, for its part, relates how the Egyptians held the Children of Israel in cruel captivity for centuries, until the latter rose up and escaped with great difficulty back to the Levant, pursued by the Egyptian army. In both cases, a group from the Levant came into Egypt, lived there for a while under hostile circumstances, and returned to the Levant. And in both accounts, as Assmann says, "the most striking feature is the strong attitude of hatred, fear, and abomination which pervades" [Assmann 1997, 367]. Each group casts themselves as the heroic victims and the other side as the despotic villains.

[2] Schudson's fourth principle, "Distanciation: The Past Recedes", falls under our Perspective Principle (chapter 11).

The problem gets even more interesting when Assmann looks at a second Egyptian tradition, that recorded by Manetho (early third century B.C.). Here a group of lepers is persecuted by the pharaoh, who hopes by cleansing the land to entice back the gods, who have disappeared. The lepers are finally resettled in northern Egypt, whereupon they invite the Hyksos back. Their leader then "makes for them laws that prescribe all that is forbidden in Egypt and forbid all that is prescribed there. The first and foremost commandments are not to worship the gods, not to abstain from their forbidden food, and not to associate with people from outside" [Assmann 1997, 368]. Finally, after thirteen years of sacrilegious and despotic rule, the lepers and the Hyksos together are driven out by the Egyptians.

Assmann makes an excellent case that we have here a mythologized memory of the twelve-year Amarna period, during which the pharaoh Akhenaten banned the traditional polytheistic state religion and set up the world's first documented monotheistic belief system.[3] As we said in chapter 7 when discussing heretics, the Egyptians so hated this new religion that when Akhenaten died, they systematically destroyed his name and monuments and utterly obliterated all direct memory of him from the cultural tradition. After much analysis, Assmann concludes:

> In Manetho's version it is clear that the presence of the lepers is the cause for the invisibility of the gods. The lepers can thus be identified as a transformation or distortion of the heretics. This becomes even more clear in the continuation of the story. The lepers are shown as religious revolutionaries. The king fears them as such because he makes his preparations by hiding the divine images and rescuing the sacred animals; and they confirm their image by destroying the temples, slashing the remaining idols, and roasting the rest of the sacred animals. The very first of their laws is a religious one: the prohibition to worship the gods. The story of the lepers is about religion. [Assmann 1997, 373]

It is fascinating that a structurally identical myth about religion grew up in Europe in the Middle Ages, in which the lepers were accused of attempting to poison the wells with leprosy, after renouncing Christianity, and of joining with the Jews, Saracens, and witches in these deeds so as to take over rule of the world from the Christians

---

[3] Akhenaten legislated the change to Aten in the fifth year of his seventeen-year rule. We also see here a (typical) conflation of events from three hundred years apart—the Hyksos and Amarna periods.

[Ginzburg 1991, 33–86]. These accusations, which began in France in 1321, led to a frantic and ever-expanding orgy of burnings and incarcerations, mostly without trial. Again we see that "hatred, fear, and abomination" dominate, and that those feared most for disease (lepers) are lumped and equated with those hated most for religious and political otherness.

We also see another widely observable principle at work. By blaming the poison conspiracy on the lepers, whom no one dared go near (and who were forced to keep to themselves), rabblerousers could say anything—and people could believe anything—without being contradicted. And since the Jewish people lived isolated in ghettos and the hated Saracens way off in Spain, the same was true of them. The Hyksos (to the Egyptians) and the Egyptians (to the Jewish people) were equally unconsultable:

ZONE-OF-CONVENIENT-REMOVE SYNDROME
People can perpetuate a vivid and seemingly plausible story by telling it of a third party who can't be consulted for verification.

This principle, in fact, generates the classic urban legend, where the third party is typically as near as possible while being unreachable: a relative of a friend, or a friend of a relative, or a Friend Of A Friend— FOAF—or simply an enemy. The locus classicus of such stories is the attribution of cannibalism to people who, because they are enemies, are never present to defend themselves against this most inhumanizing of accusations. Thus, as W. Arens says in his book *The Man-Eating Myth* [1979, vi], "in China it was believed Koreans were cannibals, while in Korea the opposite belief prevailed". Similarly, the early Christians were accused by the Romans and the Jews of eating little children, whereas later the Christians accused the Jews of same. To the extent that these groups were isolated minorities, they were all vulnerable to such calumnies.[4]

The glorification of oneself and vilification of others can even lead to portraying others as less than human: not just unclean, but demons or imps. The phenomenon is well attested linguistically as well as mythi-

---

[4] Ever-increasing distance in time (see the Perspective Principle, chapter 11) also flings particularly memorable tales into the Zone of Convenient Remove where facts can't be checked. In this way, many myths—especially those about individuals—behave like glorified urban legends, and we find the same essential story being retold of many different "heroes" [cf. Raglan 1936/79]. (See the Principle of Attraction, chapter 11, and the Centaur Syndrome, chapter 13, for principles that interlock with this one in interesting ways.)

cally. Thus the Chinese for millennia have called non-Han people "foreign devils", while the ancient Greeks called others *bárbaroi*, "barbarians", a term thought to come from an onomatopoeic *bar-bar-* for foreigners who could only "babble" instead of speaking proper Greek. The Egyptians

> made a distinction between "men," on the one hand, and Libyans or Asiatics or Africans, on the other. The word "men" in that sense meant Egyptians: otherwise it meant "humans" in distinction to the gods, or "humans" in distinction to animals. In other words, the Egyptians were "people"; foreigners were not. At a time of national distress, when the stable, old order had broken down and social conditions were upside-down, there was a complaint that "strangers from outside have come into Egypt. . . . Foreigners have become people everywhere." [Wilson 1949, 41]

Many linguistic groups, in fact, call themselves "people" (the literal translation of *Navajo*, *Hopi*, *Apache*, and *Inuit*), with the implication that all others are *not* people. Geography works the same way: China is the "Middle Kingdom", the Sumerians put themselves in the middle of their maps, and atlases printed in the United States typically put North America at top-center of the world map, although it requires splitting Eurasia.[5]

In mythology, antagonists often turn up as fiends and devils (as the Indic invaders viewed the Dravidian natives, or as the Celts viewed the prior inhabitants of Ireland [Rees and Rees 1961, 128]), and the former occupants of the territory appear as all manner of elves, brownies, and dwarves—hard to find and archaic in their ways.

The dwarves of Germanic mythology provide a particularly interesting case. Half-sized though muscular in stature, these miners with their peaked hats live inside mountains where they forge and hammer their vast treasures of gold, gems, and steel into priceless jewelry (mayhap with a curse attached) and nearly invincible weapons (usually endowed with a name and a willful spirit), which the Germanic hero of the story tries to get from them by trade or trickery. What's that all about?

Dolly the camera to the mountainsides of central Europe, where Bronze Age and Iron Age miners did the first mining in that area, and where their ancient mine shafts still turn up. Archaeologists have found that the Late Bronze and Early Iron Age mines (roughly 1300–400 B.C.)

---

[5] An Australian friend sent us a world map with Australia top-center and North America and Eurasia "upside down" at the bottom.

of Austria and Hungary were worked by men of the Hallstatt culture, the immediate ancestor of the demonstrably Celtic La Tène culture. The La Tène Celts began migrating away—primarily westward—about 400 B.C. And as the Celtic miners moved out of central Europe, the Germanic peoples moved into the vacuum. In the mines we find fragments of plaid twills (quite similar to those associated with Celts still today), tam-o-shanter style hats, and peaked hats like those traditionally depicted on the dwarves [Barber 1991, 186–92; 1994, fig. 0.1].

Now back to the camera. You, the early Germanic viewer, have not specialized in the mysteries of mining, and the miners have now left. But you know (these are the snapshots) that the former local populace, who wore pointy hats, would disappear into and reappear from small holes that you can still see in the mountainside (as in the Grimms' tale #303, "Die Zwerglöcher"—"The Dwarf Holes"), and that they obtained a seemingly unending supply of rich jewelry and wonderful weapons from the mountain. You conclude (here comes the newsreel) that they lived inside the mountain and guarded their treasures there (because that's the place associated with them), that they must have been short because the openings are only a couple of feet high, and muscular because forging all that metal required strength. They must also have known magic to be able to find the gold and gems and make all that glorious stuff; and surely they would have left—in irritation or despair—only if they had lost all their treasures.

No out-and-out proof exists for this theory of the origin of the race of treasure-forging dwarves, nor is any likely to be forthcoming; but the scenario takes care of a remarkably high percentage of otherwise weird and arbitrary details about these interesting characters, and does so by well-attested principles.

10

Metaphoric Reality: Magic and Dreams

(or Hū's on First)

PRINCIPLE OF METAPHORIC REALITY
The distinction between representation and referent—and between appearance and reality—tends to become blurred.

Your Majesty says, "Kill a gentleman," and a gentleman is told off to be killed. Consequently, that gentleman is as good as dead—practically, he *is* dead—and if he is dead, why not say so?   —W. S. Gilbert, *The Mikado*

It is not wax that I am scorching,
It is the liver, heart, and spleen of So-and-so that I scorch.
                   —Malay death charm [Frazer 1922/63, 15]

Analogy pervades our thinking. "What was it like?" we ask the survivor, the veteran, the experiencer, the expert. We continually ask for and transmit information via metaphors, similes, and comparisons, especially when the information is so new that no ready-made vocabulary exists yet to describe it. The atom with its electrons is structured *like* the sun with its planets whizzing around it. The eruption sounded "like artillery", going outside was "like sticking your head in the fireplace and stirring up the ashes" because the ash blew around "like a blizzard", and the city came to look as though "the contents of a vacuum cleaner bag" had been dumped onto it.

Suppose, however, the fact of its being a simile gets lost somehow, either through time or through interpretation. Then the eruption *is* artillery fire—an enormous battle—or the most horrendous of all storms (depending on what zone you are in). Add a dash of Willfulness and we find the Storm God engaged in an apocalyptic battle with some other, very ill-willed force. What may have started out as pure analogy can merge with the event it originally described; the representation merges with the referent. The Sumerians came to believe that lapis lazuli—deep blue like the night sky, and sometimes having tiny, bright, star-like inclusions—was the stuff of which the sanctuary of "middle heaven" was made [von Rosen 1988, 27]; some of the cultural groups living in the American southwest believed that the house of the Sun was made of turquoise, or that turquoise stole its color from the sky [Pogue 1915, 124, 126]. "It's like, therefore it is". Red liquid trails down a mountain "like red hair", "like snaky locks", "like blood"; presently it *is* the red hair or snaky locks or blood of a giant.

Perhaps the clearest example of this human propensity for blurring representation and referent comes—once again—from a well-attested linguistic phenomenon, wherein the name (verbal symbol or representation) for something comes to be viewed as tantamount to the thing itself, and power over your name comes to mean power over you yourself. For instance, Frazer reports that in central Australia

every man, woman, and child has, besides a personal name which is in common use, a secret or sacred name which is bestowed by the older men on him or her soon after birth, and which is known to none but the fully initiated members of the group. This secret name is never mentioned except upon the most solemn occasions . . . [and] spoken only in a whisper, and not until the most elaborate precautions have been taken that it shall be heard by no one but members of the group . . . [since] a stranger knowing [a person's] secret name would have special power to work him ill by means of magic. [Frazer 1922/63, 285]

Frazer then reports similar beliefs among the ancient Egyptians, the Brahmans, the Aracaunians, and the natives of Nias and Chiloe [Frazer 1922/63, 285–86]. Rumpelstiltskin too guarded his name.[1]

An ancient Egyptian document called the Memphite Theology goes further. It describes the creation of the world as a process by which the god Ptah, arising on the Primeval Mound of Mud in the waters, thinks up each part of the world to be created—himself, the other gods, and all else—then brings it into material being by naming it:

> Thus were made all work and all crafts, the action of the arms, the movement of the legs, and the activity of every member of the body, in conformance with the command which the heart thought, which came forth through the tongue, and which gives the value of everything. . . . So Ptah was satisfied [or "rested"], after he had made everything. [Wilson 1951, 60]

The very act of creation by naming had a special name, $h\bar{u}$, translatable as "authoritative utterance". Such an utterance coming from the tongue of Ptah or the pharaoh had so much power to make things happen that it too became personified as a willful being, Hū, along with its companion, Sia, the perception "in the heart" that precedes the pronouncement by the tongue (figure 12) [Wilson 1949, 66].

A rather similar statement of creation by naming comes from not far away in time and space:

> And God said, "Let there be light"; and there was light. And God saw that the light was good; and God separated the light from the darkness. God called the light Day, and the darkness he called Night. And there was evening and there was morning, one day. And God said, "Let there be a firmament in the midst of the waters, and let it separate the waters from the waters." [Genesis 1:3–6]

And so forth, until God rests. The naming makes things so. A still simpler version of the power of the word alone is, "In the beginning was the Word, and the Word was with God, and the Word was God" [John 1:1].

---

[1] In the Grimm Brothers' story of Rumpelstiltskin, the heroine must discover the little man's secret name to save herself.

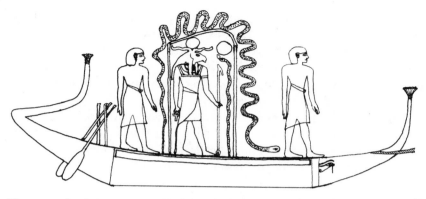

Figure 12. Sia (Magical Understanding) and Hū (Authoritative Utterance) accompanying the sun in his boat through the underworld at night. Note the Egyptian "analytic" approach to art: both of the shoulders, arms, legs, hands, and feet are drawn, although they would not normally be seen in a sideview. Tomb of Seti I, Thebes, ca. 1280 B.C.

If the spoken word has such great power over the referent, then the notion of speaking a blessing or a curse takes on very potent meaning, promising great benefits and terrifying consequences. One can create or at least influence the future with one's mouth, whether for good or for ill.

Note that knowing a name really does give one *some* special power over the person or thing with that name. Leonard Bloomfield, one of the founders of American linguistics, invites us to imagine Jack and Jill walking up the hill, when Jill sees an apple in a tree and realizes she is hungry. So she says a few words to Jack, who "vaults the fence, climbs the tree, takes the apple, brings it to Jill, and places it in her hand. Jill eats the apple" [Bloomfield 1933, 22]. Now surely that's power: by moving her mouth a little, Jill got Jack to do all the work of getting her a meal. Once you have words, you can ask for things in their absence and work on the solutions to problems before they overwhelm you. So the basic observation that language has special power is not unfounded, even if most people would not agree that language provides a one-to-one match for reality in the way that Ptah's creation myth might seem to imply.[2]

Knowing a person's name entrains some very particular powers, too. For one thing, calling people by name almost invariably makes them

[2] Courtroom lawyers often fall into the trap of treating language as an (or the) exact match for reality, then express bewilderment at the exasperation vented on them.

react to you, if only by turning to look. The use of one's personal name also elicits an emotional reaction, as you discover when someone gets your name wrong or makes jokes about the form of your name. Or try this: Next time you have to deal with a smarmy salesman, tell him your name is something else and see how deliciously detached you feel when he uses it to try to close in on you.

This power of the personal name, together with Willfulness, may account for why so many objects—particularly in Germanic mythology—have proper names: Thor's battle-hammer Mjöllnir, Heimdall's horn Gjöll, the unbreakable fetter Gleipnir, Odin's auger Rati and magic ring Draupnir (it drops eight rings like itself every nine days); Roland's sword Durendal and horn Oliphant, Oliver's sword Halteclere; King Arthur's sword Excalibur, and so on. All these objects have in common the trait that they *do* something—they have the power to smash, make noise, bind, pierce, reproduce, cut, and—in the case of the weapons—kill. Like blessings and curses, this power was taken very seriously, and swords in particular seem often to have received a name when completed, as though, like children, they were now being launched into the world to do good or ill. How close this concept hovers to the Willfulness Principle can be seen from a very early depiction of a sword, in the great rock-cut sanctuary of the Hittites at Yazılıkaya (in Turkey), dated to about 1250 B.C. (figure 13). Carved in high relief and perhaps ten feet tall, the sword has a hilt composed of animals and a ribbed blade that appears to come out of or be stuck into the stone of the cliff. At the top of the hilt protrudes a male head wearing the peaked cap peculiar to Hittite deities: the divine spirit of this Sword in the Stone.

(The Bronze Age Hittites had a monopoly on the strange new metal, iron, which differed from copper and tin, the components of bronze, in that it never occurred naturally as a metal except in rare meteorites, but always in the form of ore—"stone". The highly superior—but far more difficult to produce—iron sword may thus have been perceived as "the sword from (*ex*) the stone" and wandered off into the oral pipeline at an early date in a linguistic form as memorable and evocative as Goldilocks's porridge (chapter 7). Interestingly, the Hittites could obtain their iron only during the non-snowy season, apparently from the mountains east of the Black Sea. The resemblance of the name of the iron-smelting inhabitants of that area, the Chalybians, to the famous Arthurian "Sword in the Stone", *Ex-calibur*, is striking. This and some other parts of the Arthurian legend have been shown to

Figure 13. Hittite sword god: head with deity's hat protrudes from top, paired animals form hilt, and blade disappears into shelf of stone at the bottom—the Sword in the Stone. Relief cut into live rock, Yazılıkaya (Turkey), ca. 1250 B.C.

match Caucasian legends so exactly as to leave no doubt they originated there and moved to Britain with displaced soldiers serving Rome.)[3]

Name magic forms part of a wider analogic phenomenon known as *sympathetic magic*, in which *any* resemblance or relation to the object of the magic can be employed, not just the name. Thus in parts of the Caribbean and Africa pins stuck into a doll are intended to *become* real pain in a real person, whereas in Slavic areas all knots in the house are untied to help release the baby for a woman in difficult labor. Similarly Ovid recounts how Eileithyia (Greek goddess of childbirth) sat for days with her hands clasped over her crossed legs to prevent Alkmene from giving birth to Herakles. Alkmene's maid, recognizing this, ran to Eileithyia and excitedly announced the birth—causing the goddess to jump up in surprise and release her hold. Instantly the child was born. [Ovid, *Metamorphoses* 9.281–315]

The blurring of symbols and other representations with their referents constitutes part of a still broader phenomenon, the blurring of appearance and reality. Stage magicians work hard to entertain us with tricky appearances, but most of us leave the theater convinced we've been hoodwinked, even if we don't know quite how. Before literacy, however, the smallness of the database sometimes led to quite different results and expectations (a fact which medieval churchmen often exploited with artificially miraculous "weeping madonnas" and the like).

In particular, until very recently a dream event was taken to be quite as real and potentially as important as a waking event. Today we know that dreams result from random neural firings in the brain, as the brain degausses itself during sleep, while the analytic hemisphere desperately tries to make the unconnected images cohere somehow (remember the bird and the orange). But formerly, dream experiences were taken seriously. A text of 1893 tells us that

> the wife of a poor shoemaker in Jaraczewo [in today's Poland] died. On the day of the funeral, he wanted to be awakened early in the morning, at four o'clock, by his apprentice, in order to run some errands for the funeral. The

---

[3] Our thanks to C. Scott Littleton for the seeds of this interpretation of Yazılıkaya, which he sowed in our direction twenty years ago and then forgot about. Much more on the Caucasian origins of Excalibur, Arthur, and so forth is found in his book, written with Linda Malcor, *From Scythia to Camelot* [2000].

apprentice, however, overslept the time. Then the dead wife arrived, exactly at four o'clock, and boxed him on the ear four times with her ice-cold hand of death. Frightened, he awakened and jumped out of the bed. [Barber 1988, 185]

Note that we are not warned that the apprentice saw the woman in his dream: we are told that she arrived and boxed his ear, after which he woke up. The narrator presents her actions as being fully as real as the apprentice's. Yet the woman was dead. Here is another such from Serbia:

Jowiza reports that his stepdaughter, by name of Stanacka, lay down to sleep fifteen days ago, fresh and healthy, but at midnight she started up out of her sleep with a terrible cry, fearful and trembling, and complained that she had been throttled by the son of a haiduk by the name of Milloe, who had died nine weeks earlier. [Barber 1988, 16]

And where did Stanacka (who died soon after) see this vampire? Not, as Hollywood would have it, climbing out of a coffin in the graveyard, waving long bony fingers and a black cloak. She saw an acquaintance, recently deceased, attack her *in her house as she slept*. When we are awake (and sober), we cannot see deceased people speaking and doing things—but we can and do when we are asleep. A not unreasonable conclusion: the souls of the dead can stick around, and we can see and talk to them in dreams. As an elderly Greek woman put it,

"At death the soul emerges in its entirety, like a man. It has the shape of a man, only it's invisible. It has a mouth and hands and eats real food just like we do. When you see someone in your dreams, it's the soul you see. People in your dreams eat, don't they? The souls of the dead eat too." [Danforth 1982, 46]

So the descendants may set out actual meals and other things for the deceased, further blurring the distinctions between the quick and the dead.

These wandering spirits, however, must have at least some knowledge that we don't—at the very least they will know what the spirit world is like (see chapter 15) and will have met and conversed with other spirits. So people viewed dreams as an important source of information not available to us when awake. On the occasion of a drought,

King Gudea, a powerful ruler in late third-millennium Mesopotamia, "went to sleep in the temple in order to be instructed in a dream as to the meaning of the drought" [Frankfort and Frankfort 1949, 24]. Likewise, the Greek hero Bellerophon, according to Pindar (*Olympian Ode* 13, strophe 4), "lay down for the night on the altar of the goddess" Athena, who told him in a dream how to catch Pegasus.

In the Sumerian *Epic of Gilgamesh*, during the dangerous expedition to obtain cedar logs from the mountain guarded by the monster Humbaba, Gilgamesh and his friend Enkidu repeatedly solicit dream-messages from the gods:

> Gilgamesh dug a well before the setting sun. He went up the mountain and poured out fine meal on the ground and said, "O mountain, dwelling of the gods, bring me a favourable dream." Then they took each other by the hand and lay down to sleep; and sleep that flows from the night lapped over them. Gilgamesh dreamed, and at midnight sleep left him, and he told his dream to his friend. "Enkidu, what was it that woke me if you did not? My friend, I have dreamed a dream. We stood in a deep gorge of the mountain, and suddenly the mountain fell, and beside it we two were like the smallest of swamp flies. In my second dream again the mountain fell, it struck me and caught my feet from under me. Then came an intolerable light blazing out, and in it was one whose grace and beauty were greater than the beauty of this world. He pulled me out from under the mountain, he gave me water to drink and my heart was comforted, and he set my feet on the ground."
>
> Then Enkidu, the child of the plains, said, "Let us go down from the mountain and talk this thing over together. . . . Your dream is good, your dream is excellent, the mountain which you saw is Humbaba. Now, surely, we will seize and kill him, and throw his body down as the mountain fell on the plain."[4] [Sandars 1964, 76–77]

One purpose of talking to the spirits was to solicit advice, as when the Norse king or Slavic head of household would spend the night on his ancestor's grave. Another purpose was, of course, to obtain information about the future. In recent times, people have viewed the spirits as bringing this information unbidden and encoded in reverse, as in this case from rural Greece in the 1970s:

---

[4] The entire Humbaba episode sounds thoroughly volcanic, although which Near Eastern volcano(s) inspired it is undetermined.

Irini would discuss the dreams that she and her husband had seen prior to Eleni's accident. They now realized that these dreams had clearly foretold their daughter's death. One night Irini had seen her daughter, dressed as a bride, leaving home in a taxi. As all the dream books say, dreams of weddings are ominous signs of impending death. A week before Eleni's death, her father had seen in his sleep a herd of black goats descending the hill toward his pens at the edge of the village. [Danforth 1982, 15]

The dictum that dreams of marriage forebode death occurs already in that first "dream book" of European literature, Artemidorus's *On the Interpretation of Dreams* (second century A.D.). A millennium earlier, in a famous passage in the *Odyssey*, Homer's Penelope claims to see dreams merely as being true or untrue:

> *Stranger, dreams are intractable and hard to discern,*
> *nor are they always fulfilled for men.*
> *For double are the gates of fleeting dreams:*
> *the one constructed of horn, the other of ivory;*
> *and those [dreams] that come through the one of sawn ivory,*
> *they deceive, bearing unfulfilled words;*
> *whereas those that come from the door of polished horn,*
> *they fulfill true things, when mortals see them.*[5] [*Odyssey* 19.560–67]

Once the distinction between reality and appearance is thoroughly blurred, yet other things happen. When we paint a picture, in our Western culture, we try to paint what we see (or at least we did until Picasso, Klee, and the like led us in new directions). If I, as your model, stand sideways so that one arm and shoulder are hidden from your view, you paint me that way. That is, unafraid of separating reality (I have two shoulders) from appearance (I seem to have only one), we traditionally paint how things appear to us: the *appearance* of reality. By contrast, the ancient Egyptian painter would depict *both* shoulders frontally of a person walking sideview (figure 12), painting what he knew was there even

---

[5] Those who don't read Greek must be warned that Homer played for a chortle from his audience with this passage that modern scholars take so seriously, for it is based on a pair of puns: *elephant-* "ivory" and *elephair-* "deceive"; *kéras* "horn" and *krain-* "fulfill, accomplish". The ivory and horn should be treated as a joke—although a belief that some dreams come true and others do not requires little apology.

if he couldn't see it. (Many children and some adults draw hands this way, with all five fingers always visible.) Unable or unwilling to risk the isolation of appearance from the reality, he painted his *conception* of what was there. As a matter of fact, cognitive studies have shown that this problem arises, once again, from brain structure. The analytic or left side of the brain instigates conceptual drawings (drawing what it knows to be there, whether visible or not), whereas the opposite side of the brain (which specializes in spatial relations rather than analysis) draws eidetically—draws what it sees [Edwards 1979]. (What this says about the thinking habits of the Minoans, who alone among ancient Mediterranean peoples drew eidetically, has not been investigated.)

Let us return, now, to myth itself, to those similes that lost their "like" so that the descriptor has fused with the event or object. Some cases are stable: lapis looks rather like night sky and turquoise like daytime sky to anyone who sees them. In other cases, while the observable reality is stable, the culture has changed so much that the descriptor can no longer be understood.

In Snorri Sturluson's tale of Thor's visit to the giant Útgarð-Loki, the host challenges Thor to empty a drinking horn, saying, "We consider it good drinking if this horn is drained at one drink, some men take two to empty it, but no one is such a wretched drinker that he can't finish it in three" [Sturluson 1971, 74]. Thor takes the horn and drinks for all he is worth, but to his disgust cannot empty it in even three tremendous drafts. Later the giant catches up with Thor and his friends after they have left his hall and confesses that he had bested them by magic. "The other end of the horn was in the sea, but you didn't perceive that, and now when you come to the ocean you'll see how much you have made it shrink" [Sturluson 1971, 78].

We might dismiss the tale as cute, even clever. But Snorri, who lived soon after Iceland accepted Christianity and who wrote his book to preserve for poets the meanings of the myths that traditional Icelandic poetry referred to, had one foot in each world, the literate Christian world and the largely nonliterate "heathen" world, and he understood both symbol systems to a fair extent. So he keeps sticking in little translations for his Christian friends. Knowing that representation and referent have merged here too thoroughly for his audience, he tells us point-blank at this juncture: "That is called the ebb-tide now" [Sturluson 1971, 78]. We can see that possibility *after* Snorri tells us. But honestly, did you get it before? Too much of a gulf separates our cultures. Just because we don't understand something immediately doesn't mean it didn't have a solid meaning at one time. Nor is Snorri crazy: his other insertions, such as explaining Loki's writhing as earthquakes and things weeping for the death of Baldr as the condensation on cold objects all depend on clear analogies [Sturluson 1971, 86, 84].

Now suppose—thanks to migration or the vastness of geologic and astronomical time—that the referent can no longer be seen and only the descriptor remains. Those who have not experienced at first hand the terror of an eruption, major quake or tsunami, or a plague of locusts, or witnessed the marvel of a supernova so bright it shines in the daytime sky for weeks (as the Crab Nebula did in 1054, and others did earlier [Masse 1995, 466]) can only take other people's word for what it is like. And this they may well misinterpret, even when they belong to the same culture:

FOGGING EFFECT
Blurring of representation and referent is especially likely to occur when people no longer have direct experience of the referent.

Consider yet again volcanic eruptions. But this time imagine the quieter kind, in which molten lava flows like water from a bubbling crater and runs down the side of the mountain.

What does the lava look like—if you know no geology? When it trails down the side of the mountain: perhaps like red stringy hair, such as that of the Sky Spirit's daughter, or maybe like snaky locks adorning the "head" of the mountain, as in Hesiod's account of huge Typhoeus, on whose shoulders writhed a hundred snake-heads with flickering tongues and fire flashing from the eyes (*Theogony* 824–28); or maybe like molten bronze being poured from the crucible. When it squirts straight up in a bright fountain: like a tall, flashing sword blade, or a shower of gold. And what does it sound like? Sometimes it hisses: like snakes again. Sometimes it roars: like a lion, or a monster in pain. It can also make sharp percussive sounds: like artillery, or a smith pounding on his anvil, or tremendous footfalls. Hesiod reports of Typhoeus:

And voices were in all his terrible heads,
producing every sort of unspeakable utterance: for one time

they spoke so the gods understood, but at another
in the voice of a proud bull bellowing loudly in ungovernable rage,
and at another in that of a ruthless-hearted lion;
or sometimes yelping like puppies, a marvel to hear,
or hissing repeatedly; and the great mountains echoed with the sounds.
[*Theogony* 829–35][6]

And what is the crater like? If you can get close, you feel its over-whelming heat—as in a smithy. From a distance you see only its glow, brightest at night. And since ancient Mediterranean peoples thought vision occurred by light coming *out* of the eye, rather than into it (chap-ter 7), the volcano may be described as having a great eye. When Odysseus resents the inhospitableness of a giant with one great eye, who eats some of Odysseus's men and then hurls huge rocks at him as he tries to escape, we might at least *suspect* that we are hearing an old story of a volcano. (The episode of Polyphemus, or "Wide-renowned", who is a Cyclops, or "Round-eye", begins with Odysseus seeing smoke rising from the land, and ends with Polyphemus breaking off the mountain-top and hurling it at Odysseus's departing ship [*Odyssey* 9].)

Many years ago we watched the eruption of Mauna Ulu (figure 14), a double cone on the side of Kilauea, from a point right on its rim (pos-sible only on days with steady trade winds). Separate columns of magma fed twin lava lakes connected by a small channel and drained by a side-vent from which streams of lava flowed down the mountain to a steamy meeting with the sea. The lakes below us roiled at 2,300° F. As giant gas bubbles would raise the level of one lake, lava would cascade through a narrow corridor into the other pool with a roar like Waikiki surf, back and forth, breaking up the dark crust that constantly formed from the cooling of the surface. You had to keep reminding yourself "That's *rock*!" as great orange sheets would get sucked under, leaving a bathtub ring and slinging white-hot gobbets up to stick and darken on the black sides of the caldera. And you had to keep stepping back from the rim to cool your face. As evening fell, the hovering cloud of steam and ash glowed red underneath, reflecting the molten magma and ri-valling the sunset. During the night we drove to where we could watch the bright orange lava streams pouring down toward the sea.

Using the Mediterranean notion of vision and stating things without the "like", you could well have said that we watched two terrible mon-

---

[6] Greene [1992, 63–71] identifies this volcano as Etna, for which snaky extrusions of lava from numerous side-vents are the norm (see his figure 3.2).

Figure 14. One of twin lava lakes during nighttime eruption of Mauna Ulu, Hawaii, 1972: a rising gas bubble breaks through the congealing surface of molten lava.

sters, as alike as twin sisters, passing an eye back and forth between them, while not far away, amid the long, red tendrils that snaked and hissed their way down the shoulders of the mountain, what had been trees and houses and ancient shrines turned into a great field of stone.

Consider, now, the following famous Greek myth of Perseus, pieced together from the entry for Danaë by Hyginus (a late classical collator), plus the version by Apollodorus (2.4). Pay special attention to the phrases we have italicized.

> Danaë was the daughter of Acrisius and Aganippe. Of her there was a prophecy that whoever she bore would kill Acrisius; fearing which, Acrisius shut her up inside a *wall of stone* [Apollodorus: *bronze chamber*]. But Jove [Zeus], turning into a *golden shower*, lay with Danaë, from which union Perseus was born. Her father shut her into a chest with Perseus, because of this affair, and threw it into the sea. By Jove's will it was carried off to the isle of Seriphus. [Hyginus, *Fabulae:* 63. *Danaë*]

There the mother raised her son. Eventually the king of Seriphos, Polydektes, ordered Perseus to bring him the head of the Gorgon Medusa, a task intended to get rid of Perseus so Polydektes could marry the unwilling Danaë. Guided by Athena and Hermes, Perseus set off to Enyo and Pemphredo and Deino [*Terrible*]. They were the *offspring of* [*two monsters*] Keto and Phorkys, and *sisters* of the Gorgons: Graiai [*"Old"* fem.] from birth. The three of them had *one eye and one tooth*, and they passed these to each other by turns. Perseus got hold of these, and when [the Graiai] demanded them, he said he would give them back if they would tell him the way to the nymphs. [Apollodorus 2.4.2]

The nymphs gave him three gifts: a special bag for Medusa's head, a cap that made him invisible, and winged sandals.

After getting from Hermes an *adamantine sickle*,[7] he flew to Ocean and caught the Gorgons sleeping. These were Stheno [*Strength*], Euryale [*Wide-leaping*], and Medusa [*Queen*]. Only Medusa was mortal; for this reason, it was for her head that Perseus was sent. . . . Those that saw them they *turned to stone*. [Apollodorus 2.4.2]

Apollodorus describes them with *bronze* hands, *golden wings*, and *snaky* scales; like Pindar (*Pythian Ode* 10), most other authors—and ancient sculptors, too—insist that Medusa's head was covered with *hissing, writhing snakes*. The early pot painters, for their part, depict the Gorgons with large *cauldrons* for heads (figure 15)—a detail not previously explained.[8] Perseus avoided petrification by looking only at Medusa's reflection in his bronze shield as, hovering above her while she slept, he severed head from body with his divine weapon.

When her head had been cut off, the *winged* horse Pegasus *sprang out* of the Gorgon, and also Chrysaor [*Golden Sword*]. . . . These had been *sired by Poseidon*. [Apollodorus 2.4.2]

Escaping Medusa's angry, shrieking sisters, thanks to his invisibility, Perseus returned home just as Polydektes was closing in on his mother. By whipping out the Gorgon's head, he turned the evil king and his men to stone—where they stand to this day on the rocky isle of Seriphos—and rescued Danaë. Soon after, competing at some athletic games, Perseus *threw a discus stone* which the wind caught so it hit and

---

[7] Recall (from chapter 8) that the volcano-monster Ullikummi, too, was cut down by a divine invincible blade: Greek *a-damant-* means "un-conquerable, in-vincible".

[8] Geologists picked their name for the lava bowl of a volcano, *caldera*, from the same etymological source as *cauldron* ("heating vessel"). Wilk [2000, 186–88] makes an intriguing case that the revised (reinterpreted) artistic conventions for Medusa's terrible head originated in the horrific aspects of a bloated corpse's face.

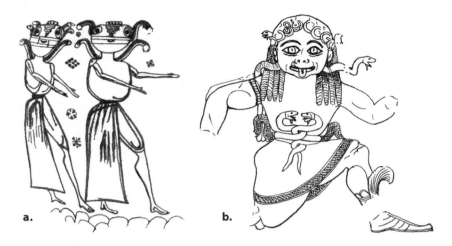

Figure 15. Gorgons in Greek art. **(a)** Early representation of Medusa's sisters with snake-surrounded cauldrons as heads; from Proto-Attic neck-amphora; Eleusis, ca. 660 B.C. **(b)** Typical later representation of Medusa with her snaky locks, from west pediment of temple of Artemis, Corfu; early 6th century B.C.

killed a spectator—none other, it turned out, than his grandfather Acrisius. The oracle was fulfilled.

It is hard to find anything in this tale that does *not* smack of volcanism. *Chrysaor* means "golden sword": compare both lava fountains, which can shoot straight up into the air like a tall, flashing blade, and the same image in a description of fiery doom that comes from Iceland, where lava fountains occur frequently: "Surt ['black, swarthy'] will ride first and with him fire blazing both before and behind. He has a very good sword and it shines more brightly than the sun" [Sturluson 1971, 87]. The name of *Pegasus*—the winged horse who becomes Zeus's thunderbolt-carrier—can now be connected linguistically with the Luvian Hittite storm god Piḫaššašši [Hutter 1995, 90–94], suggesting even more strongly that the broad-winged "creature" (Willful as always) seen rising suddenly above the mountain at the moment it loses its head/top is the ash-cloud (see chapter 17).[9]

[9] Many thanks to Joshua Katz for this reference. Both storm-clouds and volcanic ash-clouds discharge lightning and thunder, of course (chapter 8).

For petrification, compare the spontaneous remark of a child in the Congo concerning the now-active volcano Nyiragongo: "It's going to explode. . . . I'm ready to run because if it catches me it will turn me to stone. That's what happens, you know" [Lacey 2002]. As for the Gorgons' cries, consider a description of Mutnovsky, a volcano on Kamchatka: "The jets of steam so hissed and roared that it was necessary to shout in order to be heard" [Jaggar 1945, 80]. Or the 1928 eruption of Mayon (Philippines): "lava poured out through the notches in the crater wall and followed the gullies, forming snake-like trickles radiating from the summit. . . . There was a periodicity of three to five hours in the spells of roaring, hissing, cracking, and tumbling noise" [Jaggar 1945, 61]. Volcanos frequently produce far more than bangs and rumbles. Athena is said (e.g., by Pindar, *Pythian Ode* 12) to have invented the double flute in an attempt to imitate the sounds of Medusa's sisters bewailing her demise. We found this unrelatable to volcanos until we read such eyewitness accounts as that of the 1779 eruption of Sakurajima in Japan: "The noises were as of the cry of some mountain birds" [Jaggar 1945, 65]. Or Mutnovsky again: "White jets of steam shot whistling and blustering out from holes in the cliff" [Jaggar 1945, 80].

Just which volcano(s) instigated the Gorgon legend, however, may be lost forever in the mists. Seriphos, though extremely rocky, is not a volcano. Its neighbors Melos and Thera are; but the multiplicity of volcanos (the Graiai, the Gorgons, their parents, and the decapitated Medusa's two offspring) suggest a much bigger volcanic field with multiple vents like Etna, unless Thera was so configured before its decapitation in 1625 B.C. (it has two vents even today). Pindar's *Pythian Ode* 10 sets Perseus's deed in the land of the Hyperboreans, the northern "ends of the earth" (possibly the volcanos of the Caucasus?), and Pegasus's name points to Anatolia, whereas others say Perseus threw the Graiai's eye into Lake Tritonis (in Libya), and Apollonius Rhodius (4.1513–17) depicts the venomous snakes of Libya as descended from drops of blood that dripped from Medusa's head as Perseus flew homewards. Volcanos do exist in Libya (e.g., Waw an Namus), although geologic information is hard to come by. If the story has been brought in with migration from or travel to other lands, then our chances of tracing it plummet.

11

Compression: Methuselah and the Eponymous Heroes

Tell ol' Pharaoh to let my people go!
—Spiritual

PRINCIPLE OF ATTRACTION
Once the stories around something (e.g., a hero) achieve sufficient mass, that thing (or whatever) attracts yet other stories to him/her/itself, via any "significant" point of resemblance. Points of attraction include the same type of event, same place, and same name or clan name.

T he Memory Crunch problem that we identified right at the beginning—that only so much memory space is available in a nonliterate society—gets unexpected help from the Principle of Metaphoric Reality. For when the distinction between two things perceived as similar gets obliterated, such that the object or event Y is no longer merely "like" X but *partakes* of X or even *is* X—that is, when two things originally viewed as related come to be viewed as one—suddenly there is less to remember. We have achieved compression of information by a type of conflation in which likes attract each other.

Take, for instance, Theseus, the great early hero of Athens. He gained his greatest fame for killing the Minotaur and the brigand Procrustes, but many other adventures are told of him. In fact, if something happened at Athens you can be pretty sure you'll be told that Theseus did it: Attraction by Place. Storytellers still pass down the important event, but if the place is known, the doer may be automatic. (If it happened around Ohio, Johnny Appleseed must have done it.) Similarly with Herakles, famed for prodigious strength. If something occurred that would have taken enormous strength, search not for the agent, Herakles must have done it: Attraction by Quality. Thus, if a Greek river moved its channel radically in a single day (in Asia, both the Tarim and Yellow Rivers have the noxious habit of doing this), Herakles must have moved it; if a terrible beast needed killing, like as not Herakles did the job.

Others have noticed this process. Lord Raglan quotes a book from 1823, on Robin Hood lore, as commenting on "everything of a marvelous kind being attributed here [in northern England] to Robin Hood, as it is in Cornwall to King Arthur" [Ritson 1823, lxi; Raglan 1936/79, 48]. H. J. Rose, in his thorough-going *Handbook of Greek Mythology* [1959] occasionally remarks on it also. At one point he lists the children of two rather volcanic-looking monsters, Echidna (half woman, half snake, sister of the three-bodied Geryon who lives on "Red Island") and Typhon (who carries on like an explosive volcano), as including Orthros (Geryon's herd dog), "Kerberos, the hell-hound, 'with voice of bronze and fifty heads', . . . who became the watch-dog of the underworld; the [many-headed] Lernaian Hydra, the [fire-breathing] Chimaira, and finally the Theban Sphinx or Phix and the Nemean lion" [Rose 1959, 31]. The simple lion seems a bit of a come-down after all the fantastic multiheaded monsters.[1] Rose then adds, "We may be

---

[1] In fact, one gets the impression that the Greek label for volcanos and volcanic eruptions is simply "monster", and since volcanos kicking up a fuss resemble each other, they must

sure that the Nemean lion would not have figured in this group but for the fact that he, like Kerberos and the Hydra, was associated with Herakles" [Rose 1959, 32]. Call it Attraction by Association.

On the other hand, if something in the Bible happened in Egypt, Pharaoh was involved. Which pharaoh? Who knows? They have all collapsed into an undifferentiable "Pharaoh": Attraction by Title. Many scholars have suggested independently that the same thing occurred on Crete, since to the Greeks, no matter what happened on that island in mytho-history, it involved "King" Minos. "Minos" may have started as a title. It also can happen that an individual's name becomes a (magnetic) title: Russian *Tsar'* and German *Kaiser* came from Caesar, the family name of the great Roman rulers Julius and Augustus; and the Russian word for a king in general, *korol'*, came from Carolus, the Latin form of Charlemagne's name (Carolus Magnus, Charles the Great). But once the name becomes a title, those who take the title may gradually blend together in oral tradition.

Identical personal names, too, can trigger attraction. Rulers often take identical throne names, which we today carefully distinguish with numerals: Henry VIII, Elizabeth II. (Amenhotep III did not think of himself with a numeral, of course; we have numbered the pharaohs for our own convenience.) All around the world, however, yet another force works to cause Attraction by Name: many cultural groups believe that the souls of ancestors return via the newborn children of the group. Mother's new son looks like recently deceased Grandfather George (point of resemblance): it must *be* Grandpa George born to a new life, so we'll call the baby George—not just in Grandpa's *honor* (as we interpret the custom today), but in recognition of the child's identity. Now take that common custom of naming the grandchild after the grandparent (still done, for example, in Greece) and run it through six or seven generations of oral history. "George$_1$ did X; George$_2$ did Y; George$_3$ did Q; George$_4$ did Z." Lose the subscripts and George looks like a busy guy—heroically busy, with all those deeds—X, Y, Q, Z— rolled up into one lifetime.

---

belong to the same family (Kinship Principle). The parents of Geryon and Echidna are Kallirhoe ("beautifully flowing"—lava streams?) and Chrysaor, Medusa's offspring—we have just discussed those two in chapter 10. In fact, there is nothing in this big family that does *not* suggest common volcanic images.

The reader may have noticed that a loss of perspective on time has figured into several of these types of attraction. In fact, time has its own
curious modes of behavior that warrant special scrutiny. How, for example, can people just not notice that George$_1$ and George$_3$ lived a hundred years apart?

To understand the problem, first consider visual perspective. Put two
big dots on a piece of cardboard, one toward each end. When you look
straight down on them, you can see that they are several inches apart.
Now, holding the cardboard so that one dot is at your end and the other
is at the far end, move your head slowly downward past your end of the
board. Watch how the apparent distance between the dots appears
smaller and smaller, until the dots seem to coincide just as your eye finally drops below the edge of the cardboard. We call this foreshortening, of course.

Now take the following pop quiz (no peeking for answers!) and find
out at first hand how the two ends of a century can do the same trick as
the two dots:

Within the following pairs of famous people, who lived first?
(a) Lyndon Johnson or Abraham Lincoln? _____
(b) Queen Elizabeth I or Isaac Newton? _____
(c) Pliny or Vergil? _____
(d) Solon or Themistocles? _____
(e) Cheops or Sargon? _____

The first one is so obvious it seems silly: President Lincoln lived a
whole century before President Johnson. But unless your English history is pretty fresh, you may have to struggle to recall that Elizabeth
and Newton, too, lived about a century apart—Elizabeth came first. By
the time we have moved back two millennia, we feel some pride if we
know that the pair in (d) are Greeks and came before the pair in (c)
who are Romans. But who came first within each pair? The century
that separates *them* seems disappearingly small from where we sit:
Vergil before Pliny, as it happens, and Solon before Themistocles (with
some six hundred years between the Greek politicians and the Roman
authors). Squint back another two *millennia* and the images in (e) appear to coincide altogether, just as the dots on the paper did. Even archaeologists have to stop and search through their mental rolodex from
grad school to separate them: Cheops, builder of the Great Pyramid at
Giza, lived roughly a century before Sargon the Great of Akkad. And

for those who have no written history books to consult, this loss of perspective is even easier: Lord Raglan points out that English villagers a century ago "could pit St. George against Bonaparte without the least sense of incongruity" in their mummers' play.[2] That's a gap of some 1,500 years. And with not even a blink, the average moviegoer accepts cavemen like Fred Flintstone coexisting with dinosaurs—a collapse of sixty-five *million* years.

PERSPECTIVE PRINCIPLE

As we get further from an event, our perspective gets flatter, and we can no longer distinguish earlier from later events so easily: it is all "back then" some time.

What wonder is it, then, that grandfather and grandson with the *same name* get conflated a few generations later?

This predicament leads to another interesting effect. If George (George$_4$, who died recently) helped repair the temple after the big quake, but George (actually, George$_1$) also helped build the temple to begin with, then "George" lived about as long as the temple has stood. Yet the priests claim that the temple was built two hundred years ago. That means that George lived for over two centuries!

In fact, we observe this sort of thing happening sometimes in the Sumerian king-lists. The scribe sees in his records a king here and a king there with the same name and concludes it is the same man. He also knows that "this" king did various deeds for which he has recorded dates. But the dates add up to a life span of many centuries, which he duly assigns to his king of that name. (As we dig up more and more tablets from different places, we sometimes can piece together the data the ancient scribe lacked and see that this has happened.) From this phenomenon we get some of those numbers that seem so utterly fantastic to every child first hearing the "begats" in Genesis—numbers that also put Viagra to shame:

> When Jared had lived 162 years he became the father of Enoch. Jared lived after the birth of Enoch 800 years, and had other sons and daughters. Thus all the days of Jared were 962 years; and he died.
> When Enoch had lived 65 years, he became the father of Methuselah.

[2] Lord Raglan [1936/79, 7] is quoting R.J.E. Tiddy, *The Mummers' Play* [Oxford, 1923, 93]. Compare Schacter's "scale effect" in source memory [1996, 117–18] and Schudson's "distanciation" principle [1997, 348–51].

Enoch walked with God after the birth of Methuselah 300 years, and had other sons and daughters. Thus all the days of Enoch were 365 years. Enoch walked with God; and he was not, for God took him.

When Methuselah had lived 187 years, he became the father of Lamech. Methuselah lived after the birth of Lamech 782 years, and had other sons and daughters. Thus all the days of Methuselah were 969 years; and he died. [Genesis 5:18–27]

Whew.

METHUSELAH EFFECT
Deeds of identically named (or surnamed) relatives may get conflated over centuries, but if any independent gauge of time exists, then one has to ascribe centuries of lifetime to such "heroes".

If people back then could live to be many hundreds of years old, then—and the next deduction now seems obvious—they were not built like us. They clearly constituted a race of supermen, living in a Golden Age when people could live for a millennium instead of, at best, a century. Hesiod knows of them:

> *A golden race of mortal men, first of all,*
> *the deathless ones created, the deathless who have Olympian homes.*
> *These lived under Kronos, when he ruled in heaven;*
> *like gods they lived, having carefree hearts,*
> *far from toils and misery; nor was old age evident*
> *upon them, but always the same in feet and hands,*
> *rejoicing in full heartiness, away from all evils;*
> *and they died as if overcome by sleep. All worthwhile things were theirs.*
> [*Works and Days*, 109–17]

The chasm between them and us looms larger still when we consider their vast feats of strength (moving rivers, decapitating monsters, holding up the sky), and their often gigantic size. "There were giants in the earth in those days", says Genesis [6:4]. In short, the

GOLDEN AGE PHENOMENON
The past comes to be seen as different in an absolute sense from the present.

Giants, in fact, seem to have left evidence of themselves all over the place. In Sardinia, the megalithic tombs accompanying the prehistoric stone residence-towers ubiquitous on that island are called *tombe di giganti*, "giants' tombs". Archaeologists tell us that "their name derives from local legends that identified these structures as graves of an extinct race of giants" [Blake 2001a, 4]. In Greece, the classical folklorist Adrienne Mayor has shown that the notion of giants got a boost from enormous fossil bones that occasionally washed out of the earth, usually from one of the abundant beds of Tertiary fossils around the Aegean. "The widespread notion that heroes [like Ajax and Achilles] stood about 15 feet tall received confirmation whenever the isolated bones of extinct elephants or rhinos were exposed, because the femurs, shoulder blades, and other familiar bones do resemble giant counterparts of human anatomy—especially when the animals' skulls are missing. A mastodon or mammoth femur is roughly three times the size of a man's thigh bone" [Mayor 2000a, 60]. And three times five feet (ancient Greeks were shorter than we are) equals fifteen. Several ancient authors mention that giant bones were deposited in temples and the like, and in fact fossil bones have actually turned up at the Temple of Hera on Samos, at Troy, and at Nichoria, says Mayor. Such bones reinforced, of course, the notion of a former Golden Age of heroic people, gigantomachies, and the like [Mayor 2000b, 165–209].

Quite the opposite of the Golden Age Phenomenon is the modern Principle of Uniformitarianism, which postulates that geology and biology (like chemistry and physics) *have always* behaved as they do now. Thus, data obtainable from the world right around us has the potential to explain the geological and biological events of long ago. Historians of science view the formulation of this concept as a great watershed in the development of scientific thinking. But the battle for its acceptance in the life sciences began as recently as 1833, less than two centuries ago, with the publication of Sir Charles Lyell's *Principles of Geology*. This book sparked a war with the reigning "catastrophists" (who insisted on the Golden Age model), a fight that raged another twenty-five years before scholars became widely convinced of the veracity of uniformitarianism, through the rapidly growing evidence from geology and archaeology. Even today, however, many prefer the notion of Golden Ages, and the battle still continues in some of America's schools. Making the *assumption* that the overarching rules don't change—whether one is convinced of the principle or not—alters the whole game and can lead one, however slowly, to the data needed to figure out what the nonwillful "natural laws" are.

If, however, we subscribe to the Golden Age Phenomenon, we can go a step further in another direction and conclude, by the UFO Corollary, that *if certain events are not understood, according to already known ("natural") principles, they must be un-understandable—that is, "super-natural"— and there is no point in trying to understand them. They are automatically re-categorized as different in an absolute sense from the known/understood.*

That is, if things need not follow the laws we see in operation around us, then we have no basis on which even to try to figure them out. So funny lights in the sky caused by unusual (but law-abiding) meteorological phenomena could just as well be UFOs from outer space— or magical firebirds. (The colorful Russian "firebird" that flies through the air at night was almost certainly a description of the aurora borealis. In Pasadena, however, where we have lived for decades, residents and police have learned simply to assume that funny lights in the sky result either from something sent up very high from Vandenberg Air Force Base, or from some new and cleverly engineered prank launched over the city by Caltech students.) And "cattle mutilations" on the distant pastures of one's ranch can be blithely attributed to space aliens or worse, instead of to the host of small predators which have always helped themselves to unattended carcasses (see chapter 12). The shallowmindedness of television teams who put together "specials" on such subjects without learning from knowledgeable forensic experts demonstrates once again the fact that many people *prefer* the mystery and romance of the Golden Age hypothesis to reasoned logic and careful evidence.

The general collapse of earlier time and events into one indistinguishable mudpuddle is well known to cognitive scientists studying the origins of false beliefs (not to mention to people who are simply getting older). Stephen Ceci, for instance, collected the following example, from a television trivia expert:

> Dear Inman: Was there ever a TV series called "The Survivors"? I remember it was about some people who'd been stranded on an island in an airplane crash. I also remember Lily Tomlin appearing on it before she was

anybody. Could the time period be around 1969 or 1970?—Rick, Great Falls, Mont.

Dear Rick: Gee, you've managed to remember most of the ABC Monday evening lineup from the Fall of 1969 and mix all of the shows together. . . . The show you mention, "The Survivors," was a "Dynasty" style soap opera. . . . It starred Lana Turner. . . . The second show about people stranded on an island was called "The New People," and it aired just before "The Survivors." . . . And the third show, the one with Lily Tomlin, was called "The Music Scene." [Ceci 1997, 92–93]

Time interacts with analogy to compress things in other curious ways. Since every year it happens that the Nile floods its banks, then the muddy fields reappear and the crops grow and are harvested, the recurrent nature of these events may come to dominate one's worldview. People begin to ask not "On what date did it happen?" but "Where in the cycle did it happen?" Thus, the Cyclic Phenomenon: *if events at two or more points in time resemble each other strongly, they must be related or even "the same", and therefore returning. If the "same" events are seen to return many times, the observers may conclude that time is cyclical rather than linear.* Such cultures may have a linear view of immediate time but a cyclical view of large-scale time. Thus, in ancient India, the Sanskrit language had past, present, and future tenses for daily use, but one of the chief Indic deities was believed to cause a cosmic cycle of destruction and rebirth by his fiery whirling dance (figure 16): no yearly dying fertility god, this. Shiva the Destroyer seems to represent the periodic collapse and reestablishment of all the celestial coordinates—the pillars of the world—every couple of millennia, as the sun precesses relentlessly through the twelve constellations of the Zodiac (see chapter 16).

Recurrence of the "same event" across time creates one sort of analysis, but close succession in time of two different events creates quite another: that the first event made the second one happen. For example, we mentioned the scene in *Black Orpheus* in which the little boys played the guitar on the hillside to try to cause the sun to come up.

POST HOC, ERGO PROPTER HOC
("After this, therefore because of this")
Because one event occurs soon after another event, the prior event is taken to have caused the later event.

Figure 16. Shiva the Destroyer, whose whirling dance in a fiery ring cyclically destroys the "world ages". Traditional sculpture, South India.

The Klamath medicine men jumped into the erupting crater, and soon the volcano stopped erupting. "Therefore" their sacrifice caused it to stop. The town drunk died; someone else died four days later; therefore the drunk must have become a vampire and killed the second person. I smelled a funny smell, then I got a headache; so I conclude that a toxic fume caused the headache.

But however commonly we do it, as a *form of reasoning* Post Hoc, Ergo Propter Hoc is fallacious. The fume may or may not have caused the headache—we need more evidence to know. Perhaps the funny smell was merely breakfast cooking; maybe last night's five martinis caused the headache. As logician William Neblett puts it, it's like saying that because day *follows* night, therefore night *causes* day [Neblett 1985, 193].

At least with day and night, we have enough examples to determine *correlation*—one always follows the other. But if that was the first time I smelled that funny odor, I don't even have correlation yet, just temporal proximity. And spatial proximity may serve as well for jumping to conclusions: the corpse is in the kitchen, therefore the cook did it: *Prope hoc, ergo propter hoc.* The problem is that our brains are constructed to seek out patterns so avidly that they will happily pounce onto single cases and pronounce them patterns.

Attraction through various types of similarity—quality, association, name, time, location, and so on—is not the only way data get compressed in mythology.

Who cut off Samson's hair? Ask anyone. They'll all say it was Delilah—unless they memorized Bible verses as children. In fact, after Delilah had persuaded Samson to fall asleep in her lap, she ordered one of her henchmen to come cut the fatal hair:

> When Delilah saw that he had told her all his mind, . . . she made him sleep upon her knees; and she called a man, and had him shave off the seven locks of his head. Then she began to torment him, and his strength left him. [Judges 16:18–19]

The servant has gotten lost in the long chain of retellings—that is, in the oral pipeline.

DELILAH EFFECT

As a story is retold and retold, the actions of the minor char-
acters are eventually attributed to the major characters.

At the same time that we blush for getting it wrong, however, we are
saying inside ourselves: "So what? The important thing is that Samson
lost his magical hair and Delilah made it happen."

Precisely. The reduction of characters had no effect on the key elements of the story. So (unless you were the servant and this was your
one moment of fame) the loss does not matter, and in fact, this compression of information makes the story fit into the oral pipeline a little
more efficiently, a definite plus.[3]

Because the Bible and its stories have been so important in Western
tradition, they have generated a continuing oral pipeline of people recounting these stories. And because we have the Bible as a written text,
we can go back and check out the form of each story that entered the
pipe and catch this principle in operation, over and over.

Ask people about the biblical Flood and they will tell you of Noah
and his ark filled with two each of every kind of animal, just as the folk-
song says:

> *The animals came in two by two—*
> *There's one more river to cross;*
> *The elephant and the kangaroo—*
> *There's one more river to cross.*

If you press them, they may recall that Noah had a wife and three sons
on board. Typically the servants and other householders get lost—they
add nothing essential to the tale. And what about the rest of the animals that came along? (Quick, where's that mental rolodex? *What* other
animals?) God, the Bible states, instructed Noah to put in *fourteen* each
(seven pairs) of the "clean" animals and one pair each of the "unclean"
ones, plus seven pairs of each type of bird (Gen. 7). But since you need
only one of each sex for reproduction, *two* of each species constitute the
"major" characters for all practical purposes, and we can conveniently
dispense with the rest. As a practical consequence, we can appeal, for

---

[3] Schudson [1997, 347] refers to an interesting modern parallel "in the work of Robert
Merton on the 'Matthew effect' in science, where citations tend to credit the better-known
scientist of jointly authored papers, even when the scientist is the junior author of the work
(Merton, 1968, 1988)."

analytical work, to the Distillation Factor: *Stories with more characters typically have stayed in the oral pipeline a shorter time than stories with fewer characters, which have been distilled down to essentials.*

For example, the Old Testament too flowed through oral pipelines for many centuries before being committed to writing. But we have a much older written text which tells a Flood story so similar that the two must have sprung from a common source. This older text, contained in the Sumerian *Epic of Gilgamesh*, has even more people on the surviving boat than appear on Noah's ark:

> I loaded into [the boat] all that I had of gold and of living things, my family, my kin, the beasts of the field both wild and tame, and all the craftsmen. I sent them on board. . . . I looked out at the weather and it was terrible, so I too boarded the boat and battened her down. All was now complete . . . so I handed the tiller to Puzur-Amurri the steersman. [Sandars 1964, 106–7]

This multitude suggests that the Sumerian story did not stay in the oral pipeline as long as the story of Noah did—the narrators have whittled it down less. Indeed, if some sort of actual event (see chapter 16) triggered these two Flood stories, the *Gilgamesh* version, written down some 1,500 years before the biblical version, had 1,500 years fewer in the pipe.

Consider in this light the Greek myth of Deukalion and Pyrrha. When Prometheus learned that Zeus was about to destroy mankind with a flood, he warned his son Deukalion to make a boat and embark with his wife Pyrrha. As the waters subsided, Deukalion and Pyrrha landed on Mount Parnassos (above Delphi, viewed by the local culture as the center of the earth), where they received divine instructions to repopulate the world by throwing the "bones of their mother" over their shoulders, which they did by casting stones (bones of Mother Earth) behind them.

Here we are down to two humans and no animals at all—presumably a *very* long-told story.

Not all such compressions to a small number of characters function in quite that way, however. Myths, folktales, and rituals often bundle an entire class of possible individuals into a single persona who represents the class as a king or queen represents, acts, and speaks for his or her people. Thus, for example, the Eastern Orthodox wedding ritual portrays the bride and groom as a Princess and Prince who come to the church to be crowned. The ritual makes it quite clear that the two individuals represent the actions and desired attributes of *all* such couples: as it were, the kingdom of fertile males mating with the queendom of fertile females. This differs from Zeus and Hera (who as King and Queen of the gods represent all married couples) only in that the individuals are different with each "enactment"—but the titles remain the same. The English King and Queen of the May function much the same way, as do myriad other "royalty" in traditional stories: the King of the Sea (representing all its inhabitants, real or imagined), the Bear Spirit (representing all bears), and so on. We could call this type of compression the Class-Action Corollary: *The attributes and actions of a class of beings may be represented as a single individual portrayed as King or Queen of the group.*

Narrations not concerned with the regeneration of a *species*, of course, have no need to stop the whittling at two characters: one protagonist may suffice. And so we see it in story after story of yet a different type, that in which a single person makes a long journey, then begets an entire race or clan.

Thus Io, stung by the gadfly, rushed off to Egypt where she became grandmother of Libye and the Libyans, and great-grandmother of Aigyptos and the Egyptians. Perseus, after turning his enemies to stone with Medusa's severed head and being exiled for accidentally killing his grandfather, travelled to Asia where he fathered Perses and the Persians. In another story, the sorceress Medea fled to Asia from Athens after attempting to kill Theseus's son, taking along her son Medos, who fathered the Medes after killing Perses, son of Helios.[4] We know from Herodotus and other sources that the Medes and the Persians wandered around a good deal before settling in the Iranian plateau. But, like the other Iranians, they moved as nomadic tribes. Far more likely, in this case, than one person moving and then spawning is that a group of people who shared the same clan or family name moved and resettled. Hence the very frequent Eponymous Hero Syndrome, in which *the migrations of tribes are reduced to the journey of an individual—one who was, or is seen as, the leader or progenitor of the group in some sense. Conversely, a known group may be assumed to descend from such an eponymous ("named-after") hero.*

The Greeks became so accustomed to such stories that when tradi-

---

[4] H. J. Rose is at pains to keep Perses son of Perseus separate from two other Perseses [Rose 1959, 37, 264]. But we wonder, given that both stories have *Med*-s and *Pers*-s in them, whether the stories and characters are not somehow doublets (chapter 7) of each other: two slightly different versions of the origin of the Medes and Persians.

tion did *not* include a specifiable ancestor for a given tribe or clan, they provided one by back-formation from the name of the group, such that it is sometimes hard to tell which story went which way. Thus the Hellenes were later said to come from a hero, Hellen, son of Deukalion and Pyrrha, who in turn begat Dorus (eponymous father of the Dorians), Aiolus (father of the Aiolians), and Xuthus (stepfather to Apollo's son Ion, who in turn begat the eponymous ancestors of the four Ionian tribes) [Rose 1959, 257, 268]. Note that the Fairest-of-Them-All Effect has struck again, in that the Greeks here derive themselves from Hellen, the only true son of the only survivors of the Flood, whereas everyone else comes merely from the rocks thrown. (Rose tells us that eventually the Greeks became so accustomed to their poets laureate inventing eponymous heroes that "Korinthos, son of Zeus, was a person whom no one [who was] not a Corinthian believed in, and his very name [became] a synonym for a piece of tiresome nonsense" [Rose 1959, 269].)

Notice, too, that the Eponymous Hero Syndrome results from the Principle of Attraction by Name, the Perspective Principle, and the Distillation Factor all ganging up together. Since everyone of a given clan could take on the name of the perceived progenitor—Heraklidai, Danaids, Volsungs, Scyldings (yes, the Germanic peoples did this too)—it can quickly become unclear how many generations were involved in the migration or feud.[5] As offspring of X, all members of the group become reinterpretable as the immediate children of X, with a consequent compression of both individuals and time.

Reinterpretation of a data-set inevitably leaves it open to restructuring, a tool that the human brain has used for eons to compress linguistic data into something manageable. Each child must learn its first language from the data it hears, but a simple strategy of imitating so many utterances soon overwhelms the memory banks. The solution is pattern-matching so as to compress many component items into a few, over and over, layer after layer: *ride/rode* like *drive/drove* like *write/wrote*; *I pick/he picks* like *I cut/he cuts* like *I stop/he stops*. For it is these multiple layers of patterning (with patterns at the syntactic level even bearing meanings) that provide the key to language's remarkable flexibility and infinitude—the key to linguistic complexity. Linguists are

---

[5] Other Germanic instances exist. It sometimes surprises readers of the *Niebelungenlied* that King Etzel with his court is a remembrance of none other than Attila the Hun, whose warrior hordes terrorized Europe. (*Attila* became *Etzel* by two regular sound changes: the second Germanic consonant shift and umlaut.)

still documenting the successive waves of collection and compression that the young brain goes through: random sounds yield to more manageable syllable-types, the many syllables to a few phonemes, myriad speech chunks to reusable words and eventually morphemes, thousands of sentences to systematic syntactic types, and so on. Even at age twenty we still tumble to an occasional pattern we hadn't noticed before. Pattern matching, interpreting, structuring, compressing, and restructuring: these we thrive on.

But the contents of the language have changed since one's parents learned it. New words and phrases (like *karaoke*, *jihad*, *download*, and *You the man!*) have entered via borrowing and analogy, while other expressions (like *rumble-seat* and *Banana-oil!*) have dropped out; and sound change, though slow, upsets parts of the system Mama and Papa perceived, by creating, for example, new sets of homonyms. (Currently in America pairs like *where/wear*, *whine/wine*, *which/witch*, or *caught/cot*, *hawk/hock*, *caller/collar* are becoming indistinguishable; centuries earlier pairs like *beat/beet*, *creak/creek*, *peal/peel* did so.) This means that Baby not only *structures* the incoming data, but *restructures* it, from the perspective of the parents. Their systems differ.

The differences between parent and child are small enough that the two systems are mostly mutually intelligible; tangles occur more often in the classroom, where students and older teachers differ likewise. (About twenty years ago, students began coming into college with a syntactic pattern placing the adverb before the verb instead of after it: no longer *he ran quickly* but *he quickly ran*—a pattern that often sounds terrible to people over fifty.) But the obscuring differences keep accumulating, and the process accelerates enormously when major cultural changes occur, as with the Norman invasion of England in 1066 (remember the nobleman dining in his chamber). The Middle English of Chaucer is vaguely readable today; the Old English of *Beowulf* seems a foreign language. Sufficient restructuring, the result of seeking compressive patterns, makes the older language opaque. Just so will we find it with mythology.

12

Post Hocus Ergo Pocus: Space Aliens Mutilate Cows!

HUMANE SOCIETY OFFERS REWARD FOR CONVICTION IN "HEINOUS" CAT MUTILATIONS

Following reports of the disembowelment mutilation of a pet cat belonging to a Salt Lake Avenues [*sic*] resident, the Humane Society of Utah has offered a reward of $2,500 for information leading to the identification and conviction of the perpetrator or perpetrators of an act that [the Director] describes as "a heinous, revolting manifestation of the very worst impulses that human beings are capable of generating."   —www.utahhumane.org [July 2002]

T he reader may wonder by now if anyone still thinks according to the principles we've been describing. The answer is clearly affirmative, as can be demonstrated by investigating a modern "myth". Periodically, people notice that small pets—dogs and cats—are being killed and mutilated. Indeed, in the epigraph we see that the Humane Society put out a reward for information leading to the apprehension of those responsible for such a crime. Yet such events scarcely make it into the news. What would make such a story newsworthy? Well, bigger, more valuable animals.

In the late 1960s, it was reported that cattle were being killed and mutilated in the western United States. Blame was leveled variously at mysterious sects, space aliens, and government agencies using helicopters.

The helicopters were necessary because there wasn't any evidence of tracks of either humans or vehicles in the vicinity of the dead cattle. The mutilations went on for years, then ended for a long time, then were renewed in the fall of 2001 [see, e.g., Howe 2002; Oyan 2002; *Outher Limits* [sic] Internet site; www.algonet.se/~maggrand/cattle; several of these have pictures].

Let's consider the phenomena commonly associated with the cattle mutilations:

1. There was no evident cause of death of the cow.
2. There were no tracks in the vicinity, even in mud or snow.
3. Certain parts of the animal's anatomy had been cut out "with surgical precision".
4. The carcass was typically attacked at the tongue, eyes, sex organs, and udders.
5. The affected animals seemed to bloat faster than usual.
6. Cuts were often circular or oval and sometimes looked as though made with a tool resembling pinking shears.
7. The exposed flesh was sometimes blackened.
8. The carcasses were sometimes left untouched by predators.
9. The perpetrators mysteriously stopped mutilating cows for years on end.

If we subject this mystery to the kind of analysis we've been doing, we shall see some of our principles very clearly. This is because the cattle mutilations aren't really much of a mystery at all. When experts on dead animals have investigated them, they have concluded that the animals died of natural causes and that their wounds were proof that scavengers had made a meal of them. But if this is so, then the above list of phenomena should be easily explained.

And it is. Let's consider the items one by one:

1. "No evident cause of death of the cow." "Evident" here seems to mean that there wasn't a bullet hole, or bite marks from, say, a mountain lion. But in fact cattle, like people, die from a multitude of causes, many of which are not at all obvious even with a necropsy. And dead cattle are not commonly given necropsies.

2. "No tracks in the vicinity, even in mud or snow." Lack of tracks from people or vehicles doesn't mean anything more than that people and vehicles probably weren't involved in the event. Birds can, of course, alight directly on their prey. The question of animal tracks, however, is very complex. The movies have taught an entire generation of Americans that it's simple and easy to spot animal tracks—any western hero can do so at a glance. Tracking, however, is a highly specialized art that takes many years to learn; nor can you easily spot the tracks of even large, heavy animals. One tracking expert observes that he often sees beginning trackers trying to decipher tracks and signs while standing up or sitting on their haunches: he has to make them get down on their hands and knees or even on their belly [Brown 1983, 208].

Any professional tracker will tell you it means nothing at all if the average person can't see animal tracks, even of large animals, and if you want a real challenge, try tracking your cat through your yard. Many years ago one of us took lessons from a professional tracker; we followed a large wild pig that had preceded us by about two hours. (The pig had obligingly walked through a puddle, and the disintegration of the track in water enabled the tracker to estimate the time.) The tracks appeared and disappeared mysteriously. But the tracker got down on all fours and and peered sideways at what appeared to be nothing, then, pointing out details of the nothing, led us on. Our efforts to contribute information eventually led to a nice comedy: some distance ahead, we saw clear hoof-prints going up a hill. "There they are, going up the hill." The tracker, without looking up, said, "Nope, those are cow tracks, and they're coming *down* the hill. The pig will have gone up where it's not so steep." As we got closer, the tracks we had spotted became embarrassingly huge and changed shape.

So it is often not at all easy to detect tracks, even of large animals, and in some circumstances it is impossible. Moreover, there are powerful reasons for concluding that, although it is indeed animals that are responsible for the cattle mutilations, they are small animals, not large ones.

How do we know this? Large animals attack their prey in predictable ways that rule them out. It's easy to identify a mountain lion's kill, for example, because the lion bites into the neck of its prey. And it typically eviscerates large prey and feeds first on the liver. Years ago, when we asked that hunting guide if there were really lots of mountain lions around, as he claimed, he took us around the countryside and showed us several kills of blacktail deer. (One or two he knew of already; others he found by observing turkey vultures.) Quickly it became clear that a mutilated cow and a deer killed by a mountain lion have little in common.

But although we can easily rule out large predators in the cattle mutilations, it's not so easy to rule out small scavengers. Keep in mind that the creatures that "mutilated" the carcass aren't necessarily responsible for the death of the cow. All they had to do is chew on it. And small animals are light on their feet. So let's return to that dead cow and look again for animal tracks. Only now we're looking for the tracks of a badger or fox, or coyote, bobcat, or weasel.

We've been told there are no animal tracks, "even in mud or snow". But if the scavengers were nocturnal, they may well have approached the carcass at night, when it was very cold. (And here it should be pointed out that in areas with low humidity, and especially at higher altitudes, it can be quite hot in the daytime and quite cold at night.) The scavenger may have come and gone before snow turned into water and transformed the soil into mud. The mud may have been frozen; the snow may not have fallen yet. The snow may have been frozen hard enough to support the weight of the (rather small) scavenger. It's important to remember that if people had seen the footprints of scavengers, there would be no mystery. So there's a kind of natural selection for the mysterious. A carcass surrounded by animal tracks and showing clear evidence of bite-marks would never make it onto the Internet.

But let's get on to the evidence that it was in fact scavengers that did the mutilating.

3. "Certain parts of the animal's anatomy cut out 'with surgical precision'." This is not nearly so suspicious a circumstance as it seems. Carnivorous animals typically have carnassial teeth where humans have their molars—in the back of the mouth, on either side. These form a kind of shears, designed for cutting away chunks of meat. This is why your dog chews your new shoes apart with the back teeth on one side of its mouth.

Does Fido do so with "surgical precision"? Our own experiments here, performed with volunteer help from our Australian shepherds, show that animal teeth can make remarkably clean cuts. Rows of smaller teeth make yet cleaner lines.

4. "Carcass typically attacked at tongue, eyes, sex organs, udders." Here we are reminded of the remark in *Moby-Dick* that "the whale would by all hands be considered a noble dish, were there not so much of him; but when you come to sit down before a meat-pie nearly one hundred feet long, it takes away your appetite" [Melville 1851/1964, 391]. The reader has probably never pondered what a dead cow would look like to a badger or a ferret, but we suspect much of it would look overwhelming. In fact, what we see here is clearly a choice based not on bizarre rituals but on what is soft and accessible. The very task of chewing through cowhide would be daunting, let alone getting a small jaw around a large sparerib. So the smaller scavengers—the very ones least likely to leave footprints—attack the carcass at the softest, most accessible places. They attack the udders, tongue, and so forth not out of perverted blood-lust but because these are softer than anything else.

5. "Seemed to bloat faster than usual." This statement is really put backwards: it's the carcasses that bloat faster than usual that are *most* accessible to small scavengers. This is because the bloating puts pressure on the body from the inside, everting the various soft parts, thereby making them even more accessible to predators. Why would some carcasses bloat faster than others? There are various reasons, the most obvious being that bodies decompose quicker at higher temperatures than at low. A carcass in the sun will bloat faster, in general, than one in the shade. The mode of death influences the speed of decay as well.

6. "Cuts often circular or oval and sometimes looked as though made with pinking shears." To learn what such cuts would look like, it helps to experiment. Keep in mind that the scavenger is manipulating a set of shears. If you stuff a plastic bag with cotton, then cut a piece off with a pair of scissors, the result is an oval hole. Since the bag is spherical, the scissors cut deeper as they approach the middle of their cut—then shallower as they pass it. The size of the scissors limits the width of the cut, but the length of the cut depends on the persistence of the operator of the shears. In any case, both the beginning and end of the cut are invariably the pointed ends of an oval.

But what if the shears aren't cutting a rounded surface? What if the surface is flat or concave? Well, then the shears can't make a cut at all. In other words, the scavenger selects for a surface it can get a grip on.

That's one reason why a small scavenger is more likely to attack the udders or tongue than, say, a great expanse of beef-haunch bigger than its own body and armored with hair and hide.

As for the round cuts, they could be made by birds (not just vultures eat carrion; many birds do, including crows, ravens, magpies, hawks, and eagles) and also by more than one scavenger. If two predators chew on the same cow, the second is likely to start where the first had gained access to lunch. It's our guess that a round cut is more likely than a trapezoid or parallelogram.

Note that we've been given two descriptions of the cut itself: "with surgical precision" or "as from pinking shears". Neither description should come as a surprise. Carnassial teeth rather resemble pinking shears, and our experiments suggest considerable variations in the appearance of a piece of meat or hide cut by them. Chewing on beef hide, our dogs sometimes made cuts that had the pinking-shears effect. Different animals, one supposes, could leave cuts with different characteristics.

7. "Exposed flesh sometimes blackened." This is simply not abnormal. The curious reader is invited to check books on forensic pathology for examples of human corpses showing this trait, but we warn you, this is not for the faint of heart.

8. "Carcasses sometimes left untouched by predators." All the evidence suggests the carcasses were *not* left untouched by predators. Oddly, the carcasses are thought abnormal if they're eaten, yet if they're not eaten—then they're also abnormal. But perhaps the mystery is that the scavengers didn't finish all the food on their plate, or that larger animals, such as bears and mountain lions, didn't dine on the carcass. Here, as so often, it's easier to wonder than to prove. Were the larger animals not hungry? Were they suspicious of the carcass for some reason? Had they left the area for the time being? (Mountain lions and bears have very large territories.) Did they have other things on their minds? Did the smaller predators somehow make the dead cow unattractive, as with a scent marking? Many years ago we sat up over a dead cow, at the behest of our hunting guide, waiting for the arrival of *Sus scrofa*, the European wild boar. (Pigs eat anything, which is why they're called pigs.) But on that day, no wild pigs at all showed up. Were they fasting? Had they found a younger, tenderer dead cow? Had they succumbed to the blandishments of a pig with leadership qualities and vegan leanings? There was no way of knowing. But the hunting guide, whose very livelihood depended on his understanding pigs, did not find their absence remarkable.

9. "The perpetrators mysteriously stopped mutilating cows for years on end." This appears to have more to do with the fickleness of the media than anything else: dead cows, like dead movie stars, get a limited amount of exposure in the news, but they are held in reserve against a slow news day. And if we don't even know why the cows died, we're unlikely to know why more cows die, or at least are noticed by the media, in one year than in another.

This particular "myth" gives us the opportunity to observe some of the thought-transformations we've discussed in this book, since we know both the resulting story and the real-life phenomena behind it. One noteworthy transformation we've seen here is what we called Attraction (chapter 11). The central mystery—dead cows—has Attracted to it a number of minor mysteries, which are assumed to be related to it simply because of proximity (cf. Post Hoc, Ergo Propter Hoc: chapter 11).[1] In reality, the pinking-shears quality of carnassial teeth-cuts has nothing to do with the *death* of the cow, but the one mystery enfolds the other. In other words, people don't say, "Hey, in addition to the death of the cows, there's another mystery: why they have cuts on them that look as if they were made by pinking shears." Instead, our minds assimilate the two mysteries into one.

The matter is further complicated by another common phenomenon we see clearly in the cattle mutilation stories, what we called the Movie Construct (chapter 4). What was actually seen is not a process at all; it's just a single tableau that resulted from a process. Process is then deduced by the observer. This can be like trying to deduce the game of baseball from a picture of two players crashing into each other at second base. To get an idea of how far afield this kind of thinking can go, we need to cogitate on two of the common explanations for the cattle mutilations:

1. The cattle were mutilated by aliens, who avoided leaving tracks by floating down out of the atmosphere in spaceships. The motives of the aliens were unclear. (Compare the UFO Corollary, chapter 11.)
2. The cattle were hoisted off the ground by government agents in heli-

---

[1] Joshua Katz points out to us that *hocus pocus* is a mutilation(!) of the Eucharistic phrase *Hoc est corpus [meum]*, "This is [my] body."

copters, then taken off for nefarious experiments involving radiation at government installations. Finally, now dead, they were returned to where they had been abducted.

This theory requires that the cattle actually be returned to their pasture—for no apparent reason—after being mutilated, even though it is much simpler to assume the mutilations occurred where the cow lay. The gratuitous complexity of the theory reminds one of the old joke that Homer's works weren't actually written by Homer at all but by someone else of the same name.

When we first read of the cattle mutilations, we found them completely opaque, even though one of us was writing a book then on folklore based on the grislier aspects of decomposition [Barber 1988]. Our analysis kept getting waylaid by the theories, and it was a long time before we applied the Stripping Procedure (chapter 4), asking, "What if they're just dead cows? What *would* happen to a dead cow?" By that time the FBI had published an almost unreadable collection of scribbled-over letters and reports arguing this very position.

Imagine what difficulties would be presented, however, if you had nothing but the space-aliens theory to work with, and the observations were not separated out from the deductions—something like this: "Creatures from another realm came down out of the sky and attacked and killed cattle, stealthily mutilating them in horrible ways, then vanished without a trace." There is little here that would suggest a connection to actuality. Moreover, there is nothing preventing further Attractions from taking place and making this mystery into a subplot of larger mysteries.

But this suggests that stories can be opaque *from their inception* if we lack any information about the framework they come from. And that brings us back to those pets being mutilated in Utah. While working on this chapter, we strolled off for the morning newspaper and encountered a dead squirrel on the sidewalk, well off the roadway, and quite flat, as if run over by a truck. When we came back ten minutes later, a crow had found the squirrel, and we stopped to see what the crow had done in the few minutes we'd been gone. It had pecked its way into the corpse at the squirrel's mouth and had already pulled the esophagus up and was feasting on it. Later we remembered the squirrel and went back to check on its welfare. In the intervening four hours (this on a comfortably warm day in January), the squirrel had begun to bloat; it was no longer flat. The crow had eaten away the meat from one front leg, cleaned the top end of the backbone nicely, and removed pretty much all remnants of the head—and all this without the help of black helicopters and aliens. The "mutilation", in other words, was completed by purely natural means. This is not to say that human beings never torture and kill pets, only that if they once and for all ceased doing so, mutilated small animals would still appear on our streets.

Mysteries remain, however. How does a flattened squirrel end up on the sidewalk? Did the truck swerve to hit it while it was on the sidewalk? (There were no tracks.) Why did the crow stop eating? Why didn't other crows come by to finish up? If squirrels were valuable, we would probably construct a theory accounting for all these mysteries; as it is, most of us don't normally take the trouble even to look at a dead squirrel, let alone take notes on its disassembly by predators.

And this is not proof that the dead cat in Utah was mutilated by animals. Still, it is exceedingly common for scavengers to disembowel their dinner, while it is—praise be!—not common at all for human beings to do this just for fun.[2] And our veterinarian, Dr. Mary Jo Andrews, tells us that when it does happen, it is difficult to convince people it was a coyote that did it, rather than a neighbor. (One of her clients found their cat mutilated, buried it, then, becoming suspicious of its mode of death, dug it up again and brought it in to find out what had happened. She convinced them that the mutilation was surely accomplished by a coyote.) The theory of choice, then, usually involves something exotic rather than prosaic.

What all this suggests is that we have little hope of making out the real-life content of a myth unless we have a great deal of evidence, and the best evidence is people pointing at a mountain and saying, "That one is where the Chief of the Below World lived." Once we know the central phenomenon, we can approach the problem by studying up on its characteristics. This is why volcanos are useful for studying mythology: they stay put and reveal, for thousands of years, the evidence of their history.

And this is why much mythology that has slipped its real-life moorings is probably destined to be opaque, or largely opaque, forever. This is especially true when people have carried a myth with them away from

---

[2] After this book was completed, the *Los Angeles Times* [Aug. 2, 2003, A23] printed a story about forty-five supposed cat-mutilations in Colorado. Colorado animal-control officers and the local police had finally concluded that predators, not people, were the culprits, "ending weeks of suspicion that budding psychopaths and devil worshippers were killing the pets."

their homeland (Fogging Effect, chapter 10). The myth, after all, does not stop being shaped by our cognitive quirks just because we've moved from mountains to plains. If you leave the vicinity of a volcano, you take your volcano myths with you, only now there isn't a huge mountain nearby to remind you what the myth is about. This doesn't just allow changes in the myth, it speeds them. In time, the story needs revisions to make any kind of sense at all, and such reworkings bring us to our next principle.

13

Restructuring:
New Patterns for Old

RESTRUCTURING PRINCIPLE

Whenever there is a significant cultural change, at least some patterns will get restructured or reinterpreted. Successive changes on a given pattern will render the form of the pattern un-understandable to its users—it goes from a matter of logic to one of faith, and finally to a matter of disbelief.

KREON:
Take the [sisters] inside, servants; and from this they will be forced To act like women rather than running around.
                    —Sophocles, *Antigone* 578–79

Τ he Attic tragedians of the fifth century B.C. inherited a great treasure-house of antique myths from which they devised their dramas for the glorification of the gods and the betterment of the people—or at least of the men, since women other than servants were rarely let out of the house except for funerals. Yet almost half the surviving tragedies have as their titles the names of women: *Antigone, Alcestis, Hecuba, Medea, Andromache, Helena,* and two each for Electra and Iphigeneia. In myth after inherited myth, women not only caused events but performed the major actions. Antigone creates the strife in her story by going out to the battlefield and burying her brother Polyneikes (who had attacked his own city) in defiance of King Kreon's orders.

The discrepancy between how women functioned in myth and in classical Athens caused much difficulty for the playwrights as they struggled to make their heroines believable on stage. Jean Anouilh, in his redaction of the story 2,500 years after Sophocles, picks up the atmosphere of Sophocles' setting perfectly by showing Antigone tiptoeing, sandals in hand, back into the house at dawn (after throwing dust over her dead brother) and being accosted instantly by the nurse. How else could a closely watched female leave but furtively? Electra too stays close to home while plotting her mother's murder, while Medea sends messengers out to do her fatal bidding.

But the evidence from the myths themselves shows strongly that many of the pre-Hellenic communities of Greece and Crete were organized matrilineally. That is, inheritance of house and lands descended through the female line, a type of organization common among horticultural—as opposed to agricultural—societies.[1] In a matrilineal society, the woman's brothers, uncles, and sons act as military defence when necessary, while her marriage serves to strengthen external alliances and her sexual encounters to produce strong offspring. Kingship descends

---

[1] Horticulture involves garden crops (like fruit, nuts, olives) tended by hand, rather than crops like grain grown in fields plowed by large animals. Since the women with their children underfoot can manage the central food supply, the men are freed to go outside the community for long periods to obtain other resources, and the two groups develop partially independent societies. Thus Nausicaa tells Odysseus to ignore her father and ask her mother for shelter *in the household*; but after the queen accepts Odysseus, she turns to her husband (who is also her uncle, in good matrilineal form) and tells him to take the guest off to the harbor to do men's things, since she and her women are busy in the house with women's things (*Odyssey* 6). Note that matriliny is not the same as "matriarchy"—*rule* by women—for which, despite popular supposition, no anthropological evidence has ever turned up. See Atchity and Barber [1987] for more examples and discussion.

not through the king's sons but through the queen and her daughters. The childbearing woman forms the center of this social web.

By contrast, in patrilineal societies the father holds that pivotal position, and there paternity is everything. Unfortunately, since childbirth makes it quite clear who the mother is but not the father, the menfolk in strongly patrilineal societies tend to lock up their women in hopes of controlling whom the females mate with. In a matriliny, paternity is not a strong issue.

From this difference stems Sophocles' problem. The Mycenaean Greeks, who propagated the Athenian playwrights' myths, lived at a time when the patrilineal Greeks were moving in on and intermarrying with the matrilineal indigenes who controlled the inheritable land. Helen of Troy, for instance, received the rule of Sparta from her mother Leda (who had two famous sons, Castor and Polydeukes, who did *not* get to rule) and passed it on to her daughter Hermione (although Helen's husband Menelaos also had two sons, who also did *not* get to rule). This is undeniable matriliny. It also explains why Menelaos had to get Helen back from Troy if he wanted to continue as "king" of Sparta: like Prince Philip of England, he was simply consort to the hereditary queen, not king in his own right. The same held on Odysseus's isle of Ithaka, where Penelope's suitors wanted to marry Penelope in order to obtain the perks of being king, and where Odysseus's father, Laertes—a sort of "dowager king" sent out to pasture—had no say and no rights concerning what happened to his missing son's "kingship". Such a dual system of incoming patrilineal men marrying autochthonous matrilineal women generated tensions, of course, as in the following incident told in Rose's anthology of Greek myths:

> Temenos [great-grandson of Herakles], like his brother, came to an untimely end, for he favoured his son-in-law Deïphontes [that is, his daughter and her husband] at the expense of his sons; the latter therefore contrived his death. The throne, however, was given to Deïphontes *by right of his wife Hyrnetho.* [Rose 1959, 268; emphasis ours]

Eventually, strengthened by another tide of patrilineal Greek invaders at the end of the Bronze Age, ca. 1200 B.C., patriliny for the most part won out, and patriarchy with it.

No wonder Sophocles, Euripides, and the other later authors struggled so. Times had changed, the entire social structure had shifted from what it had been when the events of the Bronze Age myths had oc-curred, and the myths had become correspondingly opaque. Of course, knowing this principle we can turn it around and use it to make the myths less opaque, by means of the Environmental Clue: *Known changes in technology or location can be exploited to help disentangle restruc-tured beliefs.*

Another type of example, one we've encountered repeatedly, involves volcanos. Suppose an eruption occurs, then presently the clan migrates far from the offending volcano, taking its eruption story along. Unlike the Klamath group that could still point to Crater Lake and other local volcanos, the myth-tellers now have nothing visible—no hardened lava, no craters, no sibling volcanos, nothing to demonstrate what the tale pertains to; and the Fogging Effect sets in. How are the hearers (and, after a generation, the narrators too) now to know what the story means?

In such cases, the narrative goes from a matter of logic to a matter of faith and finally to disbelief, as some elements necessary for under-standing get silenced in the River of Forgetfulness and the remainder is restructured. One could even say that myth "declines" as follows: I have an explanation, you have a religion, he has a mythology.

Let's watch the process. People may start by describing volcanos as giants (they are indeed big) that sometimes bleed hot red liquid (not bad as a simile), are very ill-willed toward humans (witness the destruc-tion), and sometimes make the earth shake as they wiggle about (you can feel it). But if you have never seen one of these bleeding monsters kicking up a fuss and throwing rocks around while hissing and fuming, the image you form in your mind as you listen to the tale will of neces-sity be formed from what you *do* know. The only creatures that most of us have ever seen lobbing rocks are primates; thus your own image al-most of necessity ends up very, very different from that which the orig-inators of the tale had in their sights: a humongous humanoid rather than a particular species of mountain.

Once again, our brains treat language the same way. So many people, for instance, re-envisioned in their minds their elders' phrase *a napron* (originally a type of linen, along with *nap-kins* and *nap-ery*) that now we all consider it to be *an apron*. Similarly, if you ask for *an ice-cold drink*, the addressee has a fifty-fifty chance of hearing it as *a nice cold drink*. Such reanalyses are quite common in language, some resulting in forms that would be as unrecognizable to the speakers of long ago as the humongous humanoid reanalysed from a volcano. Thus Elephant and Castle, the name of a London tube stop, started out centuries ago as a public house in that area called L'Infante de Castille, that is, the Infanta of Castille: no elephants, no castles.

Restructuring turns up regularly in other ways. A change in location may make earlier stories opaque, hence prey to restructuring, but it may also make life enough different that the traditional deities (Willers) no longer cover life's contingencies. For example, when the Germanic peoples migrated far to the north, they met up with ice and snow of formerly unimaginable quantity and duration: enter the Frost Giants. When the Greeks, for their part, moved south into Greece, they encountered a wide variety of new things—from bathtubs to tsunamis, and from sophisticated architecture to fancy weaving. Some of these encounters merely left their marks on the language, in the form of loan words—often in deep strata like archaeological deposits [see Barber 1991, 260–82]. Others affected the mythology and pantheon, in any of several ways.

Notice, first, the following commonsense Power Principle that goes hand in hand with Willfulness: *The bigger the force represented, the more major the deity to represent it.* To see how it works, let's reduce it to absurdity. Tsunamis involve so much more force (especially force not controlled by humans) than bathtubs that a bathtub deity is unthinkable, whereas deities or spirits in charge of tsunamis sometimes occur where tidal waves have been a problem (as in Greece and the Philippines). By the same token, putting a thunder god like the Indo-European Zeus/Jupiter/Thor/Perun toward the top of the pantheon seems quite natural in a place like the steppes, where awe-inspiring storms roll across vast tracts of open territory, whereas rainless Egypt had no use for such a deity and chose the sun as its most powerful divinity.

The sun looms as such a huge and important force everywhere, in fact, that one can hardly blame Max Müller for finding sun gods everywhere, and powerful, central ones at that. Snow, on the other hand, has little power and no deity in a warm country like Greece, except marginally as a personification for poetic purposes. Snow and ice do not even occur in the languages of many peoples in the tropics, let alone in their pantheons, but spirits and demons of snow do occur in the Far North, such as Russian Snegurochka (Snow Maiden).

If, however, a group of people moves from a temperate climate to an icy one, or from a geologically stable area to an unstable one, the shift in importance of powers may well be discernible in the mythology. Comparison of the myths of various Indo-European groups suggests that the parent community mythologized good and helpful powers as "gods" and evil or harmful forces as "giants" or "monsters" of various sorts. But the mythologies of the Germanic and Greek subgroups ended up with gods and giants that differ systematically in interesting ways.

Greek giants show almost exclusively volcanic and seismic traits: chained under the earth, they create earthquakes by their writhing, except when they break loose and start throwing rocks and mountain tops—that is, erupt. The Greeks moved south into a highly seismic area. Germanic giants, on the other hand, have become Frost Giants— terrible ogres who live beyond where mortals can live and who bring the ice and cold. The Germanic tribes moved far to the north. (Could the allegation that the Frost Giants are no longer quite so mean as they once were reflect the gradual and continued melting of the Scandinavian glaciers?) Seismic powers in Germanic mythology are mostly reduced to the person of Loki, writhing on his bed of rocks in a single story (see chapter 17)—except in the volcanic isles of Iceland, which are still being extruded as lava from the great Atlantic Rift. There Thor, god of thunderous black clouds, expanded into the job of dealing with eruptions and quakes, and even today a huge number of Icelanders have the element *Thor* in their names.

We can enunciate this widespread phenomenon as the Diachronic Power Principle: *If a force changes in importance, its deity will change in importance too.* Such changes typically occur with a change of location or technology. Thus volcanism suddenly became important to those Polynesians who moved to Hawaii—and became even more important as strange fiery events increased:

> The famous story about the coming to Hawaii of the volcano goddess, Pele (*pele*, "eruption"), can now with certainty be correlated with a series of spectacular great meteor showers and other temporary celestial events between 900 and 934 A.D. . . . Pele was then transformed from a sky goddess to being the goddess of Hawaiian volcanoes, usurping the role of an earlier Hawaiian volcano god, Ai-laau (*ai-laau*, "destroying the forest by fire"). A more recent legendary battle between Pele and a half-man/half-hog demigod named Kamapua'a (*ka-ma-pu-a'a*, "the sparkling bundle of eyes") encodes the coincidence of the 1301 A.D. apparition of Halley's Comet with the largest rift eruption in Kilauea volcano history. [Masse 1995, 466–67]

We encountered another example of diachronic power shift in earlier chapters, when we saw how the Indo-European god of huge steppeland rivers, the Neptune figure, shrivelled upon reaching the dry valleys of Greece until he was swallowed up by the local god of vast seas and scary tidal waves, Poseidon the Earth-Shaker.

Changes of technology and even of politics can have the same effect. So, for instance, gods to do with fire often expand in scope and importance when the hot-working of metals comes along. And in ancient Mesopotamia, as a particular city-state rose in power, so did its patron deity. Thus Assur took over Marduk's place in key myths when Assyria came to power in the first millennium B.C., just as Marduk had usurped those stories from Enlil a millennium earlier, when Babylon rose and the city of Nippur declined [Jacobsen 1949, 183].

The Diachronic Power Principle pulls at least one curious little eddy behind it, tinged as well by the Golden Age Phenomenon—the phenomenon of Bumping Upstairs: *What belonged to earlier epochs is often viewed as more hallowed and entailing more power than what people do nowadays.* So what belonged to the royalty (for example) of one epoch may belong to the deities of a later one, and so on. For state occasions, kings and queens wear the dress of previous centuries, priests and academics wear medieval robes, and God is portrayed in flowing drapes more in vogue several millennia ago. Brides in Western cities still typically wear the dress of a century prior, on that special day, whereas rural brides in eastern Europe wear costumes built up from archaic elements added piece by piece over the last 20,000 years [Barber 1999]. In language, as we have seen, the name of an actual person like Caesar or Charlemagne may move up to the title of a ruler (German *Kaiser*, Russian *tsar'*, *korol'*). In architecture, the plan of the Aegean *megaron* (containing a columned portico and a room with a central hearth), which functioned in 3500 B.C. as the best house in the village and in 1400 B.C. as the Mycenaean king's palace, was bumped up yet again in the first millennium B.C. to form the basis of the Greek temple. Similarly, the location of the king's palace in Bronze Age Athens, the Akropolis, became the exclusive sanctuary of the goddess Athena in the next millennium.

Because people enjoy prestige, even little things can get bumped upstairs. Lord Raglan describes an interesting step-process whereby possibility becomes restructured as reality in what he calls

the snowball type of story, which grows as it goes. The process is somewhat as follows:

Stage I.—"This house dates from Elizabethan times, and since it lies close to the road which the Virgin Queen must have taken when travelling from X to Y, it may well have been visited by her."

Stage II.—"This house is said to have been visited by Queen Elizabeth on her way from X to Y."

Stage III.—"The state bedroom is over the entrance. It is this room which Queen Elizabeth probably occupied when she broke her journey here on her way from X to Y."

Stage IV.—"According to a local tradition, the truth of which there is no reason to doubt, the bed in the room over the entrance is that in which Queen Elizabeth slept, when she broke her journey here on her way from X to Y." [Raglan 1936/79, 30–31]

As a center of prestige, Queen Elizabeth attracts up the stairs toward herself not just stories but places and objects. Lord Raglan concludes by saying: "A man whom I asked how he knew that Queen Elizabeth had slept in his house asked in return, in a surprised and indignant tone: 'Why shouldn't she have?'" [Raglan 1936/79, 31] (Shades of "George Washington slept here".) We can abstract this process as the Snowball Effect: *A statement of possibility may be restructured as probability and then as fact, which may entrain yet other probabilities which come in turn to be told as fact.* The shift from "if" to "when" in Raglan's example, occurring as it does in a subordinate clause, makes the change about as linguistically unobtrusive as it could be.

We encountered yet other results of restructuring when we investigated how the Perspective Principle and the Methuselah Effect could alter one's view of the past. This led us to the Golden Age Phenomenon, where the past comes to be seen—restructured—as different in an absolute sense from the present. Thus, huge fossil bones as well as structures of enormous stones (such as the Sardinian megalithic tombs, or the "Cyclopean walls" of Mycenae and Tiryns: figure 17) generated beliefs in former races of giant humanoid types, a belief that still resurfaces here and there around the likes of Yeti and Sasquatch (Bigfoot). It is worth adding another, more specific corollary, that contains a touch of the Mismatch Effect, namely the Centaur Syndrome: *People of other times or other cultures come to be seen as different in an absolute sense (e.g., as nonhuman, possibly as fiends or demons).* Like the broader Golden Age

Figure 17. Mycenae, Greece: "Cyclopean" masonry (2nd millennium B.C.), named after the giant Cyclops ("Round-eye") who threw huge boulders at Odysseus.

Phenomenon, it applies to giants and monsters, but it takes its name from the centaurs, described by the Greeks as a race of creatures half horse and half human (figure 18), like Sagittarius. Many have suggested these hybrid creatures resulted from a misunderstanding of the mounted horsemen who spread rapidly across the Eurasian steppe late in the second millennium B.C., when horseriding came into vogue. Some nomadic riders seldom dismount, as if permanently attached to their horses. We need only lose the "as if" to restructure our idea of them into creatures born as hybrids.

Many cultures have subjected their perceived enemies to the Centaur Syndrome, sometimes with equally picturesque results. Thus the Celts viewed their predecessors in Ireland as fiends, often jet-black and either hairy or feathered [Rees and Rees 1961, 128], while the Chinese viewed the whole rest of the world as "foreign devils". Medieval Christians viewed those who hobnobbed with the archenemy of their religion, the Devil, as likely to sprout horns, a tail, or worse—things to watch for during religious security checks. Snowball Stories abound in this domain also, and not just about what people look like but also about what they do. Thus, people collecting rawhide playing-cards

Figure 18. Early Greeks depicted two types of centaurs, settling eventually on the second: **(a)** those with two human and two equine legs, i.e., full human frame with horse's torso and hind legs attached behind (on a Proto-Corinthian aryballos, ca. 680 B.C.), and **(b)** those with four equine and no human legs, but human head and torso in place of horse's head and neck (on an Attic neck-amphora by Nettos Painter, ca. 620 B.C.).

made by the Apache in the late nineteenth century often made such claims as this: "made from the skin of a human being who was captured, slain and skinned by the savage. The hide was then tanned and made into the playing cards" [Wayland, Wayland, and Ferg, in press]. These packs have been scientifically tested and found uniformly to consist of raw (not tanned) animal (not human) hide. Clearly what started as "this is made of skin" and "some Indians scalp people" snowballed to "I wonder if the skin used for this Apache artifact is human" and then was re-structured into "these cards are of human skin". The Apache, being out-lawed at the time, lived of course in the Zone of Convenient Remove (chapter 9).

We also encountered restructuring with the related UFO Corollary, which stated that, if certain events are not understood according to al-ready known ("natural") principles, they must be un-understandable—that is, super-natural—and there is no point in trying to understand them; so they are automatically recategorized as different in an absolute sense from the known/understood. Flitting firebirds, flying saucers, and cattle mutilations fell into this category. But we could also note that, particularly in medieval Europe, beyond-natural events and entities were strongly associated with nighttime, when it's always harder to ob-serve what's going on [cf. Ginzburg 1991]. Conversely, daybreak was thought to dispell the "unnatural" spirits (see chapter 15).

Only the collection and careful sifting of masses of data, made pos-sible by writing things down, provide the evidence to show that the past really did work the way the present does and that the night is governed by the same rules as the day. Even if some species might now be extinct, we can often still determine with some precision what they looked like, how they functioned biologically, and where they fit on the family tree of life. Unlike the classical Greeks, we can now tell a dinosaur from a mastodon from a hominid.[2]

This leads us to the great watershed in thinking methods, the Stock-pile Effect: *The invention of writing (especially efficient writing and effi-cient mathematical notation) enabled people for the first time to stockpile enough information to deduce cause-and-effect relationships other than the very simplest. Where cause-and-effect came to be seen as more closely predic-tive of natural phenomena than analogy, the function of analogy in thought processes was redeployed. Eventually it was no longer possible in the new framework to understand the previous use of analogy, and those earlier modes of thought came to be viewed—Restructured—as "untrue".*

Thus the word *myth*, originally Greek *mŷthos* "a traditional explana-tory saying", has now become synonymous with "untruth": "Oh, that's just a myth!"

It's no accident that the Greek philosophers who laid many foun-dations for modern science—Thales, Anaximander, Pythagoras, and

---

[2] See Mayor's [2000b] cogent discussion of the classical world's regular Restructuring of local mammoth fossils as bones of gigantic, Golden-Age humanoids (especially her figure 3.5).

others—began to flourish not long after the invention of the Greek alphabet around 800 B.C., since it then became much easier to start stockpiling information.

Contrary to popular belief, this was not the first alphabet, but we can learn from the earlier case. A true alphabet had been invented around 1400 B.C. by Hurrians living in Ugarit, a multilingual Syrian port where literacy was widespread among the merchants. The local Semites used a simple consonantal syllabary historically related to the Phoenician one that later jump-started the Greek alphabet. By adding or reusing three or four signs for specified vowels, the Hurrians adapted the writing system of twenty-some characters to their language, incidentally creating a true alphabet. But the widespread invasions of 1200 B.C. that marked the end of the Bronze Age destroyed both Ugarit and the Hurrian power base farther north, and the Hurrian alphabet was lost only a couple of centuries after it started.

One can speculate that the Ugaritic script did not catch on more widely because people wrote it with wedges on clay, rather than with ink on more portable substances. But we should also note that the Greeks took three or four centuries to start taking their alphabet seriously and behaving en masse like literate individuals.

As long as writing systems contained hundreds of signs, as did Mesopotamian cuneiform and Egyptian hieroglyphics, one had to devote one's life to learning and using such a script. Society supported a small number of such scribes, and mostly only the texts important to the society as a whole got written down: key religious, economic, and legal documents. The accumulated wisdom of the common man, however, died with him. The development of simpler syllabaries in the second millennium B.C. allowed more people—merchants and the like—to write. But truly widespread literacy required a script with so few signs—a couple of dozen—that a person could learn the script quickly and spell simply by sounding words out.

The first person on record as using writing to make copious personal notes of things—that is, to stockpile information regularly for his own use—was Solon, who lived in Athens around 600 B.C., a rough contemporary and friend of the philosopher-scientist Thales of Miletus. Great statesman and noted poet, Solon put into verse for his largely illiterate countrymen the things he felt citizens should know and remember [Plutarch, *Life of Solon*], verse being a more easily remembered form. In other words, two centuries after the invention of the Greek alphabet,

only a few Greeks had discovered the full power of personal literacy.
And although fifth-century Athenian law required citizens to know
how to read public notices and write their own ballots, anecdotes show
that many still fell short of this ideal—as we see from an incident during the "ostracism" (temporary banishment) of Aristides the Just in 482
B.C., recounted thus by a famous historian:

> On the day of the voting an illiterate citizen chanced to be close to Aris-
> tides who was unknown to him by sight, and requested him to write down
> the name "Aristides" on the ostrakon [potsherd, serving as ballot—hence
> our word *ostracism*]. "Why," said Aristides, doing as he was asked, "do you
> wish to ostracise him?" "Because," said the fellow, "I am tired of hearing
> him called the Just." [Bury 1913, 250]

Later still comes the first reference to someone sitting around
reading to himself: in Aristophanes' prize comedy of 405 B.C., *The
Frogs*, where an Athenian bumpkin says he was waiting on deck between naval manoeuvres, reading a play by the recently deceased Euripides and wishing that Athens still had some good dramatists to
knock sense into people and whip up communal spirit. That is, although late fifth-century Athenians mostly *could* read, they still preferred and even expected to experience their literature *orally*, in the
live communal theater.

But the glorious artistic feats of fifth-century Athens, from the Parthenon to poetry, had depended in fact upon literacy, and by the fourth
century everyone was following where the elite had blazed the way:
reading and writing independently, copiously, and for oneself. The dramas of Sophocles, Euripides, and Aristophanes gave way to the philosophical and scientific treatises of Plato and Aristotle and to a new
form, the novel, intended to be read for fun in one's own boudoir. The
literacy watershed had finally been crossed.

Literacy alone, however, does not destroy mythology. Many people
who can read nonetheless reject the stockpiled information and its logical implications, preferring the inherited stories. Others reinterpret the
old myths to fit newer trends of thought. Thus Jung restructured Greek
mythology for his own purposes in using names of Greek gods—
Apollo, Dionysus, Epimetheus, Prometheus—to represent his classifications of observable human temperament types, while Joseph Campbell restructured world mythology to serve what Jung would call an

"Apollonian" view of the human psyche.[3] Freud, for his part, completely reinterpreted the myth of Oedipus to suit his psychoanalytic theory that men desire their mothers. The core of the ancient tragedy was that Oedipus did *not* know that the queen whose throne (and hand) he was offered happened to be his birth-mother. Believing his mother was someone else entirely, he had run away from home to avoid marrying *that* lady (after hearing the fatal prophecy), and in horror repudiated his marriage when he learned Queen Jocasta was his real mother. Poor Oedipus would undoubtedly feel equally horrified to hear what (re-structured) "complex" his name now adorns.

Nor does literacy stop the processes that we have discussed. As we have seen, modern literate people repeating *orally* such stories as that of Delilah fall into the very same thought-patterns as their nonliterate ancestors. Urban legends, too, follow the old patterns. Our brains are still the same. But now we have a second option for using those brains, namely that of inching our knowledge forward by applying careful logic to recorded data. And myths themselves constitute one such type of data.

[3] Students today will most likely be acquainted with Jung's schema via the Myers-Briggs tests of temperament type commonly administered by school career centers: NF (Apollonian), SP (Dionysian), SJ (Epimethean), NT (Promethean). For a highly readable account, see Keirsey and Bates 1984.

14

Mnemonics:
Behind the Silliness

There is no room for chitchat aboard the vessel of oral
transmission.   —William Sullivan [1996, 26]

Pumas, foxes, snakes, and all kinds of birds cleaned and
fixed [the god Paria Caca's] canal.

Pumas, jaguars, and all kinds of animals vied with each
other to improve it, saying, "Who'll be the leader when we
lay out the watercourse?"

"Me first! Me first!" exclaimed this one and that one.

The fox won, saying, "I'm the chief, the *curaca*, so I'll
lead the way first."

And so he, the fox, went on ahead.

While the fox was leading the way, after he'd laid the
watercourse out halfway up the mountain over San
Lorenzo, a tinamou [partridge-like bird] suddenly darted
up, whistling "Pisc pisc!"

Startled, the fox yelped "Huac!" and fell down the slope.
          —Huarochirí myth [Salomon and Urioste 1991, 62–63]

The reader may have noticed that in the last chapters we shifted gradually back from the "what" of mythology to the "how". As we began to see through the veil of thought-processes used to cope with a condition not our own, namely nonliteracy, we came to recognize more and more myths as dealing with important matters—accounts of how the world is and functions, and how it apparently came to be that way; accounts of important events observed in the past, such as migrations and a whole host of catastrophes; and accounts of the (presumed) Willful Spirits who caused and continue to cause most of the above. Since, as we said before, you can remember only a limited amount of material to pass down, everything added to the corpus of stories to retell had better deserve its place, for it may be ousting something else. So first of all, the accounts to be transmitted have (and had) to be winnowed down to the most important. That suggests that we stand to learn much more by trying to *decode* myths than by dismissing them as empty, *no matter how silly they may seem at first.*

We also noted a number of "condensing" mechanisms at work on the material to be transmitted: ways the brain has of analysing, restructuring, and otherwise compressing the material into the small channel available for transmission. And we saw how these processes of compression, along with the Silence Principle, often (unfortunately) obscure the "original" data and events that we would like to learn about from the time capsules.

Once the information enters the channel, however, there is one more requirement, besides importance and compression, if it is to reach later generations: it must be made memorable enough to survive in the pipeline. How *can* this be accomplished cognitively—and how *was* it done?

It's no accident that so much of the orally composed literature that has come down to us has the form of poetry: Homer, Hesiod, *Beowulf*, parts of both the Bible and the *Epic of Gilgamesh*, and so on. If you memorize something constructed in a particular rhythm or meter, and you momentarily forget a bit of it, the rhythm helps you reconstruct the part you forgot.[1] The same is true of rhyme (which spread across Western literature in the Middle Ages), alliteration (the mainstay of early

---

[1] Recently one of us was asked to recite a three-page tale in rhymed verse by Hilaire Belloc, memorized forty-five years earlier and not recited for at least fifteen years. The first try was bumpy and full of lacunae, to say the least. The second try, four hours later, poured out word-perfect: in the interim, the brain had matched into the holes all the missing bits and pieces.

For an ambitious theory of how the meters of oral poetry worldwide are constructed to mesh exactly with the timing mechanisms inherent in our brains, see Turner and Pöppel 1983.

Germanic poetry), formulaic expressions (including certain kennings—another feature of Germanic verse), epithets (typical of Homeric verse), and all the other systems of formal regularities that set off poetic language from prose. Linguists such as Calvert Watkins [1995] have demonstrated, in fact, that some felicitous turns of phrase were handed down from poet to oral poet for millennia.

Memorability is not, however, the only reason for these formal structures: they also set such recitations off from everyday language and events, in the same way that special locations, like temples, or markers, like ritual textiles, set *extra*ordinary space off from ordinary space. And the propensity to find ways of marking some speech-acts as different from the ordinary may be universal. One day we overheard two neighborhood children arguing in the next garden, until one proclaimed she was not going to talk any more to her playmate. Minutes of silence ensued; then we heard the first girl chanting in a high and rhythmic sing-song voice, unlike her normal tone: "I'm not talking to you-u, I'm not talking to you-u!" Apparently she felt that using a sing-song intonation sufficed to mark these words as not in the realm of "talking"—so she could continue to verbalize her irritation!

The traditions of form are so strong that, if you combine the sense with the known traditions of rhythm, rhyme, et cetera in a given language, you can even fill out poems you may never have heard before, such as the old Burma-Shave roadside ditties (which have persisted orally in our family for decades):

> "*Road was slippery, curve was sharp:*
> *White robe, halo, wings and ..... .*"

Or:

> "*Heaven's latest neophyte*
> *Signalled left, then ....*" [*Rowsome* 1965, 103, 112]

All these regularities of form add redundancy to the language; and as we said at the very start, from the point of view of communication theory, redundancy is the answer to preserving a message intact (chapter 2). Then, if one encoding gets lost or garbled, others exist to back it up.

On the other hand, from the point of view of the human brain, an obvious redundancy like simple repetition ("I'll tell you this story twice") is such a crashing bore that the brain will likely go take a nap and miss the reruns. What gets the brain busy is novelty—something new, not something old. The magnetic appeal of newness explains the popularity of "urban legends", which—with a tiny touch of the Mismatch Effect—tickle us with their dramatically vivid twists on normal life. And the skilled storytellers of nonliterate groups enliven their traditional narratives by embroidering with new and vivid details, even while key information to be passed down forms the basic fabric—as we saw with the legend of Crater Lake.

This embroidery is also a central trait of oral poetry which, like that of Homer, was composed as it was recited or sung. The main story is traditional, as are the formulaic epithets used strategically to fill out the meter. (Milman Parry, and more recently Albert Lord, showed how Homeric and also twentieth-century South Slavic poetry was composed largely from old formulaic chunks that fit the meter and helped fill out the metrical lines.)[2] But then comes that word *hōs*, meaning "like" or "as when", which makes the poor student of Greek quail and reach for the dictionary—for here comes a simile, a vivid little vignette on any topic whatsoever that struck the poet as analogous to some (any) aspect of the story at hand. Newness knows no limits here.

Dialogue, too, brings both newness and much vividness to any story: that is its raison d'être, not historicity. As Lord Raglan points out, most of the conversations in myth and epic could not possibly have been reported, and he cites (among many other examples) an Irish tale in which "the sons of the King of Ulster spy upon the sons of the King of Iruath. We are told exactly what was said and done, yet the latter forthwith kill the former and then disappear forever" [Raglan 1936/79, 233]. And how many Greek and Trojan heroes take time out from a busy battle to boast and recite pedigrees to each other just before "darkness en-

---

[2] It is interesting that most of the "new" information that carries the story forward falls at or near the beginnings of lines, whereas the tails (which now require a particular metrical complement) are almost always filled in with the "old" prefabricated chunks. Of course, which pre-fab chunk you choose can add novelty to the poem, but Parry's work [1971] shows clearly that stock epithets of people and things were distributed according to their metrical characteristics rather than by exactness of meaning.

Paul Waters, a skilled square-dance caller, once demonstrated for us in a term paper the similarity of this structure to "calling". In calling a dance ad lib (either because the music didn't have a pre-set patter or because one square was tangled up and needed instant directions for getting unscrambled), he too had learned to put the new material—the next move—into the first part of the verse and fill the tail out with stock formulae. He said he needed the time while he was rattling off these automatic bits of patter ("Rock and roll on your heel and toe, as you did a bit ago, as you did a bit ago") to think ahead to what had to happen on the floor next.

folded their eyes" as they meet the sharp end of a sword or spear? The dialogue makes each of these repetitive events new.

Raglan sees these traits as demonstrating that all myths began as dramas associated with (and explanatory of) rituals: this is the central thesis of his forcefully argued book, *The Hero* [1936/79]. We view his interesting arguments and examples, on the contrary, as demonstrating how the human brain creates *narratives*, for whatever purpose, not necessarily just for ritual. Note that Raglan began by focusing on myths and sagas about individuals and ended by dismissing these as having nothing to do with history, whereas we investigated primarily natural events and phenomena as reflected in myth and concluded that many of them, thanks to the Willfulness Principle, came to be encoded as myths about "individuals". Thus we agree with Raglan that these mythic individuals do not (as Euhemeros would have it) reflect humans who actually lived, yet our data suggest that real events may be involved. (Note: We are *not* saying that all individuals in myth began as events.)

So one might think that from the point of view of the brain, newness is the answer to memorability. As Homer says, clearly from experience, "people praise that song most that is the newest to those listening" [*Odyssey* 1.351–52]. The poet Pindar concurs, in his ninth *Olympian Ode* [48–49]: "Praise the wine that is old, and the flowerings of the newest songs!"

And yet, as many experiments show (we discussed Ebbinghaus's "curve of forgetting" in chapter 2), things *too* new won't stick in the mind either. It is a truism of research on teaching that, to latch onto the new *and keep hold of it*, the brain must be able to hook the new material onto old things it already knows. The "likeliness" of the reported speech and thought can serve as an anchor—"Yes, that's about what I would have said"—even while the novel details of the tale unfold. Other narrative tricks for tying newness vividly to oldness are prophecy and revelation. Thus we wait in breathless anticipation for Oedipus to learn whether and how the prophecy will be fulfilled that he kill his father and marry his mother. His situation is constantly in flux—yet the endpoint of the story shines ahead of us like the pole star, fixed in advance.[3]

The Greek poet-philosopher Simonides (500 B.C.) already knew quite consciously this mnemonic principle of attaching the new to the old. His recipe for remembering a list of disconnected things (too much

---

[3] The material here about vividness in literature (oral or written) stems from research laid out fully in the book *Words of Uncommon Shape: Vividness in Language and Stories* [Barber, forthcoming].

newness there!) is to imagine each item mapped onto a point on a route or figure you are very familiar with. You could use it for your grocery list, if caught without a pencil: imagine milk on the doorstep, eggs on the hall table, celery in the umbrella stand, and so forth. If they can connect somehow or simply make a funny picture—the eggs stashed like Easter eggs, a watermelon balanced on the chandelier, bread loafing on the recliner—so much the better. The funny picture makes the item all the more memorable.

VIVIDNESS PRINCIPLE
Random or apparently patternless phenomena are best
remembered by inventing stories to connect and encode
them; but these stories must be either internally patterned
or connected to something known to be rememberable, and
the sillier or funnier they are, the more memorable.

What, for example, is more overwhelmingly random than the stars above us on a dark night? But if we shape the scattered points of light into Rorschach images of things we know, and these images into stories, we have a fighting chance of recalling which star is which, even as the hours and seasons make them shift their positions: the Dipper, the Teapot, the Cross; Bull, Crab, and Scorpion. Orion the Hunter hopelessly pursues forevermore the Seven Sisters, the Pleiades; Perseus continually intervenes between Andromeda and her vain mother, Cassiopeia. The Scorpion forever guards the Milky Way from intruders at the ecliptic.

We are now ready to understand the mechanisms behind the bizarre Andean story of Fox and Tinamou. How did such a fable rate a coveted place in the oral mythology? Because it encodes pivotal constellations—and not just their order but their behavior too.

Later in the account of Huarochirí mythology, compiled in Quechua for Father Francisco de Avila around 1600, we find a section that begins thus:

How Something Called the Yacana Comes Down from the Sky to Drink Water. We Shall Also Speak about the Other Stars and Their Names.
They say the Yacana, which is the animator of llamas [i.e., the llama "spirit"], moves through the middle of the sky. We native people can see it standing out as a black spot.
The Yacana moves inside the Milky Way. It's big, really big. It becomes

blacker as it approaches through the sky, with two eyes and a very large neck . . .

A small dark spot goes before the Yacana, and, as we know, people call it the Tinamou.

This Yacana, they say, has a calf. It looks just as if the calf were suckling. [Salomon and Urioste 1991, 132–33]

So the tinamou, like the llama and its calf, is a constellation—but not of our sort. Anthropogist William Sullivan describes the Yacana thus:

The identity of the celestial Llama is well established in both contemporary and Conquest-period literature. The "black cloud" celestial Llama runs from star epsilon Scorpius, in the "tail" of the Western constellation Scorpius, south to the stars alpha and beta of the Western constellation Centaurus. . . . These two first-magnitude stars, called alpha Centauri and Hadar in Western astronomy, are known in the Andes as *llamaq ñawin*, "the eyes of the llama."[4] [Sullivan 1996, 32; cf. Zuidema 1982]

Clouds of interstellar dust forming both large and small black patches, once you get your eye on them, invite Rorschach interpretations quite as much as star-groups (figure 19). But of course Andean peoples will see in them animals and other things that *they* know: a llama and a tinamou as well as a fox and a toad.

What, then, of their antics?

Most of us know that the stars pass overhead during the night, and that different stars will be visible at 10 P.M. on, say, July 1 and January 1. Many fewer people today are aware that over long periods of time the position of the stars in the sky shifts altogether, a little over a degree per century, in the opposite direction from the apparent daily rotation of sun, moon, and stars. This slow slippage is known as the "precession of the equinoxes" (see chapter 16). From their vantage point in the Andes, the Huarochirí people noticed that as the sun rose on the winter solstice,[5] the Fox (a fox-shaped black cloud following hungrily after the Llama's baby: figure 19) was slipping farther and farther downwards, so

---

[4] See Sullivan [1996] for numerous diagrams.

[5] The solstices and equinoxes served early astronomers as key reference days for observing long-term changes because it was relatively easy to figure out for sure where you were in the cycle of days. The solstice is (literally) the day the "sun stands still", stopping its yearly movement one direction (south in fall, north in spring) to begin moving the other way. Many ancient monuments are set up with primary reference to sunrise at one of the solstices. See chapter 16.

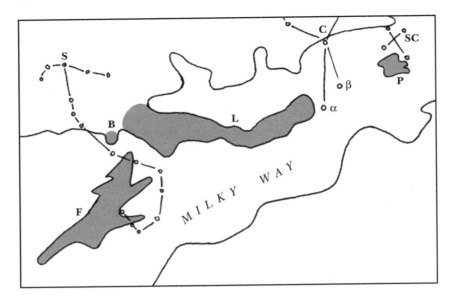

Figure 19. Constellations of dark interstellar dust seen in southern hemisphere, as named in the Andes. Fox (F: partly within curl of Scorpio, S) pursues Baby Llama (B), who follows long-necked celestial Llama (L: her eyes are alpha and beta stars of our Centaurus, C). Ahead of her is Tinamou/Partridge (P: known elsewhere as Coalsack), just below Southern Cross (SC).

that first his tail was no longer visible (that's another story, "why Fox's tail is black" [chapter 16]), then gradually more and more of his body could not be seen on the winter solstice. Meanwhile the Tinamou was flying higher, on Observation Night:

> A tinamou suddenly darted up, whistling "Pisc pisc!"
> Startled, the fox yelped "Huac!" and fell down the slope.

The "animal fable" is a mnemonic![6]

A vivid mnemonic for star position—and an apt one for movements which, though systematic, are barely discernible within a single life-time, since the stars precess only one degree (out of the 360 of the circle) in 72 years. And that slowness is why, if the fact and direction of precessional shift were to be known at all, successive positions *had* to be encoded and put into the oral pipeline for distant descendants. The

---

[6] In fact, the myth is even more complex than this, encoding yet more information; but this will do for now. It was worked out in considerable detail at great cost by Sullivan [1996, 271–74].

heavens provided the measures of time, both long and short, and time to humans is critical. This story, inconsequential though it sounded at first, is important.

Note that stories such as that of Fox and Tinamou carry themselves through the oral pipeline very slickly. The tale is both cute and apt enough that even if we don't understand it we can transmit it adequately. We are not likely to garble the story by having the bird fall down and . . . and what? The fox fly up? No, we all know that foxes don't fly, so the crucial direction of movement is safe; and there would be no story here without the animals moving, so the fact of movement is safe too. As we said before, even the village idiot can pass it on if he can remember and repeat the vivid little tale just as he heard it. He need know nothing of astronomy. Only the calendar keepers and navigators must perpetuate the true meaning.

Much the same can be said for the nursery rhymes "Hey diddle diddle, the Cat and the Fiddle" and "Mo(o)nday's child is fair [pale] of face".

Does the reader have a sudden giddy feeling? A feeling, perhaps, of tumbling like Alice down down down through a long pipe, one reaching millennia into the past and filled with unsuspected earlier knowledge? A feeling, even, that lots of quaint old myths, had they Willful Spirits, would be laughing at *us* for *our* ignorance?

15

The Spirit World: A Realm Reversed

The dead of the night's high noon!
—W.S. Gilbert, *Ruddigore*

And the spirit of God moved upon the face of the waters.
—Genesis 1:1

So far we have tried to demonstrate two things:

First, myths, as they are passed down through the ages, are inevitably distorted by peculiarities of our cognition until finally, if there is nothing nearby to remind people of the original story—a volcano, or stars, for example—they typically become unintelligible.

Second, in certain cases, we can reconstruct some of the original information by paying close attention to these cognitive peculiarities—analyzing backwards from them, in effect. But we still have little hope of finding independent verification of our reconstruction unless we too can look at the object that kept the original story more or less intact—that is, study, say, the actual volcano. Patterns alone aren't all that helpful [cf. Mason 2000]. (If we seem to pick on volcanos a lot, it's because they are both alarmingly active and relatively permanent.) We know that, throughout the world, the streams of lava pouring down the sides of a volcano have been typically portrayed in mythology as locks of hair. But this doesn't help us much if we encounter locks of hair in a myth. Claiming that all locks of hair are necessarily representations of lava casts us, too, straight into the Fallacy of Affirming the Consequent (chapter 5).

The real power of this method becomes clear when we realize what it implies about data that are suspiciously similar throughout the world. In 1915, G. Elliott Smith argued that all cultures that practice mummification had to have gotten the idea from the Egyptians. We are now pretty sure that the Australian natives didn't consult with the Egyptians before they started mummifying their dead. But then why are their methods so similar? Because animal carcasses are similar around the world: if you don't remove the viscera and dry the flesh, a body turns into a ghastly mass of decay [Barber 1995]. In other words, bodies themselves will inevitably instruct you in the methods of mummification.

But before you ask why *either* culture would mummify its dead (we'll get to that), let's consider another subject treated much the same worldwide—although too odd to seem obvious or inevitable—and try to figure out by this method where it comes from.

Why, throughout the world, do people believe there is a world parallel to ours that is made up of insubstantial versions of the objects in our world, that is, a spirit world? Not only are the objects there without substance, but they are reversed, and they are regularly accessed and appealed to by various types of reversal.

Our argument (based on what we've learned about myths) is that this universality can result only from people observing the same things and drawing similar conclusions from them. If we assume that people are simply wired in a way causing them everywhere to have common beliefs about a parallel world of insubstantial spirits, then we have begged the question: *Why* are they so wired? An evolutionary explanation would require that there be an advantage to individuals with such a predisposition. But we get nowhere when we suppose that, at an early stage in human development, survival came to depend on the propitiation of clouds of imaginary and quite insubstantial spirits.

We will make some progress if we consider carefully some traditional explanations of the spirit world. At various times, quite independently, scholars have suggested that the spirit world derives from the experience of dreaming. A. Wiedemann, the German Egyptologist, suggested this in 1900 [34]: "Presumably the belief in this doubleness of man originated in the dream-image. During life, while sleeping, one could see the person before one in corporeal form, even when the bearer of this form was distant, and the same form could show itself after the death of the person." Similarly, Edward Tylor [1871, 1:450]: "My own view is that nothing but dreams and visions could have ever put into men's minds such an idea as that of souls being ethereal images of bodies."

Although we will find the dream-hypothesis is not fully adequate, much is explained by it. For one thing, it can account for the ubiquity of belief in the spirit world: because all people dream, all cultures conceive of a world of insubstantial doubles that mimic flesh and blood. And often we see that dream-images (and their actions) are taken by people as directly related to the events of the "real" world. A century ago, a German ethnologist told of an Australian tribe that used the spirit world to determine the (Willful) cause of death: "If a Narrinyeri dies, his nearest relative sleeps next to the corpse the first night, resting his head on it. In his dreams he then believes he will see the murderer" [Eylmann 1908, 229]. When we are told, then, that in India "the spirits of the dead reveal themselves in dreams" [Crooke 1926, 187], we should not suppose that we have entered a different plane of reality: we are simply seeing a different interpretation of the dream from our own.[1]

---

[1] See also Bächtold-Stäubli 1987, 3:477 "Geist".

Like Tylor, we could easily enlarge this hypothesis to include visions from other altered states of consciousness—hallucinations.

But the dream/hallucination hypothesis, as obvious as it seems if we choose our data carefully, quickly fails us as insufficient if we look at other manifestations of the spirit world:

(1) "If you look in a mirror at midnight, you will see the devil."
(2) "If you pass a haunted house, cross a body of water and the ghosts that are following you will stop."
(3) "You must not play with your shadow because it represents the evil spirit (devil) in you, and by paying attention to him, he'll bring you calamity."
(4) "On Old Christmas (January 6) take a mirror and go backwards up the stairway, and you will see a reflection of your future wife." [Puckett 1981, 26206, 29799, 5897, 13214]

Here our "spirit as dream" hypothesis doesn't help us much. In the first example, there is indeed an insubstantial form, but it is a reflection, not a dream-image. In the second, how do we explain why imaginary spirits based on dream-images would be foiled by water? In the third, although there is again an insubstantial form, it is clearly the shadow, not the dream-image. And in the fourth, we encounter one of the common examples of reversal associated with the spirit world. But what does reversal have to do with dreams, or with spirits?

Let's try another long-standing hypothesis. Uno Harva records that

a Lappish shaman, upon awakening from his trance, recounted that "under the earth is a people that walk with their feet against ours". If one believes further that the subterranean landscape, with its forests, mountains, rivers and lakes, reflects point for point the world above, then it is clear that *the other world is thus a mirror image of the earthly one*. In one of my studies I have shown that the stated peculiarities of the Underworld seem originally to be based on *experiences with reflection in water*. Probably, also, the conception that the realm of the dead is "down below" and behind the water rests on this. [Harva 1933/38, 349; emphasis his.]

Plausible. But while our dream-hypothesis accounted for only part of the data, the reflection-hypothesis accounts for only some other parts. How to proceed?

We know that different peoples divide up the world differently (Rainbow Corollary, chapter 7). We will make further progress only if we ignore our modern notion that the various insubstantial forms we see during our lives stem from different *causes* and concentrate on the fact that all insubstantial forms share the quality of insubstantialness. (We have seen that Analogy creeps in where evidence of true causality is wanting.) *We* see mirror, shadow, dream-image, and hallucination as radically different phenomena—the first two as optical, the last two as involuntary functions of our brain during sleep or under influence of special chemicals. In the past, however, as our data show, these phenomena were lumped together, and on reasonable enough grounds: all four produce insubstantial images.

Word analysis makes this clear. In Liddell and Scott [1968], the Greek word *eídōlon*, from which *idol* is derived, is defined as "any insubstantial form; image reflected in mirror or water; image in the mind, idea; phantom of the mind, fancy". That is, one term was used for several kinds of insubstantial images. In Homer, *eídōlon* is also the term used for the dead Patroklos when he visits the sleeping Achilles—in other words, an *eídōlon* is a dream-image too. And for Greek *skiá*, which we think of as the word for shadow, Liddell and Scott give additional meanings as well: "reflection, image; shade of one dead, phantom". Any word for one type of double, in other words, is apt to serve for other doubles. Put another way: shadow, reflection, and dream-image all fall into the same conceptual bin, just as "wine-color" and "ocean-color" landed in a single Greek bin (chapter 7). As late as Middle High German, the word for "shadow" (*Schatten*) was still occasionally used to mean "reflection" [Bächtold-Stäubli 1927/87, 9:Nachträge 548].

It is not just dreams, hallucinations, and ordinary vision that undergo Conflation, but all forms of image-making or duplication, including reflections in mirrors and water, shadows, dream-images, drawings, statues, and even echoes (an echo duplicates a sound, after all). Rather than being seen in a functional way, as the effects of various causes, these are all seen as Multiple Aspects of the world of spirits. They are manifestations (prone to Willfulness), rather than effects brought about by known causes (chapter 6).

In folklore there are endless examples of conflation of the various real-life doubles. Thus, in a study of folklore from Ohio,[2] we find, "Never let a baby see himself in a mirror, or he will have bad dreams", and, "If you sleep with a mirror under your pillow, you will dream about

---

[2] Puckett's enormous compendium "from Ohio" actually documents beliefs brought in by immigrants from many regions and cultures.

the man you are going to marry" [Puckett 1981, 3087, 13209]. In both examples, two types of real-life doubles, dream and reflection, are treated as functionally related. Often the dispersal of darkness and deep shadow by the sun at dawn is seen as banishing the images of dead people who might harm you.[3] Or again: "If you place a glass of water in front of a burning kerosene lamp and look over your left shoulder into a mirror, you will see the person whom you will marry" [Puckett 1981, 13,207]. Note the extraordinary profusion of spirit-motifs here: fire and water (one casts shadows, the other reflects), a mirror, a spirit (seen in the water via the mirror), and the left, or spirit-side, of which we shall say more later.

We see, then, that Tylor's view (dreams and visions as spirits) and Harva's view (reflections as spirits) are not so much wrong as incomplete: spirits have been deduced from reflections and shadows *as well as* from dreams.

Once we recognize how people of many cultures concluded independently that there must be a parallel mirror-image world of insubstantial forms, one that may be rendered visible in several ways, many practices and beliefs start to make sense (the Logic Cross-check, chapter 4). For example, we pay tribute to an ancient conception when we toss coins into a fountain—the domain of a visible form of the double—and make a wish. The "wishing well" presumes that the spirits are aware and, given the opportunity, will act on our behalf. Fountains on the property of churches—the Santa Barbara Mission, for example—collect more than their share of such coins, for they are located at a gathering point of the spirit world.[4]

Because these doubles have a great deal of power (being generally held responsible for illness and death),[5] a specialist, the shaman, takes charge of making contact with them. Not surprisingly, we find among

[3] Because of its association with shadows, we may expect the progress of the sun to be keyed into the activities of the spirits: in the Celtic calendar, the eve of November first—Halloween—begins the dark half of the year, marking a point at which the spirit world is released. Similarly, May Day, the end of the dark half-year, signals another cosmic crack through which spirits have access to the phenomenal world [Rees and Rees 1961, 83–94].

[4] Here, as in so many instances, the modern has not supplanted the ancient: they survive side by side or even incorporated into one another. Thus, in Europe, with the advent of Christianity, churches tended to be erected where the local population had honored their previous gods [cf. Bächtold-Stäubli 1987, 9:30].

[5] The lord of the dead is even conceived sometimes as the twin (double) of the original human, having become the latter's sacrificial victim and hence the first "dead": Vedic *Yama* (and possibly Latin *Remus*) come from PIE *yem- "twin", likewise Germanic *Ymir*, the primordial being from whom the world was fashioned [Puhvel 1987, 63, 284–90].

his tools such image-generating materials as mirrors and hallucinogenic drugs, and among his practices the sorts of repetitive behaviors (drum-beating, dancing, chanting, et cetera) that lead to hallucinations.

But if the spirit world is largely compounded out of the characteristics of actual phenomena, then we should be able to find some of the peculiarities of the actual phenomena in its functionings. This leads us to ask: What are some of the most distinctive qualities of real-life insubstantial doubles?

First is reversal. Mircea Eliade, in his book on shamanism, points out that, among other cultural groups,

> The peoples of North Asia conceive the otherworld as an inverted image of this world. Everything takes place as it does here, but in reverse. When it is day on earth, it is night in the beyond (this is why festivals of the dead are held after sunset; that is when they wake and begin their day); the summer of the living corresponds to winter in the land of the dead; a scarcity of game or fish on earth means that it is plentiful in the otherworld; and so forth. The Beltir put the reins and a bottle of wine in the corpse's left hand, for the left hand corresponds to the right hand on earth. In the underworld rivers flow backward to their sources. And everything that is inverted on earth is in its normal position among the dead; this is why objects offered on the grave for the use of the dead are turned upside down, unless, that is, they are broken, for what is broken here below is whole in the otherworld and vice versa. [Eliade 1951/64, 205, citing Harva 1933/38, 343ff., for data]

But if notions of the spirit world derive in major part from reflections and shadows, its reversal follows quite logically.

Reflections reverse your image: if you stand before a mirror and hold out your right hand, your image (interpreted as someone facing you, which is what it looks like) appears to hold out its left hand. The same is true of your shadow. From this, spirits came to be seen as reversed versions of ourselves and—since most people are right-handed—seen as characteristically left-handed. Historically, left-handed people have been viewed with suspicion and worse, as though they were somehow the spirit-version made flesh. This is why terms for lefties are typically so negative: *sinister, gauche, maladroit.* Spirits are taken for reversed versions of the phenomenal world.

Further, if the reflection or shadow is a reversed image of an object or person, and if the dream is a manifestation of the same thing as reflections and shadows, then dreams too must be characterized by reversals. And in fact, dream interpretation has historically assumed this to be true: a modern informant in Ohio says, "Dreams should be interpreted in reverse, e.g., if one dreams of a misfortune, good luck can be expected" [Puckett 1981, 4850]. But the notion goes at least as far back as Artemidorus's *Interpretation of Dreams* (second century A.D.; cf. chapter 10) and probably further.

The reversed quality of the spirit world has endless consequences. Clothes to accompany the dead may be turned inside out (like First Dynasty Egyptian shirts [Landi and Hall 1979]) or upside down (like the saddle-cloth tied onto an early mummified horse in Egypt [Lansing and Hayes 1937, 10]. People may dress "in reverse" for rituals of religious origin—men as women, women as men, white face painted black, and so forth [cf. Propp 1963/87, 135]—or reverse their roles to head off the spirits, as in the practice of couvade (the custom of having a man feign childbirth and subject himself to its taboos: cf. *Argonautica* 2.1,011–14; Strabo, *Geography* 3.4.17). Shamans, who often decorate their costumes with mirrors, frequently approach the spirit world through reversals, as by entering their hut backwards, while rituals concerning the dead progress the opposite direction from the usual [Garfinkel 2003, 46]. Those suspected of planning a return from the spirit world—people who died "before their time"—were often buried prone instead of supine [Barber 1988, 46, 49].

Because the spirit world is reversed, it is also expected to respond in opposite ways. Thus, if you were to wish an actor good luck and the spirits were listening, they would give him the opposite of good luck. This is why you encourage him by saying "Break a leg!"

In his book on handedness, Ira Wile remarks [1934, 208] that "at times one is puzzled by seeming shifts in the luck values of a side [that is, right/left]". We would argue that it's not the right or left per se that determines luckiness, but the association of the left with the spirit world. This means the left is appropriate (and "lucky") when you *wish* to propitiate or consult the spirits. But you should avoid it (as "unlucky") whenever you *don't* want meddlesome spirits about. Hence the practice, common in the past, of forcing left-handed children to become right-handed. (This was not just so they could comfortably use scissors.)

For a folklorist, the derivation of reversal from reflections runs afoul of a more entrenched interpretation, the argument that such reversals derive from observations of the direction of the sun, which, in northern latitudes, appears to move from left to right in the course of the day (since there the sun is to the south) [e.g., Wile 1934]. People observed this, so the argument goes, and concluded somehow that the one direction was lucky, the other unlucky. But this theory suffers from a fatal defect.

If the reversal of the spirit world derives from the course of the sun, then in the *southern* hemisphere, where the sun (being to the north) appears to move from right to left, the side of the spirits should be the *right* side, and on the equator the leftness or rightness of the spirit world should be immaterial. In fact this is not true. The Australian natives take the same view of the left as northern people, and a wide variety of peoples on the equator hold to the common belief that the left side has to do with spirits.[6] In Borneo (which is on the equator) we are told that "the rationale that Berawan give for their antipathy toward sunsets is that it is the beginning of the day for the spirits, who are often attributed characteristics that are the inverse of human ones" [Metcalf 1982, 102]. Thus the inversion of the spirit world, including the aspect of "leftness", is a worldwide phenomenon.

In the north the direction of the sun seems to have been subsumed eventually under the larger category of the right, or correct, side versus the left—the side of the spirit world, death, and unpropitious events; in short, the wrong side. (For "left = wrong", compare "getting up on the wrong side of the bed" with informant statements like, "Get up on the right side of the bed, and you will have good luck . . ." and, "If you get up on the left side of the bed, it's bad luck" [Puckett 1981, 4670, 4673].) So it became problematic to move in the direction opposite to the sun. Thus we get the concept of *widdershins* or *withershins*, the modern meaning of which is counterclockwise movement, which is held to be unlucky. According to the O.E.D., one early meaning of *widdershins* was simply "in a direction opposite to the usual; the wrong way". The concept of mirror-image would seem to be a natural symbol for the wrong way. Attempts have been made to associate this word etymologically with German *Wiederschein* "reflection" (Dutch *weerschijn*,

---

[6] See Wirz [1928, 11] for an example of using the left hand in Bali (just below the equator) in connection with death.

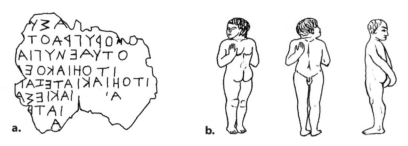

Figure 20. Reversals. **(a)** Curse written with backwards letters on lead "curse tablet", buried with corpse (to take along to the Underworld) in Kerameikos cemetery, Athens; late 5th century B.C. It is aimed at a silversmith (line 2), cursing him, his wife (l. 3), and everything he makes and does (ll. 4–6). **(b)** Late Greco-Roman tomb figurines, with some body parts backwards (left front/back, from Kephalonia; right, from Athens).

Danish *wederskin*, et cetera), which—if correct—would provide further evidence that the concept of reversal, in its relation to the spirit world, derived from observation of the reversal of our reflections.[7]

However that may be, it seems indisputable that the world of the spirits is characterized by reversal, and that reversed motion is merely a subcategory of this reversal. So pervasive is the notion of spirit-reversal that it even creeps into the *form* of language, where we find sometimes that the sounds themselves have been reversed within words pertaining to the spirits. Thus the name for one of the chief Eurasian hallucinogens was said backwards in Indic—induced hallucination being a quick and certain way to visit the spirit world [Barber 1987; Barber 1991, 36–38]. Ancient Greeks bent on vengeance often wrote their curses backwards on lead "curse tablets", reversing either the direction of reading or the letters themselves [Jordan 1985] (figure 20a). The Central and South American words for the guardian spirit of a lineage, *waka (huaca)*, and for the magical bird, the *macaw*—Quechua *akwa*—"are all metatheses of each other", says Sullivan [1996, 239]. He explains further that the Andean people "prayed to the *wakas* as *intercessors* between themselves and the divine realm", symbolized in the macaw because "macaws, large parrots, speak two different languages—human speech, and the language of the animal world. Thus, when addressing the *wakas*, the people transposed the usual order of things" [Sullivan 1996, 240].

---

[7] *Withershins* would have been the word for "reflection" in English before we replaced it with French-borrowed *reflection*.

At one time in England prayers could be used for maleficent purposes by being recited backwards [Thomas 1973, 48], a motif still reported in American folklore: "To conjure up the devil one must go to a crossroad at midnight and say the Lord's prayer backwards" [Puckett 1981, 26241; and see 31693]. In Germany reversing the Lord's Prayer could also make one invisible [Bächthold-Stäubli 1927/87, 8:1461, citing Hovorka and Kronfeld 1908–9], and in ancient Greece invisibility could be attained by reversing the Ring of Gyges on one's finger [Pliny 33.4]. The rationale seems to be that if we wish to gain access to the special powers that spirits appear to possess, we must first become like the spirits, by undergoing some sort of reversal. Behind the practice, then, is the kind of analogical thought we discussed in chapter 5.

Efficacious reversal—doing things backwards to access or propitiate the spirits—extends to yet other realms. It is efficacious reversal when one puts one's clothes on backwards in order to see whatever is hidden under the ground [Bächtold-Stäubli 1927/87, 8:1324], or to see vampires—as among certain Moslem gypsies in the Balkans, who believe that "a vampire can be seen by a twin brother and sister born on a Saturday [when vampires stay in their graves], who wear their drawers and shirts inside out" [Vukanovic 1959, 114].[8] One may wonder, too, what the Greco-Roman sculptors were up to who constructed figurines with heads and/or feet on backwards (figure 20b), but it probably wasn't nice.

Many facets of the notion that spirits inhabit the reversed world of reflections have hung on in modern Western culture, from the superstition that breaking a mirror is bad luck (mirrors "collect" spirits) to fortune-telling with crystal balls (which transmit images both upside down and backwards).

Let us turn now to some other key qualities of insubstantial doubles.

1. Because everything material has a shadow and a reflection and can appear in dreams, any object can also be said to have a spirit (one reason why trees, rocks, et cetera, are all commonly seen as having spirits). Naturally, nothing prevents people from reformulating their notions of the spirit. In the course of history, our current version of the spirit—the soul—has become something of a specialist: it is specific to human be-

[8] In many cultures, human twins are seen as the result of intercourse with spirits; often, as with Castor and Pollux, one is the expected human baby and the other somehow "a spirit".

Figure 21. Soul-bird emerging from dying warrior (Prokris); Attic amphora, early 5th century B.C.

ings. Once we lost the notion that reflections, shadows, and dreams are highly significant, we no longer saw our particular spirits as similar to those of the rest of the world. And it must be stressed that it is one thing to see spirits as partly derived from real-world phenomena, and another entirely to suppose that that is all there is to them. In fact, like everything else, the spirit world is subject to endless Restructuring.

2. Spirits move around very quickly—the spirits of distant people can appear in your dreams. This may be one reason why spirits are so persistently associated with birds (figure 21)—the fastest-moving animate objects in the preindustrial world—and why the ancients used bird-flight and bird-guts for augury.

3. Spirits are attracted to anything in their shape. Water can temporarily pull your spirit out of you—that is, you see your reflection in water[9]—but the spirit leaps back into anything that looks like it (cf. chapter 5). That's why people try to hold the spirit of a dead person in place—keep it from disturbing people's dreams—by putting either a statue of that person or a container of water at the grave. The Egyptians used the first method, the Bulgarians the second, but both were in-

[9] In the folk tradition, "If you break a mirror, you shatter your soul", and "When looking at your reflection in water, if someone breaks the image, you'll lose your soul" [Puckett 1981, 5871–72]. Writers like E.T.A. Hoffmann have altered this, by the Fallacy of Affirming the Consequent, to, "If you lose your soul, you'll lose your reflection"!

tended to accomplish the same thing. In fact, the details of Egyptian mummification practices (in which everything that will cause decay is removed and such fillers as straw are shoved in to restore the *shape*) show us that one purpose of mummification was to provide a shape-home for the spirit [Barber 1995]; by adding statues and reliefs of the deceased, they hedged their bets. In the ritual of baptism, it is surely the spirit-collecting quality of water (that is, its ability to reflect) that is a key issue. The point is that typically spirits are recycled from generation to generation—which accounts for family resemblance (cf. chapter 6)—and water-based rituals like baptism are used to prevent otherwise unemployed spirits from becoming incorporated into the wrong child.

Issues such as iconoclasm have to be viewed in the light of this belief. Imagery was eventually rejected for some fairly complex reasons, including the fact that we learned to appeal to a higher authority than the spirit world. Nowadays people in the West are so far removed from the original notion—that everything had an animate (willful) spirit—that we no longer understand why anyone would bother to break up giant statues of Buddha, as the Taliban did, or sling mudballs to cover the human faces in ancient murals, as Moslems in Xinjiang did.

4. The fickle movements of our insubstantial doubles, which can leap from person to person in the form of dreams, appear to have led to the belief that they function as a kind of servomechanism for bodies. Sleep is typically viewed as the temporary absence of the spirit, death as its permanent absence: that is, the body becomes inert when (i.e., because) the spirit has gone elsewhere. This is surely why people once believed that you can kill a witch by moving her while she is asleep. Her spirit, when it returns, can't find its way back into her body, and she suffers the usual fate of people lacking a spirit, namely death.

It is important to keep this footloose quality of spirits in mind when studying their world. They can easily move from one body to another—even to bodies that don't resemble that of their owner, such as those of animals. This seems to violate the notion that spirits are attracted to objects of their general shape, but it is usually shamans and sorcerers who (in their "ec-static" states) are thought to take over animals, and they are self-selected precisely for their ability to manipulate the spirit world. Throughout the world, animals that behave in ways not considered characteristic for their species are commonly believed to be animated by the spirit of a sorcerer. That is what a were-animal is: a wolf, say, that while looking exactly like any other wolf, is actually controlled by the spirit of a human (*were* means "man"). Were-animals, in other words, look no different from their species; the notion that they were half man, half wolf is an artifact of Hollywood's inability to give a wolf acting lessons. They just behave differently, and this is assumed to be because their spirit—the servomechanism operating the body—has been taken over by a human spirit.

If this seems like a strange notion—when the wolf behaves oddly, then it must be controlled by another entity—it is useful to keep in mind that all that is really happening is that people are dividing the world up differently than we do. The animal is fashioned from one kind of template, the behavior another, and if these don't correspond, then the animal is being controlled by someone whose behavior belongs to a different template. If a child misbehaves too badly, it too may be seen as "possessed" rather than simply ruder than other children: extremes are not deviations from the mean, but qualitatively different (cf. the UFO Corollary).

5. Spirits are often treated as residing in a world *below* ours, the Underworld, as in Aristophanes' *Frogs* (69–70), where Herakles asks his Athenian visitor (who wants to revive a famous but dead tragedian), "So you're headed to Hades down below?" and the Athenian replies, "Yes, by Zeus, and even belower if there is such!"

Why below? Several lines of reasoning appear to converge here. First, as Harva (quoted above) recognized, when you gaze into pools of water—the first reflective surfaces known to humans—there are the doubles, staring back up from below. Second, most cultures bury their dead in the ground, hence "down" is the realm par excellence of departed souls. Third, because the spirit world is thought to be the reverse of ours, our midnight will be their high noon, their night our day (cf. Eliade, quoted above). If so, one must immediately wonder whether our sun goes to light their world during our nighttime. It clearly goes *somewhere* else. And since the sun goes *down* in the west, disappears for hours, then comes *up* in the east, the obvious deduction is that it travelled back to the east by passing under our world, lighting the Nether Realm as it went. (By age two, humans master the cognitive concept of Object Permanence: things that "go away" for awhile don't cease to exist in the interim.) It's a tiny step to equate this oppositely phased Underworld with that deduced from the other two observations. All three approaches agree: the spirit world is below ours—a realm reversed in space and time (day/night) as well as function.

It's also a small step to deduce that the sun circles a world that's basically spherical, an ancient myth-encoded observation of such importance that it deserves its own chapter.

16

Of Sky and Time

A never-ending tale of positions and relations, . . . a
complex web of encounters, drama, mating and conflict.
　　　　　—Santillana and Dechend [1969/77, 177]

And you will think this strange, but the sun will have borne
a daughter no less lovely than herself, and she will follow
the paths of her mother.
　　　　　—*Gylfaginning* [Sturluson 1971, 92]

As the waters rose, the hill grew higher, so that it was never
covered by the flood; and when the waters subsided, the hill
also grew smaller.
　　　　　—Inca myth [C. de Molina, in Sullivan 1996, 15]

ctual histories of real humans don't seem to last: Lord Raglan was at least approximately correct in calculating that human history in oral culture lasts at most four or five generations (although the *names* of actual persons may live on) [Raglan 1936/79, 13–14]. Whatever stories were told in a person's lifetime soon fell prey to Compression and Restructuring within the oral pipeline: the Delilah Effect pared down the cast of characters, the Principle of Attraction added tales to the dossier or transferred events to other portfolios, and so on. All in all, stories of individuals in long-standing myths are not reliable histories of real people, even though myths can encode real events.

Mythical individuals "come about" in various ways, as we have seen—often as postulated Willers of general phenomena like wind and sun or of specific (and often verifiable) real events like eruptions. But clearly, too, not all the "people" who populate myths are volcanos or sun gods. Myth is richer and more varied than that. In fact, most of the past theories of mythology that have been propounded and then forcefully rejected—such as Euhemeros's view that myth is the history of real people Bumped Upstairs and presented as the history of gods (i.e., that gods all started as people); or Max Müller's stance that all myths are basically solar; or Jane Harrison and Lord Raglan's idea that myth invariably and merely accompanies and "explains" ritual—have been not so much wrong as limited by trying to make one size fit all.

What, then, of myths that occur over and over, the world around, yet describe something that could not actually happen in the world as we know it? Why, for example, do we find in the native cultures of both hemispheres a story of a catastrophic Flood covering the entire world, like that of Gilgamesh, Genesis, or the Andean peoples? Or of a Conflagration that destroys the whole world, as in Polynesia—sometimes even destroying the gods, as at Norse Ragnarök? A story which always ends with the entire world being renewed pretty much as it was? Geology has so far found no flood—or fire—that covered even half a continent within the existence of Homo sapiens, so a source in real experience seems barred (although stories of actual fires and floods could be *attracted* to this myth, and collisions with comets have such a potential [Masse 1998]). If not a "real" fire or flood, then what alternatives for interpretation can we deduce?

Instead of starting with a myth, this time, let's start with some very important problems that ancient people faced and do a task analysis from their Camera Angle.

Imagine a time with no TV, books, or movies, no electricity or wheeled transport, no city lights or even cities; and imagine yourself living at that time, in, say, the Near East. During the day you would go about your business, whatever that was; but at night, until you were ready to go to sleep (we don't need twelve hours of sleep), you would sit in the near-dark and do what? Most likely look at the Big Show—the endless river of stars flowing all night across the sky.

As long as you and your family were hunters and gatherers, knowing how to tell time "ahead of time" would be largely irrelevant. Like the other animals, you could eat what was ripe, catch what was there, and take temporary shelter from heat and cold as they presented themselves. Still, some aspects of timekeeping were surely useful (e.g., for knowing when the nights would be moon-bright, or for beating the other animals to seasonal food during a walkabout), and some cycles, such as the length of the moon's phases, might even be easy to count. Alexander Marshack [1971] has demonstrated that permanent notations for counting, if only as simple tallies, have been with us for over 30,000 years. But what were Palaeolithic people counting? Marshack found that these ancient tallies often fall into groups coinciding with the phases of the moon over many months.[1]

But there is more evidence for what they counted, directly from mythology—now that we know that myth can carry certain information accurately. To begin with, the Egyptians viewed their moon god, Thoth (figure 6a), as the one in charge of counting and mathematical notation, the inventor of writing, and the one who set the dates of the festivals. Thus they believed both that notation originated in counting celestial cycles and that it preceded writing. Other proof exists that this myth-encoded information is correct.

To guess when the Nile would flood, the Egyptians carefully noted the day each July when the bright star Sirius (which they called *Sothis*) rose at the same time as the sun, marking it as the start of the agricultural New Year. Ancient authors tell us, however, that the Egyptian civil-year calendar, based on 365 days (instead of the "true" $365\frac{1}{4}$: 365.2564), came into phase with the crucial Sirius/Sothis rising in A.D. 139. Now, shifting at the rate of that extra quarter day per year, it takes $4 \times 365 = 1460$ years for the error to right itself, so that New Year again falls on the rising of Sirius; so if we count back repeatedly by 1460, we find it was exactly in phase in 1321 B.C. and in 2781 B.C. But since the Egyptian calendar was already in use by 3000 B.C., we must go back an-

---

[1] See Krupp 1983, 158–63, for an astronomer's assessment.

other hop, to 4241 B.C. [Neugebauer 1938, 173–74], well before linguistic notation—writing—began. (Of course, by the same token it could have been set up at 4241 + 1460 = 5701 B.C., et cetera.) Note that because the Egyptians depended on the retreat of the annual Nile flood, not the calendar, to begin planting crops, they and they alone, in the agricultural Near East, could put up with a badly out-of-phase calendar.[2] Egypt is not the only place where one can note the antiquity of celestial counting, for astronomers have found that the Maya knew the cycles of Venus with an exactitude requiring millennia of counting.

However that may be, even the most superficial observer of the sky will notice that the sun that sets in the west each evening somehow conveys itself back to the east every morning to rise again, and does so unseen. It doesn't take much to surmise that the sun somehow passes *under* the earth we stand on—in other words, that the sun's course is circular. The Egyptians, short on data, actually Hedged their Bets by describing this phenomenon in Multiple ways (cf. figures 2 and 12): (1) the goddess Nut, who formed the sky with her overarching body, swallowed the sun as Osiris, the dying god, every evening and gave birth to him/it again every dawn in an eternal cycle of death and resurrection; and/or (2) the sun as the god Re (Ra), floating in his solar boat, "passed each night into a dangerous realm, the kingdom of death", where he "sailed through 12 perilous territories—12 hours of the night—and steered a course through the frightening creatures that inhabited them" to reach the east by morning [Krupp 1983, 63].

Such speculations rated as interesting in early epochs, but once the principle of agriculture—of raising one's own food—was discovered (10,000–8000 B.C. in the Near East), time changed its significance and the observation of celestial cycles had to begin in earnest. For in order to know when to plant one's crops, one cannot rely on the daily weather. On April 20, 2002, it was 90° F in much of New England and the Midwest—but despite appearances, summer had *not* come, and four days later the thermometer dipped below freezing. Farmers must know *reliably* where the sun is with respect to the major planting, growing, and harvesting seasons it creates. Thus, in shifting from hunting/gathering to an agricultural life, people had to work out a solar calendar, and since they were nonliterate, they had to encode this information orally into rememberable "myths".

---

[2] They must have got their 365-day *solar* calendar from those to whom solar reckoning did matter (see below)—presumably those in the Levant from whom they got their Neolithic domesticates ca. 5000 B.C.

Of course, we will not be able to recognize what their myths encode about astronomy unless we ourselves know the relevant astronomical facts—a topic most humanists, anthropologists, and archaeologists know little about, since we now rely on clocks and printed calendars to tell time and can descry very few stars above our city lights. So, instead of dismissing serious prehistoric knowledge of the stars as impossible (while dismissing myths as bizarre stories), let's turn full attention to what the ancients could see all around them in the sky and compare the information with the myths.

> Time is a fixed measure obtained from the turning of the heavens.
> —Macrobius, *Saturnalia* 1.8.7

To determine the yearly cycle of the sun, one needs permanent points of reference from which to notice and mark its motion. In fifth grade we taped a pencil vertically to an east window and one morning a week marked on the sill the position of the pencil shadow, watching it move. Or you can select a platform on which to set your chin every morning at sunrise, then note the spot on the eastern horizon where the sun appears. What you learn, if you start on January 1, is that the sun rises (and sets) farther and farther north until mid-June; it appears to stay still a few days (at the summer *solstice*—literally "sun-standing") and then heads south again until mid-December (the winter solstice), when it starts north once more (figure 22). One can easily figure out by counting that a full cycle, or year, from one winter solstice to the next, takes 365 full days (but catching the extra quarter-day is harder!). Such "chin-rest" calendars have been documented ethnographically, as in the following case from a remote district of the Caucasus Mountains (figure 23), described by E. C. Krupp:

> The place to stand in the Ossetian communities was carefully preserved in many villages [less than a century ago]. Next to the church-assembly hall, a bench marked the spot. From there, sunset was observed on the distinctive mountain profile to the west. The village's designated sunwatcher determined the passage of the year by observing the sun's return to the solstice point. Dates for all of the year's holidays were established in the same way.

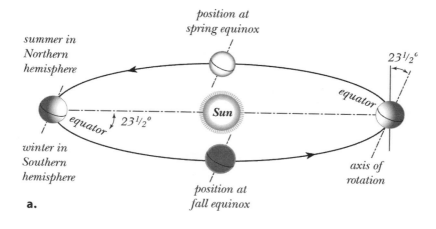

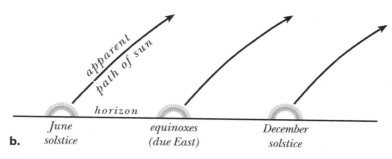

a.

b.

Figure 22. Seasonal shift. **(a)** What really happens. The axis on which Earth spins daily is tipped 23.5° with respect to the plane of its annual orbit around the sun (the *ecliptic* plane). Consequently, the northern hemisphere gets more direct sunlight during part of the year (summer) and less during another part (winter); likewise in the southern hemisphere, in opposite phases. **(b)** What we *see* in the northern hemisphere. Because Earth is tipped, the sun rises in different places during the year: far to the northeast at the June solstice (when the northern hemisphere slants sunwards), due east at the equinoxes (when the sun is "beside" the slant of Earth's axis), far to the southeast at the December solstice (when the southern hemisphere slants toward the sun).

Figure 23. Landscape of mountains and two rivers (and bear eating honey?), engraved on silver vase from Maikop, just north of the Caucasus range, ca. 2500 B.C.—the sort of highly differentiated southern horizon that facilitates calendrical observations in the northern hemisphere. (The eye-shapes are rivets.)

Between 40 and 50 of the year's 365 days were specially marked by natural horizon features, and the intervals in days between them were part of the ancient calendar lore transmitted orally from one generation to the next. [Krupp 1983, 311]

We know that many preliterate groups worked out the solstices with great precision, because they built huge stone monuments marking them. The sun at the summer solstice still rises over the Heel Stone for an observer standing in the center of Stonehenge in southern England, and at the winter solstice the rays of the rising sun enter a high transom and snake up the stone passageway to light the center of the great mound at Newgrange, Ireland. Both these monuments are now dated to the Stone Age, within a century or two of 3000 B.C., and many other ancient edifices aligned to key positions of the sun exist in Europe, Polynesia, all three Americas, China, Egypt, and elsewhere [Krupp 1983].

If you follow the angle of the sun's path during the day and the course of the planets at night, you will find they cross the sky in slanted arcs, rising and setting at roughly the same point on the horizon as each other. (You can set up another chin-rest to observe the setting points.) The moon does the same, although with more variation, since its orbit around Earth is slightly aslant to the others (which circle the sun, not earth). The sun's arching path, which slides northward and southward with the seasons (figure 22b), is known as the *ecliptic*, since it is necessarily also the path on which any eclipses will occur. That's because an eclipse happens when sun, moon, and earth line up, so that one hides another briefly. (Eclipses don't happen every day because the band within which the sun, moon, and planets appear to move is actually several degrees wide, seen from earth, and things must line up fairly exactly for an eclipse.)

Suppose, however, that you and your family are obliged to move, so you will no longer have your favorite bench or chin-rests for producing your calendar. What to do?

The sky itself contains markers: use *them* instead of peaks or standing-stones. Just before sun-up obliterates the stars, note which stars are on the horizon and where the sun rises among them. Nowadays, the summer solstice sun comes up where the constellation Gemini is rising just before it gets washed out by the dawn light. (This is called a *heliacal rising* in Gemini. Similarly, one can note *heliacal settings* at dusk.)

But to peg these heliacal risings and settings, one needs a good system of remembering the star-positions. Enter the myth-creatures.

All over the world, people remember the stars by interpreting patches of the sky as images of things they know, then making up stories about them to remember what sits where. To the extent that these "constellations" can be imagined to represent animals or people, it's easier to make up lively tales about them—as in the Andean Huarochirí myth about the Fox and the Tinamou (chapter 14). Or take, for instance, the easily recognizable constellation we know as Orion, which is followed across the sky by Sirius (Egyptian Sothis), the brightest of all stars. The Egyptians interpreted the Orion cluster as the god Osiris, who "dies"—sets and disappears—for 70 days in the summer, followed by his faithful wife Isis, who is mistress of Sirius/Sothis and is intent on reviving him [Krupp 1983, 28–29, 106].

(Note both Multiple Aspects and Analogy at play here: Osiris encompasses anything that apparently dies and returns, including Orion, the sun, and vegetation. The 70-day embalming period of the Egyptian funerary rite seems to take its cue specifically from the 70-day "death" of Osiris/Orion, and one shaft of the Great Pyramid of Khufu at Giza, built about 2500 B.C., was aimed at Orion, a celestial destination of the dead pharaoh who was to be resurrected as Osiris [Krupp 1983, 102–9].)

Among the most important constellations for timekeeping are those that fall along the ecliptic, and these are the twelve we know of today as the *Zodiac*, from a Greek term meaning "[circle] of little animals" (figure 24):

Pisces (fish)	Virgo (virgin)
Aries (ram)	Libra (scales) or Chela (the claw)
Taurus (bull)	Scorpio (scorpion)
Gemini (twins)	Sagittarius (archer)
Cancer (crab)	Capricorn (fishtailed goat)
Leo (lion)	Aquarius (water-bearer)

Not quite all of them are "animals", but the only one that today is inanimate used to be the claw of the Scorpion beside it (now restructured as the Scales of Justice—that is, of Virgo the Virgin on the other side of it). They correspond to our division of the year into twelve months, 12 being an important number in the astronomy of earthlings.

Once you can recognize the constellations of the Zodiac, it becomes

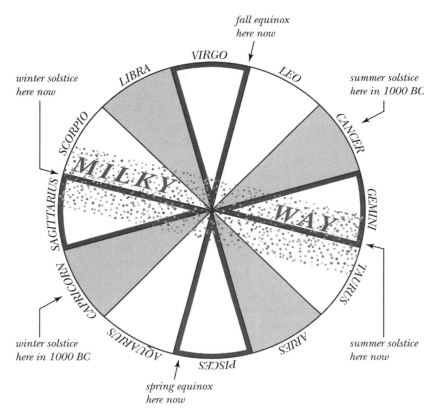

Figure 24. The Zodiac originally named a band of twelve constellations occurring along the apparent path of sun, moon, and planets (*ecliptic*), "marking" the band. The Milky Way crosses the Zodiac from Sagittarius/Scorpio to Gemini/Taurus. (For convenience, the Zodiac was later redivided into twelve *equal* sections of 30°, called *signs*, with the same names: Reinterpretation.) The sun now rises in Pisces and Virgo at the spring and fall equinoxes, and in Gemini and Sagittarius at the summer and winter solstices, respectively. But an earlier stage was frozen in the nomenclature even as the stars moved on: the Tropic ("turn") circles should now be named Gemini and Sagittarius, but the solstices (sun-turns) were occurring in Cancer and Capricorn (see figure 32) when those geographical markers were named.

apparent that they too form a circular belt that keeps coming around from under the earth, just as the sun, moon, and planets do. This is often expressed as the flowing of a gigantic river that circles the farthest edges of earth—not a bad analogy. Unfortunately, this image (unlike the competing image of a crystal sphere surrounding us) is open to Reinterpretation, by taking the flow as "around" on the same plane as the earth's surface rather than at a steep angle to that plane (figure 25).

Greek Okeanos or Ocean, for example, clearly came to be interpreted both ways [S&D, 190].[3]

Once you can recognize the constellations under any circumstances, a potentially enlightening event awaits you. For as the moon blots out the sun's disk in a total eclipse of the sun (figure 26), the constellations and planets briefly become visible, all in their proper order. This is instant proof that the stars flow perpetually around the earth.[4]

Even without eclipses it also becomes clear that things move at different speeds: all the stars at one speed, and the sun, moon, and planets each at yet other speeds. (All these cycles can of course be watched and counted.) Some of the planets, in addition to their own speeds, have strange courses, seeming to back up east to west for a while ("retrograde") before forging ahead again, as though with wills that are independent, even ornery. The sun, moon, and planets (literally "wanderers") must therefore be deities (Willfulness Principle), and pretty major ones at that (figure 27). And somebody up there must be in charge of all that motion.

The Moving Finger writes, and, having writ,
Moves on . . .
            —Edward FitzGerald, *The Rubáiyát of Omar Khayyám*
                                                    (1879) lxxi

Being the farthest away of the five planets visible to the naked eye, Saturn has the longest cycle, taking almost 30 earth-years (29.46 to be exact) to orbit the sun once (*sidereal period*). Saturn's orbit is therefore the longest single measure of time readily available in the sky, and myths of Saturn (whatever "his" name: Kronos, Wiraqocha, Ea/Enki, Ptah, et cetera) present him as the Lord of Measures, Measurer of Time [S&D, 135–36].

Jupiter, rather closer, takes not quite 12 earth-years (11.86) to circle the sun. As they orbit, Jupiter and Saturn appear to come together in

---

[3] This chapter could not have existed without the massive groundbreaking by Santillana and Dechend [1977, first published in 1969 in German]—referred to throughout this chapter as S&D—and Sullivan [1996], for Old and New Worlds, respectively. Although controversial, they have usefully flagged and collected Herculean amounts of relevant data. New "planetarium" software will help assess their interpretations.

[4] Total eclipses are known to have started religions and religious ideas: see, for example, Masse and Soklow (in press), on the Katsina cult. And compare figures 26 and 27. During eclipse, the sun will be surrounded by the same (heliacal) constellation it rose in at dawn that day.

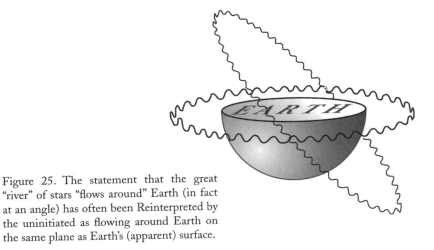

Figure 25. The statement that the great "river" of stars "flows around" Earth (in fact at an angle) has often been Reinterpreted by the uninitiated as flowing around Earth on the same plane as Earth's (apparent) surface.

Figure 26. Solar eclipse, June 30, 1973, showing sun's corona. Compare figure 27:b–d, the Egyptian and Mesopotamian winged sun-disk, which might have originated in such a spectacle. ("So that's how the sun moves—it has wings!")

Figure 27. Ancient representations of celestial bodies as deities. **(a)** Moon (Sin), Venus (Ishtar), and sun (Shamash), respectively, invoked on Mesopotamian boundary stone of Meli-Shipak II; 16th century B.C., Kassite era. **(b)** Moon, Sun, and Venus on 7th-century B.C. stele of Asarhaddon. **(c)** Egyptian divine winged sun-disk, from relief of Seti I at Abydos, ca. 1280 B.C. **(d)** Syrian winged sun-disk on stele of god El, Ugarit, ca. 13th century B.C. **(e)** Cuneiform sign originating as AN ("star," "sky") that came to signify DINGIR ("deity"). **(f)** "Scorpion Man" inlaid on Sumerian harp from Ur, ca. 2600 B.C.: presumably the mythical Scorpion Man who guards the ferry sailing to the Man who Survived the Flood in the *Epic of Gilgamesh*—as Scorpio guards the Milky Way (cf. figure 24).

the sky once every 20 years. This meeting is called a planetary *conjunction* and is easily recognizable and countable. But each time they encounter each other, they appear against a different third of the Zodiac, so that it takes them 60 years to reappear together in about the same spot among the background of stars. They actually overshoot a little, so their conjunctions move slowly through the Zodiac by triple bounces, in the same direction as the sun moves through it during the year (figure 28). It takes 40 conjunctions, hence about 800 years, for Saturn and Jupiter to meet in *exactly* the same spot in the sky as before. (These numbers, especially 40, 60, and 800, along with 12, noted earlier, keep turning up in mythology.) Viewed geometrically, it takes one angle of this triangle, or Trigon, $3 \times 800 = 2400$ years to move all the way around the Zodiac [S&D, 134a, 368a].

So Jupiter, whatever his name (Zeus, Pirua/Manco Capac, Marduk, et cetera), as the junior member of the team takes the measures "from" Saturn, allowing a systematically marked calendrical count to build up from 20 to 60 to 800 to 2400 years and beyond [S&D; Sullivan 1996, 122–23].

Mars is next, orbiting in 687 days; but because Earth moves at the same time, it takes 780 days (the *synodic period*), a bit over two earth-years, for Mars to end up in the same place in our sky again. (Vividly encoded: the Finnish super-boy Kullervo, first seen in a cradle lowered from heaven, "barked one year, another one, a little from the third . . . at the smith" Ilmarinen, maker of the continuously turning Celestial Mill [S&D, 31, 131].) The reddish color of Mars seems to have caused association with blood, hence with war and war gods.

The last two planets, Venus and Mercury, whiz around the sun in less than a year (225 and 88 days) because they lie between us and the sun. Since we would have to look right into the sun to find them much of the time, we can only see them during a total eclipse or when they happen to be off to one side near dawn and dusk, as "morning stars" or "evening stars". Then they are lit by the sun from the side and appear through a telescope as less than full circles—crescent, half, or gibbous ("humpbacked"), just like the moon. But certainly for Mercury—which is so near the sun from our perspective that it's hard to see anyway, visible only during twilight and close to the horizon—those phases are impossible to see with the naked eye. The same is said for Venus.

Venus, quite unlike Mercury, is by far the brightest object in the entire sky other than the sun and moon, shining even during the day sometimes—we have spotted it at 4:30 P.M. It hovers for almost nine months as the bright and beautiful Evening Star, nine more as the

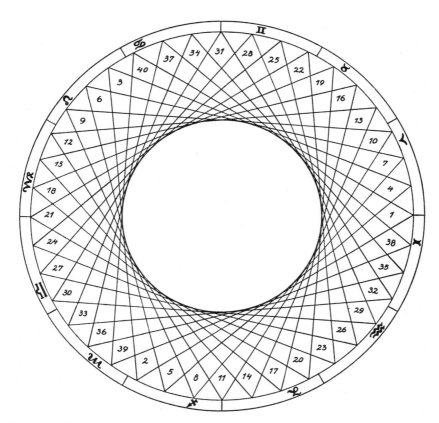

Figure 28. Johannes Kepler's Great Trigon (from the preface to his *Mysterium Cosmographicum* [1606]), showing the successive conjunctions of Saturn and Jupiter every 20 years. Because their positions against the stars shift, it takes three conjunctions (forming a rough triangle) to come back to *nearly* the same place, and 800 years to return to *exactly* the same place.

Morning Star heralding dawn, with alternately one week and seven weeks of invisibility between stints, totalling a $19\frac{1}{2}$-month synodic period. This seems to be the only planet ever thought to be a female deity (Aphrodite/Helen, Ishtar/Inanna, Anahita/Anahid, Sūryā [daughter of Sūrya, the sun; the name is etymologically the same as Helénā], et cetera).[5]

[5] Why is Venus persistently female? Could some sharp-eyed ancients actually have *noticed* that Venus has crescent phases like our moon? With 20/15 vision one of us can just make them out, but people with 20/10 vision exist. Since we associate women's "menstrual"—literally "monthly"—cycles with the moon, because they are roughly commensurate, Venus could be female by Analogy.

As a goddess among gods, and the most beautiful of all, surely Venus will be remembered by amorous liaisons as she moves about the sky. None other than Homer recounts a "silly story" [*Odyssey* 8.266–366] in which Hephaistos, tipped off by Helios/Sun, catches his wife Aphrodite/Venus in bed with Ares/Mars. Enraged, he casts an invisible net that holds them while he appeals to Zeus/Jupiter, Hermes/Mercury, Poseidon, and Apollo to come around and laugh at them, until Poseidon gravely persuades him to let them go. If the planets are gods, this stellar event, which has to have occurred before Homer (ca. 800 B.C.) and after Zeus became celestial ruler (ca. 2150 B.C., as we'll see below), must encode a massing of all five visible planets.[6] So we looked for it. One and only one such massing has occurred in the last 5000 years—a truly memorable event to long-time sky-watchers, one also noted in Chinese myth [Mosley 2002, 147]. It was visible just before sunrise throughout what we would call late February 1953 B.C. (figure 29). Homer carries baggage far older than the Trojan War.

(Santillana and Dechend [1969/77, 177] first suggested this myth was astronomical, proposing a simple conjunction of Venus and Mars in the Pleiades [a Net?]. That occurs frequently each *century* and doesn't explain the other central details; but they had no way to check their hypotheses. Fortunately, new planetarium-type software—we used Redshift and Starry Night Pro—enables anyone to generate the dates of planetary events and watch them "run" through time as viewed from a particular location. [We chose Athens for convenience.] Sullivan had to persuade operators of a *mechanical* planetarium to check a *few* key hypotheses; happily they were correct. Being able to use a PC revolutionizes star-myth research.)

So sun, moon, planets, and stars appear to circle the earth at various speeds, rising or being born in the east and setting or dying in the west each day or night, and being completely invisible for varying periods of time.

We have now dollied around to the right Camera Angle to see that, if celestial bodies "die" in the west (the sun at dusk, "shrouded" by night [Katz 2000], and the stars and planets during the night), then the west is an appropriate direction to travel to find the abode of the dead. But since the "dying" celestial bodies are easily construed as passing under the earth to rise or be reborn again hours later, the land of the dead must also lie underneath the earth (and may well be lit by the sun,

---

[6] Pre-Hellenic Poseidon appears to hold the position of solemn Saturn. Did he, like the Flood (see below), Attract celestial and "real" waters together, being lord of both "Oceans" (cf. figure 25)?

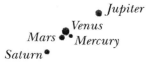

Southeast Horizon

Figure 29. Rare massing of the five visible planets in early 1953 B.C.: shown at 7 A.M., February 25, from the position of Athens.

moon, and stars while they are down there). The nether location of the dead is of course reinforced by the fact that most human cultures *put* their dead under the earth, that is, the soil. Modern scholars complain that the ancient Greeks and others vacillated as to whether one reached the land of the dead by going west or heading straight down. They miss the point: by this widespread cosmology, it was clearly in both places at once. Thus both pharaohs and Greek heroes could quite plausibly sail *west* to reach the *Under*world, just as the sun and stars do.

But if the bright celestial lights we call sun, moon, and planets are willful, then one could conclude—and many cultures did—that the stars are lesser Wills, namely the disembodied souls of ordinary people and perhaps animals waiting to be (re)born. How, then, might they get back and forth? One could presumably dispatch a dead soul quickly back to its home among the astral fires above by cremation. The Norse, in fact, often hedged their bets by cremating important persons (flame rising to flame) in a launched ship (sailing to the ocean of stars). In the Andes, as William Sullivan [1996] has shown at length, souls were thought to cross between worlds at the moments when the sun did its "standstill" (solstice) rising and setting in the Milky Way.[7]

One would wonder about this obsessive concern with the stars and their motion, were it not the case that those early thinkers thought they had located the gods which rule the universe and with it also the destiny of the soul down here and after death.

—Santillana and Dechend [1969/77, 150]

[7] Might the solstice sunray penetrating Newgrange similarly have been viewed as a pathway for dead souls—a cosmic bridge between two worlds? See below for celestial ferries and bridges.

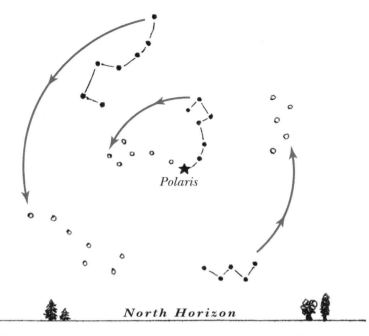

Figure 30. Current rotation from June to September (viewed about 10 P.M., from the latitude of Greece and California) of the Dippers and Cassiopeia around Polaris, the current celestial pole. The pole star is the only star that seems never to move.

The path of the Zodiac and planets is not the only circular motion observable in the night sky. The bright star-path of the Milky Way (in actuality a sideview of our own "galaxy"—from Greek *galakt-* "milk") appears to stretch between Gemini/Taurus at one end and Scorpio/Sagittarius at the other (figure 24), and to swing around the sky as the year progresses. Two more animal constellations, the Big Bear and Little Bear (a.k.a. Big and Little Dipper or Spoon; Big and Little Wain or Wagon) go round and round each other in the northern sky like the sides of a millwheel (from the viewpoint of people in the northern hemisphere), without ever disappearing into the Underworld the way the sun, moon, and most stars do (figure 30). Eternal and "undying", they seem to circle round an invisible axis or shaft, termed the *celestial pole*. At the "top" end of that shaft today we see the star Polaris, or North Star, the one star which appears immobile, thereby defining the direction North.[8]

---

[8] There are no stars near the bottom end of the celestial axis, but the second brightest star in the sky, Canopus, marks the bottom of the pole of the *ecliptic*. If you live south of 38°

Figure 31. In Hindu and Buddhist mythology, gods and demons churn the Ocean of Milk with a celestial dasher formed by the Sacred Mount (at the center of the world, resting on a tortoise), which they turn back and forth like a fire-drill by pulling on the ends of the serpent Vasuki, wrapped around the middle of the V-shaped mountain. The story is first recorded in mid-first millennium B.C. epics, the *Mahābhārata* and *Rāmāyaṇa*.

This central axis or shaft around which both earth and sky, space and time, are organized predictably figures widely in mythology. It may be Analogized as a World Tree (like Norse Yggdrasill, with heaven above, our earthly living space midway, and another more mysterious realm below; or the central Asian shaman's tree, which gives access to the multilayered spirit world; or Zeus's oak, carrying the star-mantle [S&D, 223]). Or as the axle of a Cosmic Mill (like the Finnic Sampo, or the Germanic mill of Amlodhi/Amlethus/Hamlet, or Frodhi's Grotte "the crusher") that grinds out stars, salt, and sand in turn; or as the shaft of a Churn continually stirring the Ocean of Milk (figure 31; depicted often in Asia and carefully architecturalized at Angkor Thom), or as all manner of ominous spindles, oars, steep mountains, pillars, and posts [collected and discussed in S&D; also Krupp 1983, 88–89].

If we now imagine the earth as round with a pole through it, we can either picture the earth as a disk or ball turning on this axis amid a

north latitude, it just skims the southern horizon in the keel or rudder of the ship constellation—Argo to the Greeks, and to the Egyptians "the boat that carried Isis and Osiris during a global deluge" [Chartrand 1998, 468; cf. S&D, 73].

cloud of stars (our current theory) or imagine a giant starry sphere or river that turns or flows around *us*—an older theory, corresponding more closely to how things look. If a sphere, then the stars (which move at one speed) must be affixed to a different crystalline sphere from sun, moon, and planets, which move at different paces and so must each have its own concentric crystal sphere. There must, then, be at least seven of these, carrying Sun, Moon, and the five visible planets: Saturn, Jupiter, Mars, Venus, and Mercury. Imagining that the seven heavenly bodies simply guided their boats along a stream of stars (figures 2, 12) produced a rather simpler if less deterministic theory. But the Pythagorean notion of crystal spheres carrying myriad fires persisted in Western thought into the Renaissance [Heninger 1974].

Halfway from where the pole emerges at earth's top/north and bottom/south, we can also imagine slicing in two both the earth-ball and the surrounding "crystal spheres", like cutting an onion in half. This cut-line marks the earth's equator, and, where it slices the apparent "sphere of the heavens" surrounding us, the *celestial equator* (figure 32a).

This cutting plane—the plane of the celestial equator—forms a 90° angle with the line of the pole or axis, but because the earth doesn't sit up straight, both lie at a rakish 23.5° angle to the plane of the ecliptic where the sun and planets are (figure 32b). It is tipped a bit on its side as it circles the sun, such that when the north half is facing the sun more directly, the northern hemisphere experiences summer and the southern, winter (figure 22a). The moment of maximum tip toward the sun marks the summer solstice, when daylight lasts longest, and the maximum tip away defines the winter solstice when days are shortest. Halfway between these moments, we get the *equinoxes* (from Latin for "equal night"), when night and day last exactly twelve hours each and the sun rises and sets due east and west. To look at it another way: at the equinoxes the sun shines directly down on the equator (the half-way point of its apparent north-south movement); but at the summer solstice, when its course appears to "turn" from moving north to moving south, its rays shine straight down on the Tropic (Greek *trop-* "turning") of Cancer, 23.5° north of the equator, and at the winter solstice, when it turns north again, on the Tropic of Capricorn at 23.5° south latitude (figures 22a, 32b; compare figure 24).

Now, the solstices are the easiest part of the calendar for a novice to observe, since the point of sunrise seems to stand still for a few days. But once one understands and can locate the celestial equator and the

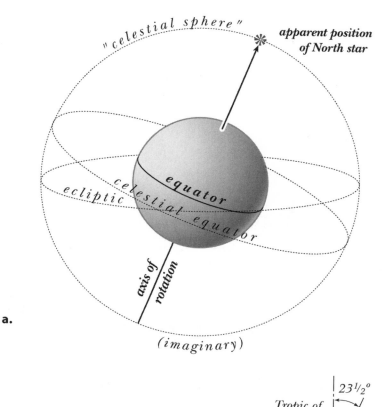

a.

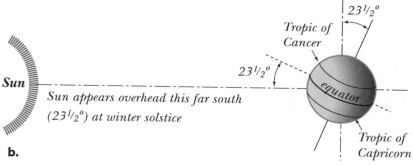

b.

Figure 32. Equator and ecliptic. **(a)** Polaris (North Star) currently sits on an extension of the axis or pole around which Earth spins. The plane slicing through Earth's equator lies at 90° to that pole; and extending that plane defines the celestial equator in what *looks* to us like a sphere of stars around us. The plane on which Earth moves around the sun—the ecliptic—crosses the plane of the equators at an angle of 23.5° (figure 22). **(b)** Because of Earth's 23.5° tilt, the sun never appears directly overhead beyond the zone lying 23.5° to either side of the equator. The limits of this zone lie where the sun appears to "turn back" (Greek *trop*- "turn") toward the equator, hence the name "Tropics" (of Cancer and Capricorn). See figures 22 and 24.

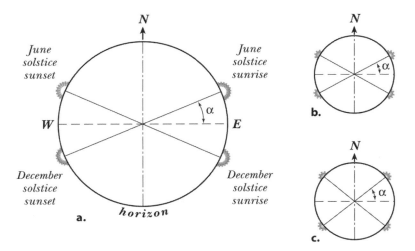

Figure 33. Observations, at three locations, of the cross made by joining the local points on the horizon where the sun rises and sets at the solstices: **(a)** at the equator, angle $\alpha = 23.5°$; **(b)** on Crete (35° latitude) $\alpha = 29.1°$; **(c)** around Kiev (51° latitude) $\alpha = 39.3°$. (Note that the farther one gets from the equator, the wider the apparent angle of north-south shift becomes.)

ecliptic,[9] the equinoxes become more accurate calendrical markers. They lie at the points where the two circles cross. This image of crossing graphically symbolized the equinox and/or solstice in many cultures (figures 33–34).

Just as the solstices and equinoxes mark time, so they also help humans orient themselves in space. Imagine yourself back in the era with no electricity, clocks, wheels, or cities: it also had no roads, no Triple-A maps, no compasses. How do you *find* north (or true east)? The sun's shadow can give you a rough idea, but the stars are far more accurate. The Egyptians of 2500 B.C. located exact north by clever observation of star alignments around the celestial pole, to orient their pyramids [Spence 2000]. Also, the sun rises and sets at the equinoxes at points due east and west, and north/south runs perpendicular to the line between those points. But how do you find any of that on some other day of the year, especially if you are a traveller, someone with no permanent markers?

[9] Five bodies—moon, Jupiter, Mars, Venus, and Mercury—lined up at nearly even intervals across the evening sky in mid-April 2002, displaying the slanting ecliptic with unforgettable clarity. See Allen [1992] and Ruggles [1997] for methods of finding the equinoxes.

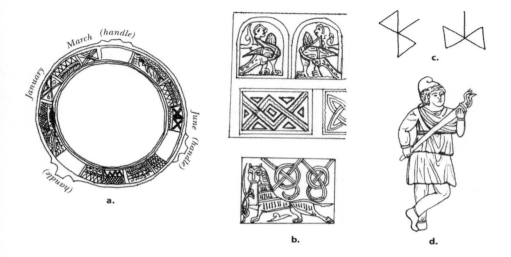

Figure 34. Crosses generated as cultural symbols of equinox and/or solstice: **(a)** single crosses marking winter solstice and spring equinox, double cross for June solstice, on fourth-century A.D. Slavic calendrical bowl from Lepesovka (Slavs ritually ignored the fall equinox, and the winter celebrations lasted far into January); **(b)** solstice/equinox figures on 12th century Russian ritual bracelets that depict Rusalii fertility spirits (see figure 8:a–b) and their festivals, held on the solstices and spring equinox; **(c)** Minoan "double axe" figure (from Mallia; second version rotated—see figure 37), possibly representing the celestial pole and cross; **(d)** Cautes, with raised torch, representing the spring equinox in the Mithraic cult, standing with legs forming the equinoctial cross (see figure 38 for context); on relief from Nersae, A.D. 172.

The trick is to learn when and where the stars rise and set, not just alone but *as a system* [cf. Kyselka 1987]. Within it, the constellations in which the sun rises and sets at the summer and winter solstices mark, at that time, the farthest north and south that the sun ever moves (with east/west halfway between), providing another set of four benchmarks from which time and direction could be reckoned (figures 22b, 33). (Stones set up at Stonehenge and elsewhere mark these key positions.) In a world before magnetic compasses, roads, and signposts, such celestial sightings were critical for travel in general and navigation in particular.

But eventually we run into trouble.

Suppose you have inherited a myth telling you that the sun rises at the summer solstice where you see the constellation Leo the Lion and the spring equinox sun rises in Taurus the Bull. Yet as you watch the sun year after year, you find it shifting ever so slowly *out* of these con-

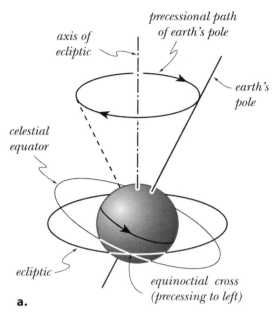

precessional path
of earth's pole

axis of
ecliptic

earth's
pole

celestial
equator

ecliptic

equinoctial cross
(precessing to left)

a.

Figure 35. Northshift. **(a)** The slow circuit of the extension of Earth's rotational pole through the stars takes almost 26,000 years, swinging the apparent North Celestial Pole from one part of the northern sky to another and causing the sun to appear against a shifting background of Zodiac stars. This shift was also noticed at solstices and equinoxes, hence its modern name, *precession of the equinoxes*. **(b)** The precessional shift of the North Celestial Pole through the northern stars as it appears from Earth ("Northshift"). When the Egyptians built the pyramids ca. 2500 B.C., the sky rotated around not Polaris but Thuban, in the constellation Draco (Dragon or Serpent). Eventually the Dragon was dispossessed of this honor, but no other star appeared to take its place at the "center" until recently. In 13,000 years, Vega will be the pole star.

stellations into the next ones, Cancer and Aries; and furthermore, the end of the rotational axis no longer sits in quite the same section of sky as before: *North has moved.*

What a catastrophe! Not so much for the calendar, but for navigation, since all the coordinates marking *direction* must now be reestablished. Travellers, remember, don't have fixed chin-rests but depend on celestial markers.

In fact, such a celestial shift actually happens: the "fixed stars" aren't quite fixed. This slippage results from a wobble in the earth's rotation (like the wobble of a top at the end of its spin) that causes the end of the

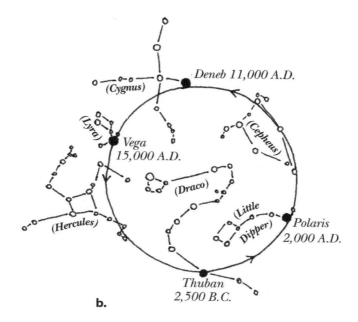

Deneb 11,000 A.D.

(Cygnus)

(Lyra)

Vega
15,000 A.D.

(Cepheus)

(Draco)

(Hercules)

(Little
Dipper)   Polaris
                 2,000 A.D.

b.

Thuban
2,500 B.C.

tipped pole to wander in a huge slow circle through the northern stars
(figure 35). When the Egyptians built the pyramids around 2500 B.C.,
the sky rotated not around Polaris at the end of the Little Dipper but
around Thuban, a brightish star in nearby Draco the Dragon (see Spence
2000 for pyramid features set on and hence datable by this difference).
After that, there was no "pole star" for millennia: the position of the pole
could only be reckoned from nearby configurations. The change in where
the axis points also causes the sunrise at the equinoxes and solstices to
move, exceedingly slowly, against the backdrop of the Zodiac.

In fact, it takes nearly 26,000 years to complete the cycle, a rate of
2160 years per zodiacal sector (if these are allotted an equal 30° apiece:
12 × 30° = 360°; 12 × 2160 = 25,920). As the pole wobbles, the positions of the equinoxes and solstices slide slowly through the Zodiac in
the *opposite* direction from everything else. Thus the sun currently
moves from a background of Gemini to Cancer during July, but about
2000 years ago the June solstice slid the opposite way, from Cancer into
Gemini. (Since the astrological system used by our newspapers was fossilized more than 2000 years ago, most people are misinformed as to
the constellation that "ruled the sun" when they were born. Thus if your
birthday is July 4, you were actually born when the sun was in Gemini,
not Cancer.) Because this slow wobble is, from our monthly point of

view, in the direction of the "preceding" constellation, the phenomenon is now known as the *precession of the equinoxes*, but it might be better called the *shift of celestial north*, or *Northshift*. In mythology it had other names.

Several other names, in fact, according to the analogies used to describe and remember this difficult yet crucial navigational information. How, for example, might one encode the relentless precession if one habitually described the heavens as rotating around a pole—whether as mill, drill, spindle, or churn? Surely some evil force—that is, some Will working against the assigned order of things—is knocking the rotating fire-drill or mill-wheel axle off its socket. Worldwide, the original owner of this vulnerable mill turns out to be Saturn, he who first gave the measures of the universe; and the mill-shaft's unseating results, in some mythologies, in a vast, open whirlpool or Maelstrom in both sky above and "Ocean" below. (Readers interested in these widespread myths can peruse the data collected by Santillana and Dechend in *Hamlet's Mill*.) Its proper seat is the "navel of the world". Thus Cuzco, name of the great Inca astronomical center, means "navel" [Sullivan 1996, 118], and the Greeks viewed Apollo's temples as the "navel of the world", both the shrine at Delphi on Mount Parnassos and that on Delos, center of the Cycladic—"wheel"—Islands.[10] (*Two* navels in one culture? Surely another Doublet syncretized from pre-Hellenic times.)

Or suppose the image is a canopy or roof propped up by the pillars of the world (figure 36)—usually four, although among Eurasian nomads, analogically to their own architecture, the sky is viewed as upheld by a central Tentpole, the world axis [Sullivan 1996, 80]. Then some great, Samson-like force comes and pulls down the Pillar(s) of the House, which will have to be reestablished [compare S&D, 165–78]. (One has to wonder whether the "cult pillars" of the Minoans signified the vulnerable pillar(s) of the earth [figure 37], marked as they are with stars and with "double axe" signs resembling the common equinoctial/solsticial sign [figures 33–34].) Santillana and Dechend [235] describe explicitly

what this "earth" is that modern interpreters like to take for a pancake. . . . "Earth" is the implied plane through the four points of the year, marked by the equinoxes and solstices, in other words the ecliptic. And this is why this

---

[10] The Cycladic culture was necessarily maritime; their sacred "navel" underscores how early the stars guided navigation [cf. Ovenden 1966].

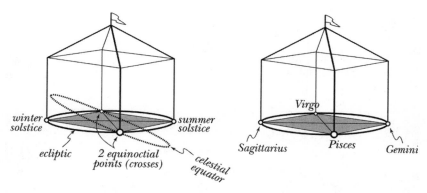

winter solstice   summer solstice

Virgo

Sagittarius   *Pisces*   *Gemini*

ecliptic   *2 equinoctial points (crosses)*   *celestial equator*

Figure 36. The mythological "pillars of the world" were the points or constellations in which the sun rose at the summer and winter solstices and the spring and fall equinoxes: these are currently Gemini and Sagittarius, Pisces and Virgo (see figure 24). Together they determine a square plane or "earth" (whence the notion that the earth is square—often misunderstood as real, not celestial) and were taken figuratively as the props of the sky. The shift of North (precession) periodically destroys these pillars (coordinates): mythically they collapse, that "earth" is destroyed (in flood or flames), and a new one—just like the former one except for its "rulers" (coordinates)—replaces it.

earth is very frequently said to be quadrangular. The four "corners," that is, the zodiacal constellations rising heliacally at both the equinoxes and solstices, . . . are the points which determine an "earth." Every world-age has its own "earth." It is for this very reason that "ends of the world" are said to take place. A new "earth" arises, when another set of zodiacal constellations brought in by the Precession determines the year points.

Or take as starting point the river of stars, flowing in endless circles round and round the earth from the unseen celestial reservoirs below.

A male llama, who was pastured on a hill with excellent fodder, knew that the Mother Sea had decided to overflow. . . . This llama became very sad; he kept crying out "in, in," and didn't eat. The llama's master, very angry, hit him with an ear of maize. "Eat, dog," he said. "You are lying about on the best pastures." Then the llama, speaking as if he were a man, told the shepherd, "Pay very close attention, and remember what I am going to tell you: Five days from now the great ocean will be here and the whole world will be flooded." And the shepherd was stricken with fear. . . . "We will go somewhere to escape. Let us go to Mount Vilcacoto; there we must save

Figure 37. "Double axe" signs and stars carved on pillars in cult room in Minoan palace at Mallia, Crete; mid-second millennium B.C. The "axe" may represent the cosmic pole and solsticial cross (figures 33 and 34); the pillar may signify the vulnerable pillar(s) of the earth (figure 35).

ourselves; bring food for five days," he ordered. And so, from that instant, he started walking, taking his family and the llama. When he was about to reach the top of Mount Vilcacoto, he found that all the animals were re-united: puma, fox, huanaco, condor, every species of animal. Hardly had the man arrived than the water began to fall in rivers; and so there they were, squeezed together at the top of Huillcacoto, in a tiny space, at the very peak, where the water couldn't quite reach. But the water did manage to reach fox's tail and get it wet, which is why fox's tail, to this day, is black. And after five days, the waters began to recede and dry up. [Sullivan 1996, 16]

Just as in Genesis, this tale—collected in two versions in the Andes in the sixteenth century—concludes with the entire world being repopu-lated by the man, his family, and the huddled animals, the sole survivors of the flood.

But this flood is located on the opposite side of the globe from the Near East, and other similar tales come from India, Greece, Indonesia, China, and so on. Consulting geologists is futile, as the second Andean version warns us: "as the waters rose, the hill grew higher, so that it was never covered by the flood; and when the waters subsided, the hill also grew smaller" [Sullivan 1996, 15]. No earthly hill can do that. The Flood is not earthly but celestial, and we must abandon seeking specific geographic sites for it (except by Attraction). The fox's tail warns us, too, where to look, since in chapter 14 we learned that Fox is an Andean con-stellation slipping tail-first down the hill and below the horizon into the "water"—the celestial river. Then again, recall that it was a boat-*constellation* that carried Isis and Osiris to safety during a global deluge.

In short, although stories of actual floods may have Attracted them-selves repeatedly to this myth (such as the sixth-millennium Black Sea flood [Ryan and Pitman 1998]), the Flood is at heart astronomical, and specifically recounts Northshift and the precession of the equinoxes, when one set of cardinal constellations, pushed by the "multitudes" be-hind it, falls below the horizon into the surrounding celestial sea, while another set rises triumphant to replace it. (Again, see Santillana and Dechend for worldwide coverage; the usual reason for the Flood is "crowding multitudes".) *Which* constellation is crowded into the drink, however, depends of course on the date and the (northern/southern) hemisphere. And because the world afterwards is much the same as be-fore, clearly (Movie Construct principle) enough humans and animals "survived" to repopulate.

Suppose, however, that the dominant image for the starry sky is that of circulating fire of some sort (Greek *Pyriphlegethon*), shining, perhaps, through little holes in the vault (and the sun through a big hole?). Then one could predict that a collapse of the old system would bring down a rain of fire destroying the "old" world; yet the net effect is the same as with the Flood, since the regenerated world, rising phoenix-like from its own ashes, resembles the previous one.[11] The Norse prediction of the death of the gods at Ragnarök (made famous by Wagner's apocalyptically fiery opera *Götterdämmerung*) includes passages asserting that each god who dies in battle when "heaven is rent asunder" by the fiery hordes will be replaced by another:

> At that time earth will rise out of the sea and be green and fair. . . . Víðar [having killed the wolf that swallows Odin] and Váli will be living, so neither the sea nor Surt's Fire will have done them injury, and they will inhabit Idavöll where Ásgarð used to be. And the sons of Thór . . . will come there and possess Mjöllnir. . . . While the world is being burnt by Surt, in a place called Hoddmímir's Wood, will be concealed two human beings . . . and from these . . . will come men after men. And you will think this strange, but the sun will have borne a daughter no less lovely than herself, and she will follow the paths of her mother. [*Gylfaginning*: Sturluson 1971, 91–92]

Compare this with a passage in the ancient royal Hawaiian Kumulipo, spotted by Santillana and Dechend [163–64]:

> *Now turns the swinging of time over the burnt-out world*
> *Back goes the great turning of things upwards again*
> *As yet sunless the time of shrouded light; . . .*
> *From out Makalii's [the Pleiades'] night-dark veil of cloud*
> *Thrills, shadow-like, the prefiguration of the world to be.*

Vikings and Polynesians alike—both adept at sailing huge distances without modern maps and instruments—paid close attention to the destruction and birth of systems of celestial coordinates. (We do not. The Tropics of Cancer and Capricorn became the Tropics—sun-turning points—of Gemini and Sagittarius 2000 years ago but, having become

---

[11] Berossos believes both: that the world is in danger from deluge when the planets line up in Capricorn, the lowest dip of the sun in his day, but from conflagration if they align in Cancer, at that time the high point and home of the summer solstice [Burstein 1978, 29].

seriously literate before that, we never bothered to change the names on our maps.)[12]

In fact, without myth to encode and transmit the critical data, preliterate societies would be hard pressed to know that precession out of one constellation into the next both *had* occurred and *would* occur again, on a regular schedule. For if precession moves 30° in 2160 years, it takes 72 years to move a single degree (about twice the apparent diameter of the moon), a rate so slow as to be barely discernible within a single lifetime. How far back, then, was the phenomenon of Northshift or precession noticed (even if not understood)?

Ask astronomers and they'll state firmly that a Greek named Hipparchos first figured it out in about 128 B.C. and calculated its cycle at about 36,000 years [Ulansey 1989, 76–78]. This is rather on the long side of the actual 25,920 years, but a small error of observation becomes enormous when one has to calculate so huge a number from a short time of measuring.

Soon after Hipparchos died, the mystery cult of Mithras began to spread across the Roman Empire, presently becoming the chief rival to Christianity. The focal point of each Mithraic temple was a depiction of the god Mithras slaying a bull (figure 38), with many other symbols around the edges such as the sun and moon, torchbearers, dog, snake, crow, sometimes a lion and a cup, and oddest of all, a scorpion beneath the bull. But this is the Zodiac—for when one equinox is in Taurus the Bull, the other lies in Scorpio, and the solstices in Leo and Aquarius (the Cupbearer). In fact, a recent book by David Ulansey on *The Origins of the Mithraic Mysteries* patiently ferrets out the tightly interlocked astral significance of each and every detail in those reliefs, and they are *all* celestial. The central motif, then, must signify that the god Mithras, in slaying Taurus, had the power to move the entire heavens off their coordinates, causing the sun, at spring equinox, to leave Taurus. As Ulansey remarks, a god with that much power was a god to reckon with:

For the possession of carefully guarded secret knowledge concerning such a mighty divinity would naturally have been experienced as assuring privi-

[12] Apparently the Sumerians set up their nomenclature when the spring equinox was in Taurus (fourth–third millennia B.C.), since they call that constellation simply MUL "star"— presumably the central reference point for the system. That also suggests they were already savvy enough to use equinoxes instead of solstices for reckoning. (See Thurston [1994, 67] for Sumerian star-names inherited by Babylonia.)

Figure 38. Typical Mithraic cult relief: Mithras, wearing Phrygian cap and looking away, holds down and slays a bull, whose blood is lapped up by a dog, while a scorpion and a serpent attack from below; a crow observes from above left. (The bull's tail normally ends as ears of wheat.) This scene is usually accompanied by sun and moon (above left and right) with two torch-bearers, dressed like Mithras, standing with legs crossed, representing fall and spring equinoxes. One (right, named Cautopates) holds his torch low, the other (Cautes; missing on left: see figure 34:d) holds his high. Stars usually decorate the background and/or Mithras's cloak.

> leged access to the favors which this god could grant, such as deliverance from the forces of fate residing in the stars and protection for the soul after death during its journey through the planetary spheres. [Ulansey 1989, 125]

Now, precession out of Taurus into Aries occurred nearly two thousand years before Mithraism became popular, and Ulansey casts about vainly to find good reasons for this archaic imagery, "knowing" Hipparchos to be the first discoverer of precession. But note that this sudden popularity immediately precedes the *next* precession—from Aries into Pisces in 6 B.C. Clearly, some Near Eastern group already knew another shift was coming.

Other evidence supports this conclusion. If Hipparchos were really first, why is it that much older Babylonian texts are working with numbers like 2160 and 4320—precisely the (rather peculiar) numbers of years associated with precession? People will tell you Copernicus was the first to realize the earth goes around the sun, instead of sun around earth. Yet we have documentation that certain Pythagorean philosophers in the late centuries B.C. developed a heliocentric view of the cosmos [Heninger 1974, 50, 127–28]. This notion was then lost until Copernicus came along nearly two thousand years later. Since, as the geologists say, "what did happen, *can* happen"— since key ideas did and therefore can get lost for a while—let's assume for the moment that Hipparchos could have been second-comer.

Then from his ambush the son reached out his left hand,
and with his right he took the gigantic sickle,
long and jagged-toothed, and from his very own father
he swiftly lopped the genitals, and threw them behind him . . .
—Hesiod, *Theogony* 178–81

The emasculation of Ouranos by his son Kronos is one of many violent episodes in ancient Greek and Near Eastern tales of how the gods battled for possession of Kingship in Heaven (tales collected by Littleton [1970]).

According to Hesiod, after the primeval Chaos came Earth, "unfaltering foundation of all", along with "murky Tartarus" (the under half of the world) and Night and Erebos. Erebos and Night united to produce Day (Post Hoc, Ergo?) and Ether (the bright upper air); then Earth produced Ouranos (the sphere of the sky) "such that he might cover her on all sides, to be the unfaltering seat for the blessed gods always" [*Theogony* 116–29]. Ouranos next begat various children on Earth, but he hated them, we learn, and as soon as they were born "he would hide them away and not let them out into the light" [156–57]. For this evil act, Earth plotted his downfall, producing a sickle of grey "adamantine" (often translated "flint" but literally "unconquerable" [161]) and begging her children to wreak vengeance. Kronos, the youngest, took up the challenge and the sickle, ambushing his father at nightfall and emasculating him.

Kronos then assumed Kingship in Heaven, and with his sister/wife Rhea begat Hestia, Demeter, Hera, Hades, Poseidon, and finally Zeus [453–57].

But great Kronos swallowed each of them down, as each
fell to the knees of its sacred mother from the womb,
intending thus that no other, none of the illustrious descendants of Ouranos,
should hold the kingly power among the immortal gods. [459–62]

But as Zeus was about to be born, Rhea begged her parents, Earth and
Ouranos, for help against Kronos's child abuse. Earth hid the newborn
Zeus in a Cretan cave, while Rhea swaddled a stone and gave that to
Kronos to gulp down in place of Zeus. Zeus grew strong (nourished, as
we learn elsewhere, by the goat Amaltheia with her Horn of Plenty),[13]
then vanquished his father, became the next King of Heaven, and
forced Kronos to disgorge his five siblings. First up, Kronos

vomited the stone he had swallowed down last,
and Zeus planted it down on the wide-pathed earth
at holy Pytho [Delphi], under the hollows of Parnassos,
to be a sign thereafter, a marvel to mortal men. [497–500][14]

To the Greeks, Zeus was still King of Heaven in their time, but a rather
jumpy king, since Prometheus was said to know the secret of a goddess
who would bear a son stronger than his father.

A vivid story indeed—but what's it all about?

These myths *say* they record long-term changes in *heaven*. The reference to Delphi confirms *which* change—Delphi, navel of the world; Delphi, on pillar-steep Mount Parnassos where Deukalion and Pyrrha, the
survivors of the Aegean version of the Flood, landed; Delphi, where the
old order was unseated and the world renewed by Apollo, destroyer of the
snaky dragon Pytho. All the details spell Precession, that is, Northshift.[15]

The myth, moreover, recounts the precession not once but twice at
least: when Zeus came to power as the spring equinox came from Taurus
into Aries around 2150 B.C., and when Kronos vanquished Ouranos as the
equinox moved from Gemini into Taurus around 4300 B.C. (figure 39).

(Time out: When the spring equinox was in Gemini, the fall equinox

---

[13] Minoan for Capella? Capricorn?

[14] We long wondered whether a meteor fell at Delphi; recently we learned that the classical *omphalos*-stone is thought to have replaced a meteorite [Cook 1940, 936–38].

[15] Pytho the Dragon (see chapter 18) is presumably the constellation traditionally named
Draco, out of which the pole was in fact dislodged late in the third millennium (figure 35).
The Delphic story is told from a Camera Angle focused specifically on "Northshift" rather
than on "Precession", suggesting a local tradition that developed before diffusion of the Near
Eastern model.

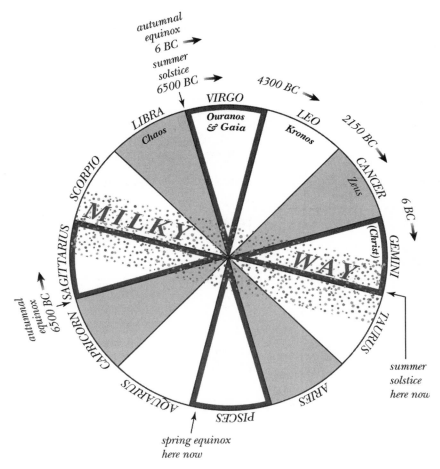

Figure 39. Zodiac wheel showing position of solstices and equinoxes in earlier World Ages. In the Golden Age, apparently equinoxes were in Gemini/Sagittarius and solstices in Virgo/Pisces; around 4300 B.C. the key sunrises moved into Taurus/Scorpio and Leo/Aquarius; somewhat before 2000 B.C. (when "Mithras" killed Taurus) they precessed to Aries/Libra and Cancer/Capricorn; in 6 B.C. they shifted to our current configuration (see figure 24).

was in Sagittarius; and the Milky Way—which spans the sky between them—formed a pathway of stars/souls aligned with the cardinal points, making it easy for the souls to move to and fro, conversing with the gods: truly a Golden Age. Later, when the sky had moved as far as the third Age, one needed a bridge across the gap, or perhaps a boatman to ferry souls to their destination. In the Golden Age, the summer solstice was in

Table 2. Change of Kingship in Heaven*

Babylonian	APSU / TI'AMAT (sweet (sea water) water) killed / divided	→ ANSHAR / KISHAR (= sky / earth)		
		→ ANU kills Apsu when he he threatens to destroy noisy crowd of gods	→ EA (ENKI) divides Ti'amat's body into world when she seeks to destroy all	→ ENLIL
Hittite/ Hurrian	ALALU 1st King in Heaven, hurled down	→ ANU emasculated by being bitten	→ KUMARBI → eats own kids?, driven out	→ Weather god (TESHUB)
Phoenician	ELIUN *Hypsistos*— 1st King in Heaven	→ SKY/EARTH driven out, then emasculated	→ EL emasculates self	→ BAAL
Greek	CHAOS (*yawning void*)	→ OURANOS/GAIA emasculated with sickle	→ KRONOS eats own kids, then driven out	→ ZEUS
Norse	GINNUNGAGAP (*yawning void*)	→ YMIR (divided into sky / earth) → BURI	→ BOR / BESTLA	→ ODIN
Corresponding Precessional Constellations: Summer solstice:	LIBRA	VIRGO	Leo	Cancer
Spring equinox:	Cancer	Gemini	TAURUS	ARIES
Approximate date of shift:		6480 B.C.	4320 B.C.	2160 B.C.

* Babylonian based on Viéyra [1963/73, 63–70] and Jacobsen [1949, 184–99]; others based on Littleton [1970]. Sumerian parallels omitted because still too fragmentary, Iranian because very late/derivative.
"→" means "beget(s) and cede(s) to".

Virgo. As the fourth World Age started, 6500 years after the Golden Age began, the *fall* equinox moved into Virgo, once again placing a Pillar of the World in that quarter. When Saturn and Jupiter came into Great Conjunction in Pisces in 6 B.C., everyone who still understood the old lore and images—the Magi (Persian "wise men" or astrologers), Pythagoreans, and

Vergil alike—took that moment as marking the precession into Pisces and the advent of a new King of Heaven to rule the New Age:

> *Now comes the final age of the Cumaean song;*
> *the great succession of ages is born anew.*
> *Now the Virgin herself returns, the Saturnian reign returns;*
> *now a new generation is sent down from high heaven.*
> *On the boy being born, under whom first the Race of Iron*
> *will cease and a Golden Race arise throughout the world,*
> *smile, chaste Lucina!* [Vergil, *Fourth Eclogue* 4–10]

"Iam redit et Virgo"—now the Virgin returns. On the strength of this passage, with its Virgin and Child, the upcoming Christians, whose creed made knowledge of star-deities subversive, dubbed Vergil an honorary Christian, whom Dante could take as spiritual guide to the Underworld. Such is the power of Restructuring. But it tells us why we no longer know any of this ancient lore: Christianity wiped its significance out of our culture.)

Structurally similar stories of the Change of Kingship in Heaven were told by Babylonians, Hittites, and Phoenicians (see table 2), by Germanic and Finnic tribes, and across Eurasia to Iran, India, and China [see S&D]. All must have diffused ultimately from the ancient Near East, since the details match far too well for coincidence. If we line up the participants according to their deeds, we see at least two clear turnovers, corresponding to Ouranos ceding to Kronos, and Kronos to Zeus. These would have to correspond to the summer solstice moving from Virgo to Leo, then to Cancer, and spring equinox from Gemini to Taurus, then to Aries. That the Virgin "returned" as one of the four cardinal constellations in the precession of 6 B.C., returning the world to the original "golden age" of man, makes full sense in this light, and only thus.

> *Una dies dabit exitio multosque per annos*
> *sustentata ruet moles et machina mundi.*
> —Lucretius, *De rerum natura* 5.96–97

One day will consign it to an end, and the bulky structure of the universe, upheld through many years, will rush to ruin. [Trans. Puhvel 1987, 284]

So the *existence* of precession was known and mythologized by some cultures before the constellational shift ca. 4300 B.C.—a Stone Age date that differs little from the latest date by which the Egyptian calendar must have been set up, 4241 B.C.[16] At that point, people in the Near East would have been settled down with permanent chin-rests more than long enough to notice that their alignments, set up to work out a solar calendar after the invention of agriculture, were sliding relentlessly out of whack.[17] To those for whom the stars were immutable, this realization must have been shattering: the very frame of the sky moved, however slow the wheels.

The ancients vacillated as to whether the appropriate mythical analogy for precession should be reciprocating motion as with the churn or fire-drill, which turns one way then an equal amount back, or continuous rotary motion as with mill-wheels and spindles. Indic myth opted for reciprocation, mythologizing the churn (in the Ocean of Milk: figure 31) and fire-drill (*pramantha*), whereas Plato, following the Pythagoreans (the Greek inheritors of the "deep" astronomical tradition), chose rotation, citing the "spindle turning on the lap of Necessity" [*Republic* 10.617b], as did Germanic and Finnic myths with their periodically upset mill-wheels, and the Harappans with Shiva's recurrent whirling dance of world-destruction (figure 16). The problem was that although people had been noting precession through several stages of the Zodiac, so they knew the frame turned and knew roughly how fast, they had observed considerably less than half a cycle (13,000 years), so they didn't know if it would keep going or turn back.

Several scholars suggest that some myth-tellers not only knew of the

---

[16] Santillana and Dechend [135] argue that the separation of Earth and Sky by the adamantine sickle mythically represents the moment of realization that earth and sky really *were* separate, that Sky (Ouranos) could turn independently over Earth (Gaia) on his earth-piercing Shaft, thereby begetting the cycle of World Ages and Time itself. We encountered this sickle in chapter 8: the gods reused it to cut the bellowing volcano-monster Ullikummi off at the ankles, when he (the ash-cloud) grew on the shoulder of Ocean and challenged the sky gods. This sickle produces space between sky and earth. (Being originally Neolithic, was it first imagined as bladed with obsidian, the Neolithic wonder-substance?)

Slippage in the Chinese "lunar lodge" calendar, apparently established ca. 2800 B.C., also instigated three precessional corrections over the next millennium [Nivison 1989].

[17] Near Eastern myth, at least, hints of yet one earlier recognized cycle of precession. That puts us into the seventh millennium—still long enough after agriculture and permanent settlement *there* for motion to be observable.

Note, however, that not all Flood/Conflagration myths show the same level of understanding of precession. Some, like Genesis, report it as an exceptional one-time event, whereas others *predict* that it may (Greek, Inca) or will (Norse, Indic) recur.

precession but even had a close idea of its cycle [Campbell 1962, 117–20]. (It moves one degree in 72 years, 30° or a twelfth of the Zodiac in 2160 years, and the entire circle in 25,920 years—72 × 360°.) These suspicions arise because of the numbers associated with "Flood" myths. For example, the five approaches to Angkor Thom in Cambodia, constructed as a cosmic map, each depict 54 gods and 54 demons— 540 in all—tugging on the serpent-cord wrapped around the celestial mountain-pillar (represented by the temple) that serves as dasher to churn the Milky Ocean: 540 × 4 = 2160. (The temple is twelfth century, but the story goes back to the *Mahābhārata* and *Rāmāyaṇa*, epics composed 2500 years ago.) Similarly, the *Grimnismal* says Valhalla has 540 doors, from each of which 800 warriors will emerge at Ragnarök [S&D 162]: remember that the Trigon of Saturn and Jupiter, crucial to timekeeping, revolves completely in 800 years; 540 × 800 = 2160 × 200 = 432,000. But 432,000 is the astronomical number of years which Berossos (the Babylonian priest who tried to summarize his country's accumulated wisdom for the conquering Greeks in 281 B.C.) ascribes to the combined reigns of the ten mythical kings who preceded the Flood. A quarter of that number (540 × 200, or 2160 × 50) equals 10,800, the number of stanzas in the Rig Veda, of bricks to be laid in an Indic fire-altar, of years said by Heraclitus to constitute an Eon, and so on [S&D, 162]. These numbers keep recurring.

More myth-borne evidence of clocking the cycle comes from a cuneiform "king-list" written about 1700 B.C. (Weld-Blum tablet 62) that totals the ten antediluvian kings' reigns at 456,000 years [Jacobsen 1939; Campbell 1962, 119]. If Berossos's 432,000 reflects knowledge that it takes 72 years to move one degree, then 456,000 would exactly reflect a belief that it takes 75 years. This earlier and slightly less good approximation (amounting to 27,000 years per round, rather than 25,920) must then have been refined further before Berossos wrote nearly 1500 years later; but it is still far better than Hipparchos's crude estimate of 36,000 years, suggesting a much longer period of noting the shift than he had access to. Hipparchos worked almost alone; the Babylonians passed down traditional knowledge in myth over millennia.

Πάντα ῥεῖ.
"Everything flows."
—Heraclitus

Why do the same numbers keep coming up?—especially multiples of 6, like 60, 360, and 2160, not to mention 12, 24, 30, 72, 540, 10,800, 432,000, and so on?

Most of them turn up in ancient measures of sky and time that diffused widely from the Near East: 12 (Zodiac constellations or months/ year), 24 (hours/day), 30 (days/month), 60 (minutes/hour, minutes/ degree, seconds/minute), 72 (years/degree), 360 (degrees in circle). But in a way, we load the dice in saying it thus, because the Mesopotamians clearly used an arithmetic *based* as much on 6 as on 10, and we see this as soon as we can read their tablets, around 3000 B.C. [Schmandt-Besserat 1992; Nissen, Damerow, and Englund 1993]. Presumably they *chose* to divide the day into 24 hours, the hour and minute into 60 parts, and the circle into 360 degrees because they *already* worked with bases 6, 10, and 60. Base 10 is obvious: ten fingers. But why base 6 or 60? We need to locate their Camera Angle.

The closest thing to 360 is the year, which both Egyptians and Mesopotamians treated as having 360 days plus an extra 5-day holiday. But was that (slightly forced) congruence a cause or an afterthought? Then again, the moon cycles through four quarters in $29\frac{1}{2}$ days. One could chop it to 28 as we do, evenly quarterable into 7-day "weeks"; but the extra day and a half will make hash of staying in phase with the moon. Or one could lengthen it to 30, which divides the year nicely into 12 months ($12 \times 30 = 360$)—but the extra half-day will throw the moon-phases off and the year actually has a few more days. In short, 365 days a year doesn't lead clearly to these numbers as sacred: we need a different Angle.

As part of an attempt to understand the prehistoric system of accounting with shaped clay tokens,[18] Denise Schmandt-Besserat summarizes what is known of the cognition and linguistics of simple counting. Briefly, young children and many economically simple societies recognize readily only the numerical abstractions "one, two, many";[19] counting above two is managed by matching the objects to a pile of "counters" (pebbles, sticks, notches, whatever). The clay tokens have

[18] Tokens start in the newly agricultural Near East, Syria to Iran, before 7000 B.C. [Schmandt-Besserat 1992, 36]), appearing as far west as Romania by the fourth millennium.

[19] The Indo-European languages show inflectional vestiges of an earlier system in which one counted "1, 2, 3, (4?), all/many". And Carol Justus [1999; 2000, 190–91] gives evidence that 6, 7, and perhaps 4 were borrowed as common sequencers in both Indo-European and the Caucasian languages, once the idea of sequencing was invented in Mesopotamia ca. 3000 B.C. (see below).

proved to be just such one-for-one counters, different shapes serving for different commodities, with no means of showing abstract numbers. Numerals seem to turn up exactly when the token system is Restructured into the first true writing system shortly before 3000 B.C. The Sumerian language itself shows vestiges of the old way, having several different sets of counting-words that depend on what is being counted and that contain basic words only for "one", "three", and sometimes "two". Higher numerals are compounded of these (4 being literally "three-one", 7 "three-three-one", et cetera) [Schmandt-Besserat 1992, 184–88]. Despite the invention of number signs, the cuneiform system was about as clumsy as Roman numerals for computation (try multiplying MCV by XIII), and scribes depended on looking up the needed figures in laboriously compiled tables of numerical relations, such as times-tables, to find such things as the areas of plots of land from measurements of two sides. Integers (whole numbers) and integral factors (divisors with no left-over fractions) dominated the approach, avoiding coping directly with fractions.

Now imagine yourself back in that leisurely era with no TV, and contemplate one by one the wonderful qualities of each integer:

1	unity;
2, 3	primes;
4	$= 2 + 2$ *and*
	$= 2 \times 2$, a square;
5	prime (also $2 + 3$);

but

6	$= 3 + 3$ (Sumerian "three-three") but also
	$= 1 \times 2 \times 3$—all of the first three digits as factors;
7	prime;
8	$= 2 \times 2 \times 2$, the first cube;
9	$= 3 \times 3$, the next square;
10	$= 2 \times 5$;
11, 13	primes;

but

12	factorable (evenly divisible) by 1, 2, 3, and 4 (the first four digits) as well as by 6.

To get a number with all of the first *five* digits as factors you must jump to 60, factorable by 1, 2, 3, 4, and 5, plus 6 for good measure, as well as by 10, 12, 15, 20, 30, and of course 60: a whopping 12 possibilities. The next winner in the factor derby is none other than 360 (6 × 60), with 24 possible factors: surely a number to conjure with (along with 6 and 60).[20]

In short, the multiples of 6 and 60 end up being the most "flexible" for a system accessed by integral factors. And 360 is close to the all-important number of days in the year, is integrally divisible by the roughly 30-day lunar cycle, and so on. The universe now begins to take on orderliness! Humans may then follow divine suit and *assign* 360 degrees as a measure of the encircling horizon, and assign convenient multiples of 6 to all those other measures of time and space.[21] (No one disputes that this handy system diffused across the world; it's why your

---

[20] 30 is a multiple of the first 4 primes ($1 \times 2 \times 3 \times 5$), while 36 (the square of 6) equals $1 \times 4 \times 9$, the squares of the first 3 primes. One must jump to $210 = 1 \times 2 \times 3 \times 5 \times 7$ to get the first 5 primes as factors, to 420 for the first 7 digits as possible factors, and to 900 for the first 5 squares as possible factors.

That factoring *was* the linchpin of early Mesopotamian mathematics is confirmed by the odd structure of what Neugebauer [1957, 31–33] describes as tables of reciprocals, but which (where not fractional) are also tables of the factors of 60:

2	[×]	30	[$60 = 2 \times 30 = 30 \times 2$, hence the term "reciprocal"]
3		20	
4		15	
5		12	
6		10	et cetera

After listing the sexagesimal reciprocals through 6, the tables thereafter *skip* all primes *and their multiples* from 7 on (i.e., 7, 11, 13, 14, . . .), with such comments as "7 does not divide". That is, 7 is not a *factor of 60* (or 360, the next sexagesimal unit, et cetera).

Other directions of number-inquiry led, by Pythagoras's time, to dimensionality (1 establishes a point, 2 a line, 3 a surface, 4 a solid), to the 5 regular solids (taken to represent the universe and four elements), and to theory of harmony [see Heninger 1974].

Further insight into nonliterate abilities with numbers can be gained from two sources. First, Oliver Sacks [1985, 185–203] describes twins with *savant* syndrome whose favorite game was to locate (in their heads!) prime numbers of six to ten digits; but recognizing primes depends on also recognizing factors. Second, the Atharvavedas, composed orally in India in the first millennium B.C., contain simple sutra algorithms for doing such things as multiplication and division of pairs of very large numbers and solving quadratic equations *rapidly and in the head* [Bhārati 1992]. (One of us attended at Caltech a remarkable presentation of this oral method by Bhārati in 1958, just as computers—ironically—were taking over.)

[21] Going by this theory, one must suspect that the neat commensurateness of the precessional years with 60 was a happy accident that merely reinforced the belief that a divine architect or Demiurge had constructed the cycles of the sky. Attempts to zero in on the *length* of the cycle can almost certainly be dated to the Bronze Age (once people had numbers), not the Neolithic.

watch divides time into multiples of 6 whether you buy it in Geneva, Hong Kong, or Los Angeles.)

Surely, then, number would be a principal manifestation of the divine and permanent, and we are now at the right Camera Angle to see why the early Greek philosophers who inherited the ancient tradition insisted on this point. Everything around us constantly changes—we are born, grow, and die, the moon waxes and wanes, tides ebb and flow, weather shifts, time and the sky move on—but the qualities of Number remain constant [cf. Heninger 1974, 74–75]. That profound insight must go back to the star-gazers of protoliterate Mesopotamia.

Just as the royal Hawaiian chants transmit more than a millennium of often verifiable celestial events [Masse 1995], so the followers of Pythagoras, Orpheus, Socrates, Plato, Mithras, and others piped down to us many records of ancient astronomical observation, encoded into mythical language that becomes increasingly clear to those "initiates" willing to ferret out the deeper-than-surface meanings. We do well not to underestimate the intelligence and knowledge of our remote ancestors.[22]

[22] Well after this chapter was completed, we discovered Michael Ovenden's 1966 article, "The Origins of the Constellations", in which he demonstrates by a careful analysis of the geometry of the constellations of Eudoxos (ca. 350 B.C., known through Aratos) that these are aligned on a center that, thanks to precession, *was last the center shortly after 3000 B.C.*, and therefore that this system must have been codified at that time. He further concludes that the purpose was chiefly navigational, and specifically for seafarers plying the Mediterranean (but not the Persian Gulf, which is too far south to account for what was and was not named). Using an ingenious but (necessarily) nonmathematical argument for the longitude of the inventors [cf. Sobel 1995], he suggests that the system is specifically Aegean, not Levantine, in origin. Of course, since the island folk had to cross seas just to reach their homes, they had more at stake in navigation, right from the start, than people of the Levant.

17

Prometheus

And with unbreakable shackles [Zeus] bound wily Prometheus,
with painful bonds, driving a shaft through the middle;
and he set on him a long-winged eagle; and it ate at
his immortal liver, which would grow back exactly as much
at night as the spread-winged bird would eat during the whole day.
—Hesiod, *Theogony* 521–25

Long ago men were hungry and unhappy. They were cold.
The only fire in the world was on a mountain top, watched
by three Skookums. They guarded the fire carefully. Men
might steal it and become as strong as they.
—Pacific Northwest myth [Judson 1910/97, 40]

Quis hoc credat, nisi sit pro teste vetustas?
Who would believe this, except that it has age as a witness?
—Ovid, *Metamorphoses* 1.400

P rometheus holds an important position in the Greek pantheon because he brought Fire to Mankind, either from heaven or from the forge of Hephaistos, depending on whom you believe; in punishment for this and other outwittings, Zeus chained him to a mountain, tormenting him with an eagle. But if the God of Fire is attached to a mountain, we might venture a guess that we are looking at another old story of a volcano. And with this as our hypothesis, we should be able to puzzle out the details in Hesiod's narrative.

Instead of dismissing the account because we wouldn't have told the story that way, we may start by asking if there is anything in it that suggests the story has any connection at all with reality. This approach draws our attention to Hesiod's distinction between the scene at night and that during the day. At a distance, a fire typically shows itself as smoke by day and as flame at night. As we see from Exodus, with its alternating pillars of smoke and fire (chapter 8), even God stays with this rule. So the distinction between nighttime and daytime appearances makes perfect sense if the story of Prometheus is an account of a fire— hardly unlikely, considering his function in Greek myth. The regrowth of the bloody liver by night may then be an image suggesting the startling and obvious redness of the fire when surrounded by darkness.

Opaque though Hesiod's story seems, the conclusion that it indeed concerns a volcano is strengthened by volcano myths from around the world. Typically they involve giants (especially with one eye, like Cyclops), flying stones, battles, loud noises, overwhelming darkness, lightning, mountaintops, the discovery of fire, three typical colors (black, red, and white), and a lot of bizarre but consistent imagery, including hair (red, snaky, et cetera). We explored numerous geological parallels to the noises, darkness, lightning, and so forth in chapter 8.

But eagles? If the reader finds it difficult to see a story about a fire or volcano in a story about an eagle (see frontispiece), try visualizing the scene: figure 40. The "long-winged eagle" would serve nicely as an image for the volcano's ash-cloud spreading across the sky. This may seem far-fetched to us, but we must remember how common it has been for people to relate major weather systems to the beating wings of giant birds—the Thunderbird in the Americas is viewed thus, for example [Alexander 1916, 60–61]. Indeed, Prometheus's eagle is eventually Reinterpreted in the Caucasus as the source of storms, which it causes by the beating of its wings [Olrik 1922, 160].

Has anyone *seeing* an eruption ever thought it was really a giant eagle feeding on a liver? We think we can safely doubt this, but the very ques-

Figure 40. Mount St. Helens erupting, March 1847 (as painted by Paul Kane): compare eruption cloud to myth-image of eagle pecking at "Prometheus" on Elbrus.

tion obscures the immense difficulty confronting the person who sees a volcano erupt for the first time and lacks any grasp of tectonic theory. A more useful question is, "How did the first human beings talk about a volcano, the first time they saw one erupt?"

The answer is that, once they could talk, they probably wove together a group of images that created a coherent whole, which is what *we* do [see Bartlett 1932, 83–89]. This is easiest to see if you try the alternatives.

But what are the alternatives? We can't even say that the mountain exploded—not without such a concept and word. If we say that "rocks flew about" we have violated the Willfulness Principle: something has to have thrown the rocks. We can say that a giant on the mountain flung rocks about, but that is pretty much what people *did* say, and now we find it all but unintelligible. The following is from a later version of the Prometheus story:

> *You [the Prometheus figure] aim at the bird with a stone*
> *And try to throw it at her,*
> *But your chains wind more tightly,*
> *And your pillar sinks deeper into the earth.* [Colarusso 2002, 168]

Human cognition, moreover, simply won't allow major events to be reported without being put into an overall worldview (or minor events either: remember the bird and the orange in chapter 2). Physicists don't just seek a unified field theory, they demand it. So it's not as if the story could have been told as a series of disconnected images. It's difficult even to make up an example of disconnected images, and when we do, it's annoying and seems deliberately idiotic or giddily humorous:

> Apparently Zeus attached a Giant to a mountain. Then it was as if a huge eagle came by every day and started to devour a slab of dark, glistening liver. And at night it looked as though an immense fire-red abalone lay there in the Giant's lap, heaving and growling. Then one day the Giant, or maybe even Zeus, started to throw stones and fling dust up into the air, and there was as much lightning as in twenty rainstorms put together, but no rain. At the same time, it was as if a thousand demented hell-hounds began to bay all at once, the noise was so great. And when those of us who survived came back later, the Giant was gone and the river had dried up.

Try working *that* into your worldview.

If you find this example even more preposterous than Hesiod, then you have grasped the difficulty. Besides being incoherent, such a version leaves out everything important: *why* the events happened and what they mean. Yet coherence and meaningfulness are central to human thought-patterns. Sir Frederic Bartlett's classic experiments in having people retell later a simple but foreign folktale showed that, where the Silence Principle had caused the original "narrators and hearers to take much for granted that is not expressed" (so the narration seems "jerky"), "the subject, acting almost always unwittingly, supplies connecting links" [Bartlett 1932, 86].[1] (Ideally, of course, you would link your vol-

---

[1] This penchant for linking of course underlies our Movie Construct Principle and Schacter's "hindsight bias". Bartlett elaborates:

Sometimes . . . reasons were definitely and explicitly formulated and introduced into reproductions to account for material which had been presented without explanation. Sometimes, without any definite formulation of reasons, the material was so changed that it could be accepted by the observer without question and with satisfaction. . . . The effort stops when it produces an attitude best described as "the attitude in which no further questions are asked". The end state is primarily affective. Once reached, and it is generally reached very quickly, it recurs very readily, and it is this, more than anything else, which accounts for the persistent sameness of repeated reproduction. [Bartlett 1932, 84–85]

That is, Bartlett appears also to have learned how such stories reach a *stable* state—but we must add that this stability depends on the outlook of the repeaters of the story remaining constant.

cano story to a context that makes it a unique event—unless, that is, you want to worry constantly about the local mountains exploding. And indeed our ancestors, when a mountain did explode, had no way of knowing that this doesn't actually happen very often.) Note the causal links in the following narrative:

> Up to that time, Pahto [Mount Adams] had had a high head. Wyeast [Mount Hood] hit her from the east side and knocked her head off. Today on the north side of Pahto there is a pile of fine rocks about half a mile long. These rocks were once Pahto's head . . .
>
> [Pahto became difficult.] The Great Spirit was watching. He saw all that happened. At last he said, "I shall make a new head for Pahto. Then she will not be so mean."
>
> So he sent down a big white eagle with his son, a red eagle, riding on his right shoulder. He put the two eagles on top of Pahto, to be her head. [Clark 1953, 18]

And here we are back to eagles in volcano stories. Why eagles? Well, to paraphrase George Leigh Mallory, because they're there. They are animate and they hang around mountains. In fact, the folklorist who collected this story, Ella Clark, points out that eagles nest in the caves atop Mt. Adams. So if you need an image involving something animate and powerful at the top of a mountain, the eagle is surely your first choice. No abalones need apply. And suddenly the story of Prometheus becomes a bit less bizarre.

It is also clear that high volcanos can have both red and white—fire and snow (or ash)—at their tops. But another story collected by Clark [1953, 20] gives the eagle two children, which "sit at either side of White Eagle's topmost crown". Here the two young eagles are clearly the two points that rise, slightly lower, on either side of the top of Mt. Adams; this version could represent a later Reinterpretation. (This is no more surprising than the town of Eagle Rock, California, being named for an outcropping that's supposed to resemble an eagle—though it's hard to tell whether it's the wings or the beak that people see in the outcrop.)

Now, if we think we know what Prometheus is, how do we test our hypothesis?

We began, years ago, by looking for volcanos where the Greeks themselves located Prometheus. Although Hesiod says nothing about location, Aeschylus puts him among the Scythians, who lived in the steppes north of the Caucasus and Black Sea. More specifically, the Argonauts encounter Prometheus at the east end of the Black Sea:

> *And then as they travelled on, a recess of the sea appeared,*
> *and the crags of the Caucasus Mountains sprang up,*
> *steep ones, where, his limbs bound to the mighty rocks*
> *with unbreakable bonds, Prometheus*
> *fed with his liver the swift and ever-returning eagle.*
> *At dusk they saw it high above the ship, with a shrill whistling*
> *flying near the clouds; but nonetheless*
> *it shook all the sails with its wings as it passed.*
> *For it did not have the form of a bird of the air,*
> *but shook its swift wings to and fro like polished oars.*
> *Not long after, they heard the much-groaning voice*
> *of Prometheus having his liver ripped out; and the air*
> *resounded with his cries . . .* [Apollonius Rhodius, *Argonautica* 1246–58]

Here the eagle is enjoying supper rather than lunch on Prometheus's liver, and there is a great deal of noise from the victim's screams and groans.

We also see that the story maintained itself in its essentials for many years within the Greek world, which favors the theory that it is connected to an actual site that people could point to. And indeed, there is a spectacular volcano, Mount Elbrus, over 18,000 feet high, in the Caucasus at the east end of the Black Sea. Depending on where you draw the boundary line, it is either Europe's highest mountain or a nondescript hump in Asia (where there is at least one *pass* that high, the Karakoram).

Furthermore, we find that the Prometheus myth is alive and well among the local Caucasian inhabitants, a fact that has long been known to scholars in the field [e.g., Olrik 1922]:

> Legend tells us that a giant has been chained to the summit of snowy Elbruz for committing sins of some sort. When he awakens, he asks his guards, "Are rushes still growing on the earth? Are lambs still being born?"
>
> His pitiless guards respond, "Yes, rushes still grow and lambs are still born."

Then the giant grows furious. He breaks his shackles, and the earth then shakes as he moves. His chains give off lightning and a roar like thunder. His heavy breathing is the blizzard's gust. His moaning is the underground drone of a raging river, and his tears are its waters as it emerges into daylight at the foot of Elbruz. [Colarusso 2002, 169]

Here the only clear tectonic activity is an earthquake, and everything else attributed to the giant is simply weather. The myth, in other words, has adapted to the fact that Elbrus doesn't erupt all that often (see below), but earthquakes are common in the region. Also, it won't do to argue that we have lost the eagle with a taste for giant's flesh, because in other versions the eagle has maintained its importance for millennia.

For example, in one of the great Caucasian sagas, the Nart hero Nasran rides to the Blessed Peak (Elbrus) to fetch fire from the giant Paqua:

Suddenly he heard a voice like thunder resounding from the top of the mountain, as though someone were talking, and to him it seemed that the sky had split into two. It was Paqua saying, "You, little man! What have you come here to do? If you do not go back, you shall perish at my hands."

"You stand in God's place, and they say you are benevolent," said Nasran, trying to flatter Paqua. "If that is so, then why have you taken fire away from the Narts? Why have you sent bitter cold so that we will freeze to death?"

"If you want to return home, then go! Don't make my head hurt! If you continue in this way . . . I shall chain you to the highest peak. I shall hold you prisoner until you die!"

Paqua bound Nasran's body all around in chains and then fastened him to the summit of the Blessed Peak. Paqua had an enormous eagle. This ravening beast was greedy for human flesh. The wicked Paqua was enraged and set loose his huge eagle. The eagle's wingspan was so great that it could not fly down in the valleys. When it flew, it blocked out the sun so that the earth became enshrouded in darkness. It flew up and landed on the chest of the mighty Nart Nasran. It tore open his chest with its powerful beak. It drank his heart's blood and pecked at his lungs with its razor-sharp beak. . . . Chained to the Blessed Peak, Nasran roared and moaned, his cries being carried by the winds to the Narts.

The Narts try to rescue Nasran but fail. Finally Nart Pataraz offers to go and bring back both fire and Nasran. From the foothills he cries to Paqua:

"Call off your giant bloodthirsty eagle from Nasran and send it down here from the mountain!"

Then the sky grew very dark. This meant that the great eagle had arisen from the mountain. The wings of the wicked bird brought darkness everywhere. The horse on which Pataraz sat grew frightened. . . . Pataraz laid another lash on Little Black. Thereupon Little Black gave a snort and leaped up into the sky, and they began to fight with the monstrous eagle. . . . It was a great ordeal for Pataraz to fight with the wicked bird, but despite this he was finally able to shoot an arrow through one of its wings. When he did this it was as though someone had opened a window; the sun shone through the eagle's wing, and it became light once more. . . . In this way Nart Pataraz vanquished Paqua's eagle.

Pataraz then fights off one monster after another, who shake the ground as they fall, until Paqua flees, leaving Pataraz free to unchain and rescue Nasran [Colarusso 2002, 159–62].

If the eagle started out as an image for the ash-cloud, it really did "bring darkness everywhere" (see chapter 8). And here it helps to think back on why Prometheus is the particular mythological figure who brings fire. It is not just because fire is associated with certain mountaintops; it is also because eruptions cause static electricity—that is, lightning, another real-life "bringer of fire" (see chapter 8). Throughout the world, fire is often thought to have made its way "into wood" by lightning strikes on trees. And who is Prometheus's enemy—indeed the one who attached him to the mountain? Zeus, the wielder of thunderbolts. So the story has a kind of internal consistency (Logic Crosscheck) that is largely lost on the modern reader.

The modern Nart versions include virtually everything in Hesiod: the eagle [Colarusso 2002, 159–62], the chains [Colarusso 2002, 159], and the shaft [Colarusso 2002, 168]. The liver has been transmuted into heart and/or lungs [Colarusso 2002, 160: heart's blood and lungs; Olrik 1922, 152: heart]. Olrik points out that the local inhabitants insist that the existence of Amiran (another local name for this Prometheus figure) "is not something one is expected to believe in, but something one can actually see".[2] *Actually see.* And it is this mnemonic

---

[2] Olrik 1922, 258: "Die Entschiedenheit, mit der der heutige Bergbewohner antwortet, dass Amirans Dasein nicht etwas ist, woran man glauben soll, sondern etwas, was man beobachten kann—diese Entschiedenheit muss eine frühere Menschheit in noch höherem Grade besessen haben." Puhvel notes that the name Amiran(i) was borrowed from the evil Iranian deity Ahriman [Puhvel 1987, 217], with metathesis (cf. chapter 15).

quality of the mountain that makes it possible for the stories to remain more or less intact, and that holds the Fogging Effect somewhat at bay.

If you look at all the "Prometheus" stories, in fact, you find that it is only the imagery that is unusual; the events are hard-edged, actual events, and quite indisputable. There was once a fire attached to Elbrus, eruptions do shut out the sun, storms do occur in the vicinity of high mountains, and earthquakes are not uncommon in the local fault zone.

Consider another major Promethean tradition, that of the Georgian epic hero Amirani, treated splendidly at length (both analytically and comparatively) by Georges Charachidzé [1986].

Amirani is born in a torrent of red, being ripped prematurely from the belly of his mother, gold-haired Dali, a divine protectress of wild animals. God becomes his godfather and gives him superhuman strength, then hands him to a peasant to raise with his own two sons. The three boys amuse themselves attacking everyone who passes by, until Amirani attacks a three-headed giant. As he cuts off each head, each exudes a worm that grows into a serpent—one white, one red, one black. Amirani kills the white and red ones, but the black one swallows him. In desperation, he cuts open its belly from inside and issues back into the world. He then attacks and massacres a fortressful of demons— but again he almost drowns, this time in the rising lake of their blood that he has shed. Suddenly one wall of the black fort breaks and the red lake pours out. Thus he escapes.

During an attempt to abduct the demon-king's daughter, the two foster-brothers are killed; and although Amirani manages to slaughter the entire demon-army, king and all, he is so distraught by his brothers' deaths that he commits suicide. But the demon-girl revives all three.

Amirani now fares forth alone, encountering a half-dead giant whose leg falls on him, pinning him down. God sees his despair and grants him yet more strength, so he escapes again. But now there is none strong enough to oppose him, as he lays waste to the world— except God himself. So he challenges God. Although the details of the contest vary, it always involves trying to pull out a pillar or post that God has rooted all the way through the earth and then some. It always ends with Amirani chained to the pillar and God shutting Amirani under a dome of rock "like a cap". Amirani's winged hunting dog, Q'ur-sha ("Black Ears", a "puppy born of eagles"), tries to lick away his master's chains, but whenever he almost succeeds, they renew themselves. (This renewal is aided by human blacksmiths hammering ritually on their anvils on a particular day of the year, for fear the destructive Amirani will return.) [Charachidzé 1986, 26–28, 102–3, 107, 143, and passim.]

Again, there is little here that doesn't smack of volcanism, with a liberal sprinkling of Willfulness: birth and "rebirth" by bloodily bursting forth; a red lake pent up in a fortress of black rock; a tremendous power and its "kin" dying, then starting up again; repeated laying waste to everything around; a still greater power doming rock over the nuisance, which is suddenly attended by a black, winged "creature"; and finally blacksmiths (compare Etna as Hephaistos's smithy).

Charachidzé struggles to account for the close resemblance between Greek Prometheus and the Georgian myth of Amirani (including the closely related Abkhaz, Svan, Circassian, and other myths, some of which were written down 1,500 years ago). He suggests the Greeks and Caucasians must once have lived as neighbors (a fact deducible on several other grounds), yet he is obliged to point out the many internal details making it impossible to assume *either* that the Greeks took the myth from a Caucasian group *or* the Caucasians from the Greeks [Charachidzé 1986, 311–33]. Since the details are much too similar for chance, he understandably rejects independent invention; yet he comments that it is almost as though the Greeks took the same basic story of "one who challenged God" and built *their* version around their cultural preoccupation with challenges between intellects, while the Caucasians built *their* story around their preoccupation with challenges of physical strength [Charachidzé 1986, 311]. He would have liked the two language groups to have had a common ancestor, but understands that they didn't—at least not recently enough to account for these stories; in the end he finds no satifying solution.

Yet it takes only a tiny step to solve his dilemma (and that of Wilhelm [1998], who fares no better with the problem). The Greeks and Caucasian-speakers need only have watched the same spectacular eruption of Elbrus, from their own vantage points, and each mythologized this challenge of the mountain to the sky above according to their own cultural patterns, starting from similar Late Neolithic and/or Bronze Age cultural stages and the cognitive principles by which myths develop.

Recent dating of the eruptions of Elbrus offer a possible time-frame for the original eruptions that led to the mountain's truculent reputation. Bogatikov and his fellow geologists have "tentatively distinguish[ed]

three eruptive events of different ages" for Elbrus: 5500–5200 B.C., 3300–2600 B.C., and A.D. 0–100 [Bogatikov et al. 1998, 1094]. The last of these postdates the earliest accounts, so it is the middle eruptive sequence, also the longest and most complex, that seems most likely to have inspired the story.[3]

These geological findings strengthen the hypothesis that the story of Loki [Olrik 1922, 269 ff.] is a changed later version of the same myth as Prometheus, since for that to be true, the events would have to have antedated the breakup of the Indo-European tribes, whom archaeologists and linguists widely reconstruct as still living more or less together near the Caucasus around 3000 B.C. [e.g., Mallory 1989; Barber 1999, 191].

In fact, Loki and Prometheus share enough peculiar features that we can now puzzle out Loki's nature, long since obscured by the Silence Principle. (1) Both are of the race of "giants" or the equivalent. Technically in Greek myth the "giants" form one brood of children of the Titans, the "gods" another, and in the squabbles the giants side with the Titans against the gods. Prometheus is the son of Titans and classed as a Titan; yet (2) he lives with and generally sides with the gods—just as Loki, who is of the race of giants, generally lives with and works for the gods. (3) Both are noted for their clever craftsmanship (Prometheus using especially clay, and Loki repeatedly instigating the dwarves to forge metal treasures). (4) Both betray the gods they live with— Prometheus by stealing fire from the gods for mankind, and Loki by a whole series of pranks, such as destroying the beautiful golden hair of the grain goddess Sif.[4] That is, (5) both Loki and Prometheus are

---

[3] Recent work on dating eruptions registered in the Greenland ice sheets shows a spate of eruptions between 3200 and 3154 B.C. [Zielinski et al. 1994, 950]. But the much-needed Russian geological work on Elbrus is so recent that the ice-core team did not have that data for identifying particular eruptions with Elbrus. Future work in this domain may prove enlightening.

A sequential analysis in the style of Mott Greene [1992] suggests: (1) initial lava flow; (2) numerous small eruptions from three vents; (3) major eruption (nearby?) with triple lava flow, one of which creates a lava tube that flows out lower down; (4) major eruption with build-up of a huge lava lake that bursts its walls and flows to(ward) the Black Sea; (5) quiet; (6) small eruptions resume; (7) huge eruption blows sky-high; (8) enormous ash-cloud; (9) relative quiet, with some smoking from a new dome-shaped summit. (The superior deity may be connected with the unusual clusters of spectacular celestial events in 3300–3100 and 2850–2650 B.C. [Masse 1995, 474; 1998].)

Once the volcano stopped erupting (or the group moved away), the stories became open to Reinterpretation: for the locals, as storm-clouds, blizzards, glaciers, fossils, and so forth.

[4] In one Caucasian version, Amirani's jealous stepmother also cut off the golden hair of his goddess/mother Dali [Charachidzé 1986, 166].

sometimes good/helpful (like gods) and sometimes evil/destructive (like giants). (See chapter 7.) (6) Loki and Prometheus suffer the same punishment, being chained to rocks while being tortured daily in punishment for their misdeeds. (7) The writhings of Loki and of the Caucasian Prometheus-figures cause earthquakes.

Now let's recast the problem like a Sphinx's riddle. What active (Willful) element is the most ambiguous, being among the most useful to humans ("good") and yet among the most destructive ("evil")? Data: it is used in metalworking and with clay, can destroy an entire crop of ripe grain in no time, and sometimes appears on mountainsides in conjunction with earthquakes.

Surely the answer is fire. Loki, like Prometheus, must have once been some kind of fire deity. When Loki accompanies Thor to visit the giant Útgarð-Loki (who lives in a sort of "antimatter" world) and is nudged out in an eating contest by the giant's henchman, Logi (who ate not just the meat but the bones and the trencher too), it eventually turns out that "the man called Logi was 'wildfire' and he burned the trencher as quickly as he did the chopped meat" [Sturluson 1971, 77]. Domestic fire was paired to fight against wildfire and just barely lost.

So Prometheus—the god of fire chained to a mountain—is fire-spitting Elbrus. And now we must get down to the heart, or liver, of our argument. First, myths and folklore typically make no distinction between observations and interpretations. Once an event is interpreted, the observations and interpretations are jumbled together (Rationalization Syndrome, Movie Construct). Second, the original story had to have been told by people who reasoned that, if something happened, it had to be willed. But then it was transmitted down through history to people who no longer believed that—people for whom things could happen without a conscious Will being involved. But those people, looking at the original story, could only conclude that the "actor" in the story must have been something animate by their new standard: a person, or perhaps a god or a giant. So by the time of Aeschylus, Prometheus turns up as a person in a play, chatting up various figures who come around to see him; and we, in modern times, have typically taken our cue from Aeschylus. The Fogging Effect has rolled in.

A real event can be transformed by explanations that force it into a current worldview, and this worldview, once it is abandoned, leaves the hearer of the myth with nothing but a beguiling story—beguiling because the story wouldn't even survive if it lacked interest. Among the Romantics, Prometheus became a symbol of hubris (as in Mary Shelley's famous title, *Frankenstein, or the Modern Prometheus*), because he defied Zeus, but thousands of years ago, "he" was certainly a mountain that distinguished itself by especially dramatic tectonic activity.

18

Fire-Breathing Dragons

The invisible worm,
That flies in the night
In the howling storm . . .
    —William Blake, "The Sick Rose,"
        Songs of Innocence and of Experience

We English-speakers all know that dragons—or at least Germanic ones—look like gigantic scaly salamanders, that they have bad breath, belch fire, guard treasure inside dank caverns, and can fly. Recent fiction from *The Hobbit* to *Shrek* trades on this knowledge (not to mention Gary Larson's cartoon of two dragons in bed, one shrinking from the other saying, "It's your breath. It's . . . it's fresh and minty!" [Larson 1984, 151]). The two most famous sources for the attributes are the early Germanic literary works *Beowulf* and the *Volsunga Saga*. First let's examine *Beowulf*.

After slaying two bog-monsters (the Old English epic recounts), Beowulf reigned prosperously for fifty winters,

> *until a dragon began*
> *in the dark nights to rule—*
> *one that watched over its hoard in a heap,*
> *in the steep stone-mound.* [31.2210–13][1]

A last lone survivor of some ancient clan had hidden the family riches in a great stone burial mound on a coastal headland, and after the man died, a dragon, which "flies in the night enveloped in fire" [32.2273–74], sniffed out the treasure for his own and guarded it for three hundred winters. Then a nameless bondsman, hiding from his angered master, found entry into the mound and stole a golden cup to win back his lord's favor. The great Worm (serpent, or dragon) awoke to find himself robbed. Inside and out he hunted for his missing "precious" and its taker, but in vain.

> *The hoard-watcher waited*
> *with impatience till evening;*
> *then the barrow's warden was wrathful—*
> *then would he, hostile, with flame requite*
> *for his dear drinking-bowl. Day departed,*
> *as the Worm wished, nor would he long*
> *abide in his lair, but with burning fared forth . . .* [32.2302–8]

The fire-dragon flashed out across the fields, vomiting fire, razing the countryside, terrorizing the people, and returning at daybreak to his se-

[1] Our translations, using Klaeber 1922, Chickering 1977, and Thorpe's text in Hopper 1962.

cret hoard. As Beowulf's own favorite hall burned down, the hero vowed vengeance.

The aging king ordered an iron shield made, since wooden ones would be useless. Then he addressed his men, saying that he would not take a sword to this battle if he knew how else to grapple with the creature, but that he expected much heat and venom and so had armed them all with shields and corselets. They could watch in safety from a nearby hill while he attempted to settle accounts and win the hoard.

Nearing the mound of stones, he saw a stone arch, from which issued a stream of flame so hot he could not approach closer, so he cried a battle challenge. The gold-guarder responded. From the stones first came a blast of evil breath, then more flame, as Beowulf wielded his great sword from behind his shield. But the shield protected him "for a lesser while than his mind wished" and his sword blunted faster on the dragon's bones and "bit less strongly than its ruler had need of" [35.2571–72, 2578–79]. As he vainly fought the dragon's flames, his kinsman Wiglaf ran to his aid with shield and sword. In ire, the Worm belched flames anew, incinerating Wiglaf's linden shield so the youth had to take refuge under his lord's iron one. Beowulf struck once more, but his sword Nagling snapped in two, and the Worm flashed forth a third time, wrapping his fangs around Beowulf's neck, scorching him horribly and burning Wiglaf's hand. Ignoring the dragon's head, Wiglaf

> struck a little lower
> . . . so that the sword dived down,
> hostile and ornate, and the fire began
> to die away afterwards. [37.2699–2702]

Beowulf roused himself, pulled his dagger, and plunged a final blow deep down into the dragon's middle.

The battle over, Beowulf sat down, knowing himself mortally wounded, and surveyed the stone entrance. He asked Wiglaf to enter the dead dragon's lair and bring out some of its treasure, so that, seeing it, he might die content. Wiglaf obeyed. Inside, he found piles of gold and jewels, empty vessels, rusty helmets, arm-rings, and bright golden hangings. But

> not of the Worm was there
> any sign, for him the [blade's] edge had destroyed. [38.2771–72]

Wiglaf chose out many things and hurried back to his lord. Beowulf looked at them, grateful that his death had purchased such wealth, and asked that, after the funeral pyre, his people pile a high mound on the headland, to be called Beowulf's Hill, so that passing seafarers might see it and remember him always.

Such is Beowulf's fight with a dragon, who indeed guards gold inside a dark mound, flies, and spews fire and bad breath. We just don't know what the beast itself looked like.

To understand what is behind this story, we must begin with the Stripping Procedure (chapter 4), removing explanations (newsreel) and singling out the observations (component snapshots):

(1) Someone steals a cup from an old barrow (figure 41).
(2) Fire erupts from the barrow and spreads.
(3) Near the stone entrance, our hero stabs blindly at the source of flames while shielding himself (ineffectively) from them.
(4) It smells bad.
(5) People stab deeper, and eventually the flame goes out.
(6) Inside the barrow is treasure but no trace of a dragon's body.

People do steal from tombs; tombs can smell bad and can contain valuables. Fire, once started, can spread as wildfire (and loss of one's home may be long remembered); fires go out when the fuel is exhausted or suppressed. So far: reality.

We don't know the dragon's appearance, however, because while it's alive all you can see is flame and once the fire is out *there is nothing left*. No one ever saw it—they saw only flames and smelled a bad smell. The dragon must be a figment of Explanation: a Willer invisible except for its fiery exhalations, postulated to explain the presence of that barrier of flames. If you can't get to the treasure, *something* must be willfully, even malevolently, guarding it (so when the bondsman first got in, the guardian must have been snoozing). The storykeepers are so sure that a tangible creature *must* have existed that, four hundred lines later, the poet hedges his bets by explaining the lack of dragon bones a second and contradictory way. When the frightened retainers returned, he says, they pillaged the mound, "shoved the dragon, the Worm, over the cliff,

Figure 41. Field of five ancient barrows (burial mounds), near Jelling, Jutland, Denmark.

let the wave take—the flood enfold—the guardian of the treasure" [42:3131–33], then they carried the dead king to his pyre.

So whence the flames?

We learn more of them from the Icelandic *Grettissaga*, which follows the career of Grettir, a blustery Icelandic outlaw who reputedly lived in the eleventh century. At one point Grettir sojourned with a Norwegian farmer named Thorfinn, becoming friends with his tenant, Audun.

> It happened late one evening . . . that he saw a huge fire burst forth on the headland below Audun's farm. Grettir asked what was happening, but Audun said there was no need for him to worry about it.
>
> "If such a thing were seen in my country," said Grettir, "it would be said that the flame came from a buried treasure."
>
> The farmer said, "The owner of this fire, I think, is one whom it is better not to enquire about."
>
> "Still, I wish to know," said Grettir.
>
> "There on the headland stands a gravemound," said Audun, "and Thorfinn's father, Kar the Old, was buried in it . . ."
>
> Grettir said he had done well to tell him. "I shall be back tomorrow, and then you must have digging tools ready for me." . . . Early the next morning the digging tools were ready, and the farmer went with him to the mound. Grettir began to break open the mound, and worked hard without stopping

until he reached the rafters. . . . Then he tore them up. Audun did his best
to discourage him from entering the mound. Grettir told him to watch the
rope, "for I am going to find out what inhabits the barrow."

Then Grettir went into the mound. Inside it was dark, and the air not
very sweet.[2] He groped about to find out how things were arranged. He
came upon some horse bones, then he knocked against the carved backpost
of a chair, and he could feel someone sitting in it. A great treasure of gold
and silver was gathered together there. . . . Grettir took all the treasure and
carried it towards the rope, but as he was making his way through the barrow he was seized fast by someone. He let go of the treasure and turned to
attack, and they set on each other mercilessly, so that everything in their
way was thrown out of place. The mound-dweller attacked vigorously, and
for a while Grettir had to give way, but finally he realized this was not a
good time to spare himself. Then they both fought desperately . . . but in
the end the mound-dweller fell backwards, and there was a great crash.
Then Audun ran away from the rope, thinking that Grettir must be dead.
Grettir drew his sword—[named] Jokul's Gift—and struck with it at the
mound-dweller's neck so that it cut off his head. He placed the head against
Kar's buttocks and brought the treasure over to the rope: he found Audun
gone, so he had to climb up the rope, hand over hand. He had tied the
treasure to the rope and he hauled it up afterwards. Grettir, who was very
stiff after his dealing with Kar, made his way back to Thorfinn's farm, carrying the treasure. [Fox and Pálsson 1974, 36–37]

So here we have a burial mound spouting flame, just as in *Beowulf*,
and learn that Grettir immediately associates that pairing with treasure.
We also find stinky air and an unseen malevolent guardian, whom
Grettir takes to be the spirit (and body) of the man buried there. We
learn this when Grettir decapitates the "mound-dweller", then sets the
head against *Kar's* buttocks. (Removing the head and setting it by the
feet or thigh is an age-old prophylactic against the deceased coming
back, represented already on an Egyptian battle monument of 3100
B.C.: figure 42.) The fight itself is best understood knowing that *every*
valorous battle that Grettir claims he fought occurred when no one else
could actually see what was going on—as when he singlehandedly battled a giant under a waterfall. All Audun could observe was much
crashing around inside a dark hole.

Applying the Stripping Procedure, we find that someone breaks

---

[2] Icelandic sagas are noted for humorous understatements.

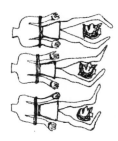

Figure 42. Decapitated enemies lying with their heads placed between their feet, on the victory palette of Narmer, possibly the first king to unify Egypt, ca. 3100 B.C.

into an old burial mound and removes its treasure, after being alerted to its existence by a sudden flame—as in *Beowulf.*

Archaeology shows that Indo-European tribes, from the late Stone Age into the Iron Age (and through the Viking period in Scandinavia), buried their important dead in a chamber over which they heaped a mound (barrow, tumulus, kurgan: figure 41). Both Beowulf and Homer describe the purpose of mounds as reminding people of important ancestors and their exploits.[3] Many such mounds have been excavated, and their chambers, if intact, can be so well sealed that perishables like textiles and carved wood often survive. The flesh—that of the owner, and of the horses often buried alongside—has generally rotted.

Decomposition of so much flesh in an anoxic environment like a sealed tomb creates a lot of poisonous-smelling methane ("marsh gas"), captive in the tomb until the seal is broken. Chinese grave-robbers in the Yangtze region often learned this the hard way. Elite tombs there of the late first millennium B.C. are often so effectively sealed that "when first broken open, a wave of highly inflammable marsh gas rushes out, which has occasionally incinerated the nocturnal robber unwise enough to carry a torch or lamp", giving them the nickname "fire-pit graves" [Hay 1973, 94]. (But how else could one explore inside an enclosed tomb, before the days of electricity, if not with a torch or lamp?) In 1972 at Mawangdui, "when Tomb 1 was opened, a spark from a metal spade ignited methane held within"; furthermore "Wang Ch'ung (A.D. 27–ca. 100) records an instance in which flames shot out of a burial chamber and burned to death several hundred persons nearby" [Thorp 1980, 68].

So the source of the fire that alerted both Grettir and Beowulf *is* the

___

[3] *Iliad* 23 describes Patroklos's mound, built by the shore where sailors would see it. Repeatedly in Indo-European mytho-history we hear that the most important thing to a warrior or king is his "renown" (Gk. *klé(w)os,* Skt. *śráva-,* OCS *sláva,* et cetera, "what is *heard* about one"). But how will anyone hear of your exploits if people forget to tell the tale? The barrow serves as a permanent, visible mnemonic for nonliterate people, especially wanderers like sailors and pastoral nomads, reminding them that the tale exists: "That was the mound for X, who . . ." (much like "That, children, is the memorial for Washington, who . . .").

mound-dweller—but in gaseous form.[4] Once the methane starts to escape (from digging or internal collapse), one needs only a spark—from
lightning, torches, or a digger's iron tool striking rocks. Hence the
mound and its buried treasure are indeed "protected" by something that
smells bad and tends to burst into flame; we need only add Willfulness
and then try to deduce the form of the creature with that evil will.

What sorts of creatures do we *know* that slither in and out of rock-
piles? Snakes, salamanders, lizards, and the like, all of them long, thin,
and scaly, as the confined habitat demands: ergo, by Analogy, fire-
dragons probably look snaky too. (Old English *worm* simply means
"snake".)

We now have the right Camera Angle to decode Fafnir, the other
great Germanic dragon, whose killing is recounted in Snorri Sturluson's
Poetic Diction [Sturluson 1971, 112–13] and at greater length in the
Volsunga Saga (sections 14–20) as follows.

The father of Otr, Fafnir, and Regin acquired an enormous heap of
(accursed) gold as recompense for Otr's death, but Fafnir murdered his
father for the gold and cheated Regin of his share of the inheritance.
Fafnir then "grew so malevolent that he went off to live in the wilds and
allowed none but himself to have any pleasure in the riches, and later on
he turned into a terrible dragon and now," says Regin to the young and
gullible hero, Sigurd, "he lies on the treasure" [section 14: Finch 1965,
26]. Sigurd promises he will attack the dragon if Regin, a smith, forges
him a first-rate sword for the purpose, which Regin eventually does.
"Now Sigurd and Regin rode up to the moors, to the track along which
Fafnir used to crawl when he went to drink . . ." [section 18: Finch
1965, 30]. (Newsreel from snapshot: all living animals must drink,
therefore so must the dragon, but he will have to crawl to the stream
from the mound.) Sigurd digs pits (!) along the crawlway and settles
into one to wait, while Regin runs away in terror.

> And when the dragon crawled to the water, . . . he breathed out poison all
> over the path ahead, but Sigurd was neither frightened nor dismayed by the
> noise. And when the dragon crawled across the pit, Sigurd thrust in the
> sword under the left shoulder, and it sunk in up to the hilt. [Section 18:
> Finch 1965, 30–31]

[4] A medical examiner told us his professor would demonstrate this methane build-up in
class by slitting a bloated cadaver a few inches and lighting a match, whereupon a foot-high
flame would shoot up.

Figure 43. Rock drawing at Ramsund, Sweden, of Sigurd slaying the gold-guarding dragon Fafnir by stabbing him from below (bottom right). This early Viking-era dragon is depicted as a mere ribbon with heads—presumably no one knew exactly what dragons looked like. In the center we see Sigurd with his burnt thumb in his mouth as he roasts the dragon's heart over a fire and turns to listen to the birds (in the tree to which Sigurd has tied his horse) remarking that Regin intends to kill him. At far left lies the beheaded Regin.

The dragon, after a leisurely conversation and some ill wishes, dies. (Translation: A rush of noxious marsh gas comes out of the burial hill after Sigurd, like Beowulf, starts piercing the ground. This abates.)

Our earliest written forms of this tale date to the thirteenth century, but we have earlier pictorial sources, as the next scene proves. In the *Volsunga Saga* Regin soon returns from safety, like Beowulf's retainers, but—shifting to a quite different type of tale—he asks Sigurd to roast the dragon's heart for him to eat (by Analogy to known creatures, the dragon presumably *has* a head and heart). "Sigurd went and roasted it on a spit. And when the juice sputtered out he touched it with his finger to see whether it was done. He jerked his finger to his mouth, and when the blood from the dragon's heart touched his tongue he could understand the language of birds" [section 19: Finch 1965, 33]. He hears the nearby birds saying Regin means to kill him, so he kills Regin first.

These singular details are carved into a rock at Ramsund, Sweden (figure 43): we see birds in a tree watching a man with his thumb in his mouth who holds a heart-shaped object on a stick over something flame-like.[5] This scene is surrounded by a "ribbon" with a couple of heads (no legs; maybe some flames) which a man stabs from below with

[5] Hilda Davidson [1967, 126–27, and pl. 36] lists several other early depictions from Britain.

a sword. This can only represent Sigurd's slaying of Fafnir. But again, no one knew what a dragon *looked* like—just a nondescript ribbon with snouts.[6]

We tend to assume the word "dragon" always refers to the same thing. But not all dragons are the same. Chinese dragons were beneficent rain-bringers, playfully swallowing up and spitting out their celestial moon-pearl as they cavorted in the sky [Newman 1979, 110–15]. No dank and smelly caverns for them. Other dragons seem to represent rainbows [Blust 2000]. Then there was the cosmic dragon of early Mesopotamia and Greece, the dragon that ruled the center of the world (the celestial pole) until a new deity fought it for ownership and won. (In chapter 16 we saw that when the north celestial pole, crucial for orientation and navigation, shifted out of Draco or "Dragon"—the long snaky constellation between the two Dippers—toward the Little Dipper where *our* "Polaris" is today [figure 35b], some Willful force had "killed" the Dragon or driven it off—why would it give way unless it had been bested in a fight?—and appropriated the navel of the world for himself, as Apollo did to Pytho[n] on Parnassos.)

The details are what provide the clues to the various origins.[7]

Generic "dragons" form the topic of several academic books—for example by Joseph Fontenrose [1959/74], Paul Newman [1979], Calvert Watkins [1995], and David Jones [2000]. The very name "dragon" Attracts the beasts together. Some of these treatises, however, begin from Camera Angles that obscure the different origins instead of elucidating them. Thus the "motif" approach to myth and folklore pioneered by Antti Aarne, Stith Thompson, and Vladimir Propp purposely reduces all narratives to basic plots, the skeletons of storytelling: Roger Schank's "scripts" [1995]. Such work produces an index for locating

---

[6] We suspect that Western dragons came to resemble Chinese ones because westerners (who, like Wiglaf, had never actually seen a dragon) concluded that dragons probably looked like other creatures found under rocks: snakes, lizards and the like; and this mental "search image" (a useful cognitive term reintroduced by Mayor [2000b, 21] from palaeontologist Jack Horner) caused them to home in on the dragons embroidered on imperial Chinese silks that began entering Europe in the first millennium A.D. ("So *that's* what dragons look like!") Mayor also cogently argues that certain fossils added to people's notions of how dragons looked.

[7] Colarusso [2002, xv] discovered this principle quite independently while tracking Caucasian mythology.

similar simple events and sequences, but obliterates unique and telltale relations to the real world. Fontenrose, for instance, reduces the story of Pytho and Apollo—and much else—to:

(1) The Enemy [Dragon] was of divine origin.
(2) The Enemy had a distinctive habitation.
      . . . He lived in a cave, hut, or tree. . . .
(3) The Enemy had extraordinary appearance and properties.
(4) The Enemy was vicious and greedy.

And so on, until "(7) The Champion fought the Enemy" and "(9) The Enemy was finally destroyed" [Fontenrose 1959/74, 9–11]. But these are so general as to constitute narrative *techniques*. Without contrasts (Enemy vs. Champion, divine vs. mortal, gigantic vs. normal) there is no story, nothing to "resolve". What is the Champion to do with the Enemy, if not fight him? Sit down at a negotiating table? Fill out environmental-impact reports?

Watkins [1995, 299–301] compresses the themes even further to "hero slays serpent"—a base useful for his examination of linguistic formulae for recounting dragon-slaying, but one that obscures the fact that some "slain dragons" originated as methane, others as lava, rain-clouds, or stars. It's not that differences stem from "*elaborations* of a single theme" [Watkins 1995, 299; emphasis ours] but that scholars have *reduced* different events until everything sounds similar. Dragons, indeed, are typically transient ("slayable") nuisances, but there the similarity stops. With all differences obscured, his question, "Why does the hero slay the serpent?" [Watkins 1995, 299] leads nowhere except back to the basic human fantasies that empower fiction: we enjoy identifying with heroic success [Barber, forthcoming].

Robert Blust [2000] also reduces "dragons" to a series of typical traits which he organizes from a worldwide survey.[8] But since, like us, he believes such ideas "arose through processes of reasoning which do not differ essentially from those underlying modern scientific explanations" [Blust 2000, 519], his meticulous treatment makes it fairly easy to extract those "dragons" not originating from rainbows (his principal theory).

Not everyone is seeking origins, of course. The point is that motifs

[8] The carefully collated data-lists of Blust [2000], incidentally, repeatedly contradict and thus make hash of the sweeping generalizations on which Jones [2000] bases his theory that dragons are a universal figment of early hominids' primal fear of predators.

won't show them to you and in fact will Blur together stories of quite different function that happen to share some surface forms. Not all dragons had the same parentage.

Saint George's dragon makes the point well. The original George lived in the eastern Mediterranean, apparently tortured and beheaded by the Romans around A.D. 300, but his dragon "does not make its first definite appearance until the twelfth century" [Coulson 1958, 196]. This dragon, for all that it fits Fontenrose's themes, was born from neither decomposing bodies nor celestial events, but from a "mistake": an analogical Reinterpretation of an image. Cornelia Hulst, in researching St. George, came upon the key Camera Angle. For over a millennium, the often illiterate Christians used visual images to teach and remember aspects of their faith (figure 44); in these images, sin or evil was encoded as a serpent—as in the Garden of Eden—while the church was represented as a chaste virgin, the Bride of Christ (the word *ekklēsía* "church" was feminine). Hence, as Hulst put it, the early Eastern Orthodox representations of St. George showed him "with a dragon under his feet and a crowned virgin at his side, a symbolical way of saying that he overcame Sin" in the service of the church [1909, quoted in Newman 1979, 193]. This image has an interesting and traceable genesis. According to Fox [1983, 40],

> The Roman emperors frequently had themselves portrayed mounted on horseback and lance in hand, spearing a prostrate figure; but in their case, although the attitude is very similar to that of St George himself, their victim is not a dragon but their defeated foe. Constantine, however, the emperor whose conversion early in the fourth century made the empire safe for Christianity, provided a significant exception, for Eusebius records that the first Christian emperor had himself depicted piercing with the labarum the serpent or dragon of paganism.

It was a short step from there to the imagery surrounding George. But the Greeks, seeing this tableau, already knew from their inherited mythology that heroes like Perseus had rescued maidens like Andromeda by slaying serpents. What was allegorical thus came to be Reinterpreted as actual (Principle of Metaphoric Reality), as in the Snowball stories: St. George actually killed a (real) dragon/serpent by force of arms, just like Perseus. Is it an accident that (the Restructured) St. George became particularly popular in England, a land with its own early history of "dragon" combats?

Chere begynnyth the lyfe of the gloryous mar=
tyr saynt George/patrone of the Royalme of En=
glonde/traflate by alexander barclay/ at cõmaun
dement of the ryght hyghe/ and myghty Prynce
Thomas/duke of Norfolke/trefozer ⁊ Erle mar=
chall of Englonde.

Figure 44. Saint George slaying the Dragon. Woodcut, ca. 1515, from English edition
of B. Spagnuoli's life of St. George.

Camera Angle is crucial, and figuring out camera placement comes from observing, not obscuring, the details. Belief in dragons is perceived today as nearly universal not because the *belief* is the same everywhere but because we use the same *word* for a variety of beliefs with a scattering of surface resemblances. Apparently the Principle of Attraction still lives, operating in modern times around words which pull to themselves such diverse creatures as Germanic gold-hoarding mound-dwellers, Basuto waterfall-dwelling rainbow-serpents [Blust 2000, 524], and the long skinny Sumerian star-constellation that held back the Celestial Flood until the next precession. Similarly, our word "vampire" attracts to itself anything anywhere that is thought to suck blood, from bloated corpses to Romanian princes to bats [Barber 1988]. *Faute de mieux* we give them the same name, then—following the Principle of Metaphoric Reality—turn around and believe the referents are all the same.

Throughout this book, we have argued that "myths" were not intended as fiction in our sense, but as carriers of important information about real events and observations. We have also given much evidence that, contrary to prevailing belief today, this information can sometimes survive intact for thousands of years. But, bombarded as myth is by Silence, Compression, Restructuring, and so on, the conditions must be right for survival.

In 1936, Lord Raglan published a very influential calculation of about 150 years maximum for "how long an incident that is not recorded in writing can be remembered" [Raglan 1936/79, 13]. After this, he claims, "we are in a period of events which have been completely forgotten, and which is therefore available for the myths. These, being ageless, can be allotted to any period" [Raglan 1936/79, 14]. We agree that the time-scale gets lost, or at least compressed, and many details of events as well, but not that *all events* or even all details are lost, for reasons we have set forth throughout the book. Most particularly we disagree with Raglan's (very astutely argued) stance that "since history depends upon written chronology, . . . the savage can have no history. And since interest in the past is induced solely by books, the savage can take no interest in the past" [Raglan 1936/79, 8]. As with Crater Lake and the stars, a major and still-present mnemonic can foster remembrance of clan history and celestial affairs for millennia. Our task is to decipher the contents of these precious time capsules.

APPENDIX
Index of Myth Principles

1. MEMORY CRUNCH   5

When all accumulated wisdom must be stored in the brain and transmitted orally (as in a nonliterate society), people reserve the formal oral tradition for transmitting the information they consider most important, often for survival.

RELEVANCE COROLLARY   9

Formal oral mythologies are neither unimportant and "off the wall" nor random in their content.

REDUNDANCY STRATEGY   11

Because of the importance attached, particular information will tend to be encoded with a high degree of redundancy and/or vividness, *except* where the piece of knowledge is believed to be universal. [Cf. Silence and Vividness Principles.]

EXPLANATION COROLLARY   15

Where permanent record-keeping is unavailable, so that there is not enough memory-space to accumulate the data needed to demonstrate cause and effect for complex phenomena, other types of "explanation" may be proffered or sought. [Cf. Analogy Principle.]

2. SILENCE PRINCIPLE   17

What everyone is expected to know already is not explained in so many words.

LETHE EFFECT   19

What is never said may eventually be forgotten entirely. [Remainder subject to Restructuring.]

SOCIALIZATION ANTIDOTE   25
Information on the basic and otherwise unstated assumptions of a culture may be teased out of those statements and stories by which adults socialize children.

RATIONALIZATION SYNDROME   26
What is not known but only surmised may nonetheless be perceived and stated as known, in explanation of things observed. [Cf. Restructuring Principle.]

BABY-WITH-THE-BATHWATER REFLEX   27
Heavily literate cultures tend to disregard the truth of the earlier events reported in myths and legends, because they can't brook the explanations—that is, they ignore the phenomena described because they reject the mechanisms indicated.

STRIPPING PROCEDURE   29
In order to understand the true original events, we have to see clearly what the events are. In order to do that, we must strip the explanations from the story.

LOGIC CROSS-CHECK   29
Investigating the logic of the actions of the participants serves as a useful cross-check that we have suitably separated their explanations from their observations.

MOVIE CONSTRUCT   31
Explanations that were derived from seeing only the result of an event (as in a single snapshot) tend to be presented as an integral part of a story that moves through time (as in a movie reel). [Cf. Restructuring and Silence Principles.]

3. ANALOGY PRINCIPLE   34
If any entities or phenomena bear *some* resemblance, in any aspect, they must be related. (Points of resemblance include form, behavior, cause, significance, name, location, and so forth.)

FALLACY OF AFFIRMING THE CONSEQUENT   37
I know that "if P, then Q" is true; I have Q (not P); so I assume— fallaciously—that P must always be true.

CONTAINER COROLLARY 38

A source container and a resident "thing contained" may be assumed where scientists consider cause and effect the appropriate relation.

WILLFULNESS PRINCIPLE 41

Humans will things to happen, then set about to make them happen. Therefore if something happens, it must have been willed. [Cf. Fallacy of Affirming the Consequent.]

KINSHIP PRINCIPLE 44

If two (willful) phenomena are perceived as alike, they must be kinsfolk. (Scientists say, like effects imply like causes; but myths say, like effects imply kinship between the willful beings.)

ADVERSARY PRINCIPLE 49

If two phenomena are perceived as the opposite of each other, they must be bitter enemies.

ADVERSARY METHOD 51

To help determine the domain of a deity, investigate the nature of his or her enemies.

MULTIPLE-ASPECTS PRINCIPLE 53

A phenomenon may be explained mythically as many times as it has "significantly" different aspects.

CAMERA-ANGLE PROBLEM 56

To understand what a story is talking about, we may have to observe the situation from a very particular viewpoint.

GOLDILOCKS PRINCIPLE 61

Key words or phrases may evoke an entire narrative complex to the members of a particular culture.

RAINBOW COROLLARY 61

Different peoples divide up the same world differently, as they fasten onto different aspects within the multiplicity.

HEDGING YOUR BETS 62

If someone else is worshipping a different (willful) aspect than you, add or graft it onto your pantheon to be safe.

DOUBLET CLUE   65

Double terminology or doublets within a belief system (especially en masse) indicate that one culture has absorbed another culture and/or changed its environment or technology. The doublets can be milked accordingly for information about the former natures of these cultures and the changes that occurred.

HERETIC SYNDROME   66

Treat as heretics those who wish to *reduce* the pantheon: it threatens your security.

MISMATCH EFFECT   71

The same real event reported by two different sources may be reported in wildly different forms, which may therefore seem unrelated at first glance.

"FAIREST OF THEM ALL" EFFECT   89

People tend to select and pass down the view or version of events that puts themselves in the best light—and enemies in the worst light.

ZONE-OF-CONVENIENT-REMOVE SYNDROME   93

People can perpetuate a vivid and seemingly plausible story by telling it of a third party who can't be consulted for verification. (In the classic urban legend, the third party is typically as near as possible while being unreachable: a relative of a friend, or a friend of a relative, or a Friend Of A Friend—FOAF—, or an enemy.)

4. COMPRESSIVE/CONFLATIONARY PRINCIPLES

PRINCIPLE OF METAPHORIC REALITY   96

The distinction between representation and referent—and between appearance and reality—tends to become blurred. (Includes sympathetic magic and name magic.)

FOGGING EFFECT   107

Blurring of representation and referent is especially likely to occur when people no longer have direct experience of the referent.

PRINCIPLE OF ATTRACTION   113

Once the stories around something (e.g., a hero) achieve sufficient mass, that thing (or whatever) attracts yet other stories to him/her/itself, via any "significant" point of resemblance. Points of attraction include the same type of event, same place, and same name or clan name. [Cf. Perspective and Analogy Principles.]

PERSPECTIVE PRINCIPLE   117
As we get further from an event, our perspective gets flatter, and we can no longer distinguish earlier from later events so easily: it is all "back then" some time.

METHUSELAH EFFECT   118
Deeds of identically named (or surnamed) relatives may get conflated over centuries, but if any independent gauge of time exists, then one has to ascribe centuries of lifetime to such "heroes". [Cf. Restructuring Principle.]

GOLDEN AGE PHENOMENON   118
The past comes to be seen as different in an absolute sense from the present. [Cf. Restructuring Principle.]

UFO COROLLARY   120
If certain events are not understood, according to already known ("natural") principles, they must be un-understandable—that is, "super-natural"—and there is no point in trying to understand them. They are automatically recategorized as different in an absolute sense from the known/understood.

CYCLIC PHENOMENON   121
If events at two or more points in time resemble each other strongly, they must be related or even "the same", and therefore returning. If the "same" events are seen to return many times, the observers may conclude that time is cyclical rather than linear.

POST HOC, ERGO PROPTER HOC
("After this, therefore because of this")   121
Because one event occurs soon after another event, the prior event is taken to have caused the later event.

DELILAH EFFECT   124
As a story is retold and retold, the actions of the minor characters are eventually attributed to the major characters. [Cf. Restructuring Principle.]

DISTILLATION FACTOR   125
Stories with more characters typically have stayed in the oral pipeline
a shorter time than stories with fewer characters, which have been
distilled down to essentials.

CLASS-ACTION COROLLARY   126
The attributes and actions of a class of beings may be represented as a
single individual portrayed as King or Queen of the group.

EPONYMOUS HERO SYNDROME   126
The migrations of tribes are reduced to the journey of an individual—
one who was, or is seen as, the leader or progenitor of the group in
some sense. Conversely, a known group may be assumed to descend
from such an eponymous ("named-after") hero.

5. RESTRUCTURING PRINCIPLE   139
Whenever there is a significant cultural change, at least some patterns will
get restructured or reinterpreted. Successive changes on a given pattern will
render the form of the pattern un-understandable to its users—it goes from
a matter of logic to one of faith, and finally to a matter of disbelief. [Cf.
Golden Age Phenomenon.]

ENVIRONMENTAL CLUE   142
Known changes in technology or location can be exploited to help disentangle restructured beliefs. [Cf. Doublet Clue.]

POWER PRINCIPLE   143
The bigger the force represented, the more major the deity to represent it.

DIACHRONIC POWER PRINCIPLE   144
If a force changes in importance, its deity will change in importance
too. (Such changes typically occur with a change of location or technology.)

BUMPING UPSTAIRS   145
What belonged to earlier epochs is often viewed as more hallowed
and entailing more power than what people do nowadays. (So what
belonged to the royalty, for example, of one epoch may belong to the
deities of a later one, and so on.)

SNOWBALL EFFECT   146

A statement of possibility may be restructured as probability and then as fact, which may entrain yet other probabilities which come in turn to be told as fact. [Cf. Fallacy of Affirming the Consequent.]

CENTAUR SYNDROME   146

People of other times or other cultures come to be seen as different in an absolute sense (e.g., as nonhuman, possibly as fiends or demons). [Cf. Perspective Principle and UFO Corollary.]

STOCKPILE EFFECT   149

The invention of writing (especially efficient writing and efficient mathematical notation) enabled people for the first time to stockpile enough information to deduce cause-and-effect relationships other than the very simplest. Where cause-and-effect came to be seen as more closely predictive of natural phenomena than analogy, the function of analogy in thought processes was redeployed. Eventually it was no longer possible in the new framework to understand the previous use of analogy, and those earlier modes of thought came to be viewed—Restructured—as "untrue".

6. VIVIDNESS PRINCIPLE   158

Random or apparently patternless phenomena are best remembered by inventing stories to connect and encode them; but these stories must be either internally patterned or connected to something known to be rememberable, and the sillier or funnier they are, the more memorable. [Cf. Memory Crunch, Redundancy Strategy, and Fogging Effect.]

BIBLIOGRAPHY

Aldred, Cyril. 1984. *The Egyptians*. London: Thames and Hudson.

Alexander, Hartley B. 1916. *The Mythology of all Races*, vol. 10: *North American*. Boston: Marshall Jones Co.

Allen, Charles. 1980. *Tales from the Dark Continent*. London: Futura.

Allen, David A. 1992. "Solstice Determination at Noon," *Archaeoastronomy* 17: S21–31.

Anouilh, Jean. 1946. *Antigone*. Paris: Table Ronde.

Arens, W. 1979. *The Man-Eating Myth*. Oxford and New York: Oxford University Press.

Arias, P. E., and Max Hirmer. 1962. *A History of 1,000 Years of Greek Vase Painting*. New York: Abrams.

Assmann, Jan. 1997. "Ancient Egyptian Antijudaism: A Case of Distorted Memory," in Schacter 1997: 365–76.

Atchity, Kenneth and E.J.W. Barber. 1987. "Greek Princes and Aegean Princesses: The Role of Women in the Homeric Poems," in *Critical Essays on Homer*, ed. K. Atchity. Boston: G. K. Hall, 15–36.

Aveni, Anthony, and Gary Urton, eds. 1982. *Ethnoastronomy and Archaeoastronomy in the American Tropics*. New York: New York Academy of Sciences.

Bächtold-Stäubli, Hanns. 1927/1987. *Handwörterbuch des deutschen Aberglaubens*. Berlin: de Gruyter.

Bagley, Clarence. 1930/1991. *Indian Myths of the Northwest*. Brighton, MI: Native American Book Publishers (reprint).

Barber, E.J.W. 1987. "Metathesis and Ancient Pot-heads," paper delivered to Linguistic Society of America, Dec. 1987.

———. 1991. *Prehistoric Textiles*. Princeton: Princeton University Press.

———. 1992. "The Peplos of Athena," in *Goddess and Polis: The Panathenaic Festival in Ancient Athens*, ed. J. Neils. Princeton: Princeton University Press, 103–17.

———. 1994. *Women's Work: The First 20,000 Years*. New York: W. W. Norton.

———. 1997. "On the Origins of the *vily/rusalki*," in *Varia on the Indo-European Past*, ed. M. R. Dexter and E. C. Polomé. Washington, DC: Institute for the Study of Man, 6–47.

———. 1999. "On the Antiquity of East European Bridal Clothing," in *Folk Dress in Europe and Anatolia: Beliefs about Protection and Fertility*, ed. L. Welters. New York and London: Berg, 13–31.

Barber, Paul T. 1988. *Vampires, Burial, and Death: Folklore and Reality*. New Haven: Yale University Press.

———. 1990. "The Real Vampire," *Natural History* (Oct.) 90: 74–82.

———. 1995. "Mummification in the Tarim Basin," *Journal of Indo-European Studies* 23: 309–18.

———. Forthcoming. *Words of Uncommon Shape: How Writers Create Vividness in Language and Stories*.

Bartlett, F. C. 1932. *Remembering: A Study in Social and Experimental Psychology*. Cambridge: Cambridge University Press.

Berlin, Brent, and Paul Kay. 1969. *Basic Color Terms: Their Universality and Evolution*. Berkeley: University of California Press.

Bhāratī Kṛṣṇa Tīrtha. 1992. *Vedic Mathematics*. 2nd ed.; Delhi: Motilal Banarsidass Publishers.

Blake, Emma. 2001a. "Detecting Nuragic Places," *Backdirt* (Spring/Summer) 1: 4–5.

———. 2001b. "Reconstructing a Nuragic Locale," *American Journal of Archaeology* 105: 145–61.

Bloom, Lois. 1970. *Language Development: Form and Function in Emerging Grammars*. Cambridge, MA: MIT Press.

Bloomfield, Leonard. 1933. *Language*. New York: H. Holt and Company.

Blust, Robert. 1981. "Linguistic Evidence for Some Early Austronesian Taboos," *American Anthropologist* 83: 285–319.

———. 1999. "The Fox's Wedding," *Anthropos* 94: 487–99.

———. 2000. "The Origin of Dragons," *Anthropos* 95: 5519–36.

Bogatikov, O. A., I. V. Melekestsev, A. G. Gurbanov, L. D. Sulerzhitskii, D. M. Katov, and A. I. Puriga. 1998. "Radiocarbon Dating of Holocene Eruptions of the Elbrus Volcano in the Northern Caucasus, Russia," *Doklady Earth Sciences* 363.8: 1093–95.

Bourne, Lyle, Roger Dominowski, and Elizabeth Loftus. 1979. *Cognitive Processes*. Englewood Cliffs, NJ: Prentice-Hall.

Bright, William. 1993. *Coyote Reader*. Berkeley: University of California Press.

Brown, Tom, Jr., with Brandt Morgan. 1983. *Tom Brown's Field Guide to Nature Observation and Tracking*. New York: Berkley Books.

Burstein, Stanley M. 1978. *The* babyloniaca *of berossus* (*SANE* 1.5). Malibu, CA: Undena.

Bury, J. B. 1913. *A History of Greece*. New York: Modern Library.

Campbell, Jeremy. 1982. *Grammatical Man*. New York: Simon and Schuster.

———. 1989. *The Improbable Machine*. New York: Simon and Schuster.

Campbell, Joseph. 1962. *The Masks of God*. New York: Viking.

Caubet, Annie, and Patrick Pouyssegur. 1998. *The Ancient Near East*. Trans. P. Snowdon. Paris: Terrail.

Ceci, Stephen. 1997. "False Beliefs," in Schacter 1997, 91–125.

Charachidzé, Georges. 1986. *Prométhée ou le Caucase*. Paris: Flammarion.

Charbonneaux, Jean, Roland Martin, and François Villard. 1971. *Archaic Greek Art*. New York: George Braziller.

Chartrand, Mark R. 1998. *National Audubon Society Field Guide to the Night Sky*. New York: Knopf.

Chickering, Howell D. 1977. *Beowulf.* New York: Anchor Books.

Clark, Ella. 1953. *Indian Legends of the Pacific Northwest.* Berkeley: University of California Press.

Clausen, Henrik, C. Hammer, C. Hvidberg, D. Dahl-Jensen, J. Steffensen, J. Kipfstuhl, M. Legrand. 1997. "A Comparison of the volcanic records over the past 4000 years from the Greenland Ice Core Project . . . ," *Journal of Geophysical Research* 102: 26707–23.

Colarusso, John, ed. 2002. *Nart Sagas from the Caucasus.* Princeton: Princeton University Press.

Cook, Arthur Bernard. 1940. *Zeus,* vol. 3. Cambridge: Cambridge University Press.

Cook, Robert. 1960. *Greek Painted Pottery.* London: Methuen.

Coulson, John. 1958. *The Saints: A Concise Biographical Dictionary.* New York: Hawthorn Books.

Costello, Chris, and Raymond Strait. 1981. *Lou's On First.* New York: St. Martin's Press.

Crooke, William. 1926. *Religion and Folklore of Northern India.* Oxford: Oxford University Press.

Danforth, Loring M. 1982. *The Death Rituals of Rural Greece.* Princeton: Princeton University Press.

Darkevich, V., and A. Mongait. 1967. "Starorjazanskij klad 1966 goda," *Sovetskaja arkheologija* 2: 211–23.

Davidson, Hilda R. Ellis. 1967. *Pagan Scandinavia.* New York: Praeger.

———. 1969. *Scandinavian Mythology.* London: Paul Hamlyn.

———. 1981. *Gods and Myths of the Viking Age.* New York: Bell.

Decker, Robert, and Barbara Decker. 1981. *Volcanoes.* San Francisco: W. H. Freeman.

Deloria, Vine, Jr. 1995. *Red Earth, White Lies.* New York: Scribner.

Diószegi, Vilmos. 1960/1968. *Tracing Shamans in Siberia.* Trans. A.R. Babó. Oosterhout: Anthropological Publications.

Dixon, R.M.W. 1984. *Searching for Aboriginal Languages: Memoirs of a Field Worker.* Chicago: University of Chicago Press.

Dumanoski, Dianne. 1991. "Under the Volcano," *Honolulu Star Bulletin* Aug. 18: D1.

Edwards, Betty. 1979. *Drawing on the Right Side of the Brain.* Los Angeles: Tarcher.

Eliade, Mircea. 1951/1964. *Shamanism: Archaic Techniques of Ecstacy.* Trans. W. Trask. Princeton: Princeton University Press.

Eylmann, Erhard. 1908. *Die Eingeborenen der Kolonie Südaustralien.* Berlin: Dietrich Reimer.

Finch, R. G., ed. and trans. 1965. *The Saga of the Volsungs.* London: Nelson.

Findley, Rowe. 1981. "Mount St. Helens," *National Geographic* 159, no. 1:3–65.

FitzGerald, Edward. 1879/1997. *Rubáiyát of Omar Khayyám: A Critical Edition.* Ed. C. Decker. Charlottesville: University Press of Virginia.

Fontenrose, Joseph. 1959/1974. *Python.* New York: Biblo and Tannen (reprint).

Fox, David Scott. 1983. *Saint George.* Shooter's Lodge, Windsor Forest, Berks., UK: Kensal Press.

Fox, Denton, and Hermann Pálsson. 1974. *Grettir's Saga*. Toronto: University of Toronto Press.

Frankfort, Henri. 1948. *Ancient Egyptian Religion*. New York: Harper and Row.

Frankfort, Henri, Mrs H. A. Frankfort, John A. Wilson, and Thorkild Jacobsen. 1949. *Before Philosophy*. Harmondsworth, UK: Pelican.

Frankfort, Henri, and H. A. Frankfort. 1949. "Myth and Reality," in Frankfort et al. 1949, 11–36.

Frazer, Sir James G. 1922/1963. *The Golden Bough*. Abridged; New York: Macmillan (reprint).

Garfinkel, Yosef. 2003. *Dancing at the Dawn of Agriculture*. Austin: University of Texas Press.

Gazzaniga, Michael. 1985. *The Social Brain*. New York: Basic Books.

Gazzaniga, Michael, Richard Ivry, and George Mangun. 2002. *Cognitive Neuroscience*. 2nd ed.; New York: W. W. Norton.

Gelb, I. J. 1963. *A Study of Writing*. 2nd ed.; Chicago: University of Chicago Press.

Gimbutas, Marija. 1982. *Goddesses and Gods of Old Europe*. Berkeley: University of California Press.

Ginzburg, Carlo. 1991. *Ecstasies: Deciphering the Witches' Sabbath*. Trans. R. Rosenthal. New York: Penguin.

Greene, Mott T. 1992. *Natural Knowledge in Preclassical Antiquity*. Baltimore: Johns Hopkins University Press.

Grice, Paul. 1989. *Studies in the Way of Words*. Cambridge, MA: Harvard University Press.

Grimal, Pierre, ed. 1963/1973. *Larousse World Mythology*. Trans. P. Beardsworth. Secaucus, NJ: Chartwell Books.

Groenwegen-Frankfort, H. A., and Bernard Ashmole. 1977. *Art of the Ancient World*. Englewood Cliffs, NJ: Prentice-Hall; and New York: Harry Abrams.

Güterbock, Hans. 1952. "The Song of Ullikummi," *Journal of Cuneiform Studies* 6: 135–61.

Hall, Edward T. 1959. *The Silent Language*. Greenwich, NY: Fawcett.

———. 1969. *The Hidden Dimension*. Garden City, NY: Doubleday Anchor.

Hartmann, Franz. 1896. *Premature Burial*. London: Swan Sonnenschein.

Harva, Uno. 1933/1938. *Die religiösen Vorstellungen der altäischen Völker* (FF Communications No. 125). Helsinki: Söderström.

Hay, John. 1973. *Ancient China*. New York: Henry Z. Walck, Inc.

Heninger, S. K. 1974. *Touches of Sweet Harmony: Pythagorean Cosmology and Renaissance Poetics*. San Marino, CA: Huntington Library.

Henle, Jane E. 1973. *Greek Myths: A Vase Painter's Notebook*. Bloomington: Indiana University Press.

Hoffner, Harry. 1990. *Hittite Myths*. Atlanta: Scholars Press.

Hopper, Vincent F., ed. and trans. 1962. *Beowulf*. Woodbury, NY: Barron's Educational Series.

Horton, Robin. 1967. "African Traditional Thought and Western Science," *Africa* 37: 50–71, 155–87.

Hovorka, O. von, and A. Kronfeld. 1908–9. *Vergleichende Volksmedizin.* Stuttgart: Strecker and Schröder.

Howe, Linda M. 2002. "More Cat and Cow Mutilations," http://www.earthfiles.com /Environment, Nov. 16.

Hulst, Cornelia S. 1909. *St. George of Cappadocia.* London.

Hutter, Manfred. 1995. "Der luwische Wettergott *piḫaššašši* und der griechische Pegasos," in *Studia Onomastica et Indogermanica,* ed. M. Ofitsch and C. Zinko. Graz: Leykam, 79–97.

Hynes, William J., and William G. Doty, eds. 1993. *Mythical Trickster Figures.* Tuscaloosa: University of Alabama Press.

Ivashneva, L. L., and E. N. Razumovskaja. 1981. "The Usviat Wedding Ritual," *Soviet Anthropology and Archaeology* 20: 25–54.

Jacobsen, Thorkild. 1939. *The Sumerian King List.* Chicago: University of Chicago Press.

———. 1949. "Mesopotamia," in Frankfort et al. 1949, 137–234.

Jaggar, T. A. 1945. *Volcanoes Declare War.* Honolulu: Paradise of the Pacific, Ltd.

Jamison, Stephanie W. 1996. *Sacrificed Wife/Sacrificer's Wife: Women, Ritual, and Hospitality in Ancient India.* New York: Oxford University Press.

Jaynes, Julian. 1976. *The Origin of Consciousness in the Breakdown of the Bicameral Mind.* Boston: Houghton Mifflin.

Jennings, Duffy. 1980. "Treacherous Cloud Moves Across U.S.," *San Francisco Chronicle* May 20: 1, 4.

Jones, David. 2000. *An Instinct for Dragons.* New York: Routledge.

Joos, Martin. 1967. *The Five Clocks.* New York: Harcourt, Brace and World.

Jordan, David. 1985. "A Survey of Greek Defixiones," *Greek, Roman, and Byzantine Studies* 26: 151–97.

Judson, Katharine B. 1910/1997. *Myths and Legends of the Pacific Northwest.* Lincoln: University of Nebraska Press (reprint).

Justus, Carol F. 1999. "Indo-European Numerals since Szemerényi," in S. Embleton, J. Joseph, and H.-J. Niederle, eds., *The Emergence of the Modern Language Sciences* (Philadelphia, Amsterdam: John Benjamins) Vol. 2: 131–52.

———. 2000. "On Language Grouping and Archaeology," *General Linguistics* 37: 183–213.

Katz, Joshua. 2000. "Evening Dress: The Metaphorical Background of Latin *uesper* and Greek ἕσπερος," in *Proceedings of the Eleventh Annual UCLA Indo-European Conference,* ed. K. Jones-Bley, M. Huld, and A. della Volpe. Washington, DC: Institute for the Study of Man, 69–93.

Keirsey, David, and Marilyn Bates. 1984. *Please Understand Me: Character and Temperament Types.* 4th ed.; Del Mar, CA: Gnosology Books and Prometheus Nemesis.

Kepler, Johannes. 1606. *Mysterium Cosmographicum*. Prague.

Klaeber, F. 1922. *Beowulf and The Fight at Finnsburg*. Boston: D. C. Heath.

Krupp, E. C. 1983. *Echoes of the Ancient Skies*. New York: Harper and Row.

Kyselka, Will. 1987. *An Ocean in Mind*. Honolulu: University of Hawaii Press.

Lacey, Marc. 2002. "Under Congo Volcano, Rebel City Trembles," *New York Times*, Nov. 10.

Landi, Sheila, and Rosalind M. Hall. 1979. "The discovery and conservation of an ancient Egyptian linen tunic," *Studies in Conservation* 24: 141–51.

Lansing, Ambrose, and William C. Hayes. 1937. "The Egyptian Expedition 1935–1936: The Museum's Excavations at Thebes," *Bulletin of the Metropolitian Museum of Art* 32 (Jan. pt. 2): 4–39.

Lanzone, R. V. 1881/1974. *Dizionario di Mitologia Egizia* I. Amsterdam: John Benjamins (reprint).

Larson, Gary. 1984. *The Far Side Gallery*. Kansas City, MO: Andrews McMeel Publishing.

Lévi-Strauss, Claude. 1969. *The Raw and the Cooked*. Trans. J. and D. Weightman. New York: Harper and Row.

Liddell, Henry George, and Robert Scott. 1968. *A Greek-English Lexicon*. 9th ed.; Oxford: Clarendon Press.

Lieberman, Philip. 1975. *On the Origins of Language*. New York: Macmillan.

———. 1991. *Uniquely Human*. Cambridge, MA: Harvard University Press.

Littleton, C. Scott. 1970. "The 'Kingship in Heaven' Theme," in *Myth and Law Among the Indo-Europeans*, ed. J. Puhvel. Berkeley: University of California Press, 83–121.

———. 1973. "Poseidon as a Reflex of the Indo-European 'Source of Waters' God," *Journal of Indo-European Studies* 1: 423–40.

Littleton, C. Scott, and Linda Malcor. 2000. *From Scythia to Camelot*. 2nd ed.; New York: Garland.

Luce, J. V. 1969. *Lost Atlantis*. New York: McGraw Hill.

Luria, A. R. 1968. *The Mind of a Mnemonist*. Trans. L. Solotaroff. Cambridge, MA: Harvard University Press.

Malinowski, Bronislaw. 1927. *The Father in Primitive Psychology*. New York: W. W. Norton.

———. 1948. *Magic, Science and Religion and Other Essays*, ed. R. Redfield. Boston: Beacon Press.

Mallory, J. P. 1989. *In Search of the Indo-Europeans*. London: Thames and Hudson.

Mallory, J. P., and D. Q. Adams, eds. 1997. *Encyclopedia of Indo-European Culture*. London and Chicago: Fitzroy Dearborn.

Mansfield, John M. 1985. *The Robe of Athena and the Panathenaic Peplos*. PhD diss., University of California, Berkeley.

Margueron, Jean-Claude. 1965. *Mesopotamia*. London: F. Muller Ltd.

Marshack, Alexander. 1971. *The Roots of Civilization*. New York: McGraw Hill.

Mason, Ronald J. 2000. "Archaeology and Native North American Oral Traditions," *American Antiquity* 65: 239–66.

Masse, W. Bruce. 1995. "The Celestial Basis of Civilization," *Vistas in Astronomy* 39: 463–77.

———. 1998. "Earth, Air, Fire, and Water: The Archaeology of Bronze Age Cosmic Catastrophes," in *Natural Catastrophes During Bronze age Civilisations*, ed. Benny Peiser, Trevor Palmer, and Mark Bailey. BAR International Series 728, 53–92.

———. In press. "Sky as Environment: Solar Eclipses and Hohokam Cultural Change," in *Environmental Change and Human Adaptation in the Ancient Southwest*, ed. D. E. Doyel and J. S. Dean, Salt Lake City: University of Utah Press.

Masse, W. Bruce, and Robert Soklow. In press. "Black Suns and Dark Times: Cultural Responses to Solar Eclipses in the Ancient Puebloan Southwest," in *Fifth Oxford Conference in Archaeoastronomy*, ed. J. Fountain and R. Sinclair. Raleigh, NC: Carolina Academic Press.

Masters, Anthony. 1972. *The Natural History of the Vampire*. New York: G. P. Putnam's Sons.

Mayor, Adrienne. 2000a. "A Time of Giants and Monsters," *Archaeology* 53, no. 2: 58–61.

———. 2000b. *The First Fossil Hunters: Paleontology in Greek and Roman Times*. Princeton: Princeton University Press.

McCoy, Floyd W., and Grant Heiken. 2000a. "Tsunami Generated by the Late Bronze Age Eruption of Thera (Santorini), Greece," *Pure and Applied Geophysics* 157: 1227–56.

———. 2000b. "The Late-Bronze Age explosive eruption of Thera (Santorini), Greece: Regional and local effects," in *Volcanic Hazards and Disasters in Human Antiquity*, ed. Floyd W. McCoy and Grant Heiken. Boulder, CO: Geological Society Special Paper 345, 43–70.

Meillet, A. 1958. *Linguistique historique et linguistique générale*. Paris: Librairie H. Champion.

Melville, Herman. 1851/1964. *Moby–Dick*. Indianapolis: Bobbs-Merrill.

Menges, Karl H. 1983. *Materialien zum Schamanismus der Ewenki-Tungusen . . . von I. M. Suslov 1926/1928*. Wiesbaden: Harrassowitz.

Merkelbach, Reinhold. 1984. *Mithras*. Koenigstein: Hain.

Metcalf, Peter. 1982. *A Borneo Journey into Death*. Philadelphia: University of Pennsylvania Press.

Mosley, John. 2002. *Starry Night™ Companion*. Toronto: Space Holding Corp.

Neblett, William. 1985. *Sherlock's Logic*. Lanham, MD: University Press of America.

Nelson, Harry. 1975. "Tidal Wave Terror," *Los Angeles Times*, Dec. 1: 1, 11.

Neugebauer, Otto. 1938. "Die Bedeutungslosigkeit der 'Sothisperiode' für die älteste ägyptische Chronologie," *Acta orientalia* 17: 169–95.

———. 1957. *The Exact Sciences in Antiquity*. Providence: Brown University Press.

———. 1983. *Astronomy and History: Selected Essays*. New York and Berlin: Springer-Verlag.

Newman, Paul. 1979. *The Hill of the Dragon*. Bath: Kingsmead Press.

Nissen, Hans, Peter Damerow, and Robert K. Englund. 1993. *Archaic Bookkeeping*. Chicago: University of Chicago Press.

Nivison, David S. 1989. "The origin of the Chinese lunar lodge system," in *World archaeoastronomy*, ed. A. F. Aveni. Cambridge: Cambridge University Press, 203–18.

Olrik, Axel. 1922. *Ragnarök: Die Sagen vom Weltuntergang*. Berlin: de Gruyter.

Ovenden, Michael. 1966. "The Origin of the Constellations," *Philosophical Journal* 3: 1–18.

Oyan, Katie. 2002. "Cattle mutilations back—Ranchers, lawmen baffled by crime wave," *Great Falls Tribune*, Jan. 3.

Parry, Milman. 1971. *The Making of Homeric Verse*, ed. Adam Parry. Oxford: Clarendon Press.

Peek, Werner. 1941. *Kerameikos, B. 3: Inschriften, Ostraka, Fluchtafeln*. Berlin: de Gruyter.

Pellegrino, Charles. 1993. *Unearthing Atlantis*. New York: Vintage.

Perdrizet, Paul-F. 1899. "Les pieds ou les genoux à rebours," *Mélusine* 9 (May–June): 194–96.

Petit, Charles. 1980. "The Volcano Blows Up," *San Francisco Chronicle*, May 19: 1, 20.

Pinker, Steven. 1995. *The Language Instinct*. New York: HarperCollins (reprint).

Pogue, Joseph. 1915. *The Turquois*. National Academy of Sciences 12, pt. 2.3.

Propp, Vladimir. 1963/1987. *Les Fêtes agraires russes* (*Russkie agrarnye prazdniki)*. Trans. L. Gruel-Apert. Paris: Maisonneuve et Larose.

Puckett, Newbell Niles. 1981. *Popular Beliefs and Superstitions*, ed. Wayland Hand, A. Cassetta, and S. Thiederman. Boston: G. K. Hall.

Puhvel, Jaan. 1987. *Comparative Mythology*. Baltimore: Johns Hopkins University Press.

Race, William H. 1997. *The Odes of Pindar*. Cambridge, MA: Harvard University Press.

Raglan, Lord Fitzroy Richard Somerset IV, Baron. 1936/1979. *The Hero*. New York: Meridian (reprint).

Rees, Alwyn, and Brinley Rees. 1961. *Celtic Heritage*. London: Thames and Hudson.

Rice, Tamara T. 1965. *Ancient Arts of Central Asia*. New York: Praeger.

Ritson, Joseph, ed. 1823. *Robin Hood: A Collection of All the Ancient Poems, Songs, and Ballads. . . .* London.

Rose, H.J. 1959. *Handbook of Greek Mythology*. New York: Dutton.

Rosenfeld, Charles, and Robert Cooke. 1982. *Earthfire*. Cambridge, MA: MIT Press.

Rowsome, Frank, Jr. 1965. *The Verse by the Side of the Road*. Lexington, MA: Stephen Greene Press.

Ruggles, Clive L. N. 1997. "Whose Equinox?" *Archaeoastronomy* 22: S46–50.

Ryan, William, and Walter Pitman. 1998. *Noah's Flood: The New Scientific Discoveries About the Event That Changed History*. New York: Simon and Schuster.

Rybakov, B. A. 1968. "The Rusalii and the God Simargl-Pereplut," *Soviet Anthropology and Archaeology* 6.4: 34–59.

———. 1981. *Jazychestvo drevnykh Slavjan.* Moscow: Nauka.

———. 1987. *Jazychestvo drevnej Rusi.* Moscow: Nauka.

Sacks, Oliver. 1985. *The Man Who Mistook His Wife for a Hat.* New York: Summit Books.

Salomon, Frank, and George L. Urioste. 1991. *The Huarochirí Manuscript.* Austin: University of Texas Press.

Sandars, Nancy, trans. 1964. *The Epic of Gilgamesh.* 2nd ed.; London: Penguin.

San Francisco Chronicle. 1980. "Climber Tells How Mountain Blew Up on Him," May 19: 1, 20.

Santillana, Giorgio de, and Hertha von Dechend. 1969/1977. *Hamlet's Mill: An essay on myth and the frame of time.* Boston: Nonpareil/Godine (reprint).

Schacter, Daniel. 1996. *Searching for Memory.* New York: Basic Books.

———. 1997. *Memory Distortion.* Cambridge, MA: Harvard University Press.

———. 2001. *The Seven Sins of Memory.* Boston: Houghton Mifflin.

Schank, Roger C. 1995. *Tell Me a Story: Narrative and Intelligence.* Evanston, IL: Northwestern University Press.

Schmandt-Besserat, Denise. 1992. *Before Writing, I: From Counting to Cuneiform.* Austin: University of Texas Press.

Schudson, Michael. 1997. "Dynamics of Distortion in Collective Memory," in Schacter 1997, 346–64.

Shannon, Claude E. 1949. "Communication Theory of Secrecy Systems," *Bell System Technical Journal* 28: 656–715.

Simkin, Tom, and Richard Fiske. 1983. *Krakatau 1883: The Volcanic Eruption and Its Effects.* Washington, DC: Smithsonian.

Smith, G. Elliott. 1915. "On the Significance of the Geographical Distribution of the Practice of Mummification," *Manchester Memoirs* 59: 13–143.

Snodgrass, Anthony. 1998. *Homer and the Artists.* Cambridge: Cambridge University Press.

Sobel, Dava. 1995. *Longitude.* New York: Penguin.

Spence, Kate. 2000. "Ancient Egyptian chronology and the astronomical orientation of pyramids," *Nature* 408: Nov. 11: 320–24.

Stannard, Martin. 1986. *Evelyn Waugh: The Early Years 1903–1939.* New York: W. W. Norton.

Sturluson, Snorri. 1971. *The Prose Edda.* Trans. J. Young. Berkeley: University of California Press.

Sullivan, William. 1996. *The Secret of the Incas.* New York: Three Rivers Press.

Thomas, Keith. 1973. *Religion and the Decline of Magic.* Harmondsworth: Penguin (reprint).

Thorp, Robert Lee. 1980. *The Mortuary Art and Architecture of Early Imperial China.* Ann Arbor: University Microfilms.

Thurston, Hugh. 1994. *Early Astronomy*. New York and Berlin: Springer-Verlag.

Turner, Frederick, and Ernst Pöppel. 1983. "The Neural Lyre: Poetic Meter, the Brain, and Time," *Poetry* 142: 277–307.

Tylor, Edward. 1871. *Primitive Culture*. London.

Ulansey, David. 1989. *The Origins of the Mithraic Mysteries: Cosmology and Salvation in the Ancient World*. New York and Oxford: Oxford University Press.

Ursulet, Léo. 1997. *Le Désastre de 1902 à la Martinique*. Paris: L'Harmattan.

Vansina, Jan. 1985. *Oral Tradition as History*. Madison: University of Wisconsin Press.

Vermaseren, M. J. 1982. *Mithriaca III: The Mithraeum at Marino*. Leiden: Brill.

Viéyra, M. 1963/1973. "Empires of the Ancient Near East: Hymns of Creation," in Grimal 1963/1973, 55–83.

Vitaliano, Dorothy. 1973. *Legends of the Earth*. Bloomington: Indiana University Press.

von Rosen, Lissie. 1988. *Lapis Lazuli in Geological Contexts and Ancient Sources*. Partille: Paul Åströms förlag.

Vukanovic, T. P. 1959. "The Vampire," *Journal of the Gypsy Lore Society* 38: 111–18.

Vygotsky, Lev S. 1934/1962. *Thought and Language*. Trans. E. Hanfmann and G. Vakar. Cambridge, MA: MIT Press.

Walle, B. van de. 1963/1973. "Egypt: Syncretism and State Religion," in Grimal 1963/1973, 25–54.

Walter, Chip. 1988. *The Infinite Voyage: Fires of the Mind*. Video for WQED, Pittsburgh, and the National Academy of Science. Santa Barbara: Intellimation.

Washburn, Sherwood. 1960. "Tools and Human Evolution," *Scientific American* 203 (Sept.): 63–75.

Watkins, Calvert. 1995. *How to Kill a Dragon*. Oxford and New York: Oxford University Press.

Wayland, Virginia, Harold Wayland, and Alan Ferg. In press. *Playing Cards of the Apaches: A Study in Cultural Adaptation*. Santa Barbara: Perpetua Press.

Weicker, Georg. 1902. *Der Seelenvogel in der alten Litteratur* [sic] *und Kunst*. Leipzig: Teubner.

Wiedemann, A. 1900. *Die Toten und ihre Reiche*. Leipzig.

Weiss, Harvey. 1985. *Ebla to Damascus*. Washington, DC: Smithsonian.

Wile, Ira S. 1934. *Handedness*. Boston: Lothrop, Lee, and Shepard.

Wilhelm, Christopher. 1998. "Prometheans and the Caucasus: The Origins of the Prometheus Myth," in *Proceedings of the Ninth Annual UCLA Indo-European Conference*, ed. K. Jones-Bley, M. Huld, and A. della Volpe. Washington, DC: Institute for the Study of Man, 142–57.

Wilk, Stephen. 2000. *Medusa: Solving the Mystery of the Gorgon*. Oxford: Oxford University Press.

Willetts, Ronald F. 1967. *The Law Code of Gortyn*. Berlin: de Gruyter.

Williams, Howel. 1954. *Crater Lake: The Story of its Origin*. Berkeley: University of California.

Wilson, John A. 1949. "Egypt," in Frankfort et al. 1949, 39–133.

———. 1951. *The Culture of Ancient Egypt*. Chicago: University of Chicago Press.

Winokur, Jon. 1986. *Writers on Writing*. Philadelphia: Running Press.

Wirz, Paul. 1928. *Der Totenkult auf Bali*. Stuttgart.

Wood, Robert. 1775. *Essay on the Original Genius of Homer*. 2nd ed.; London.

Zdanowicz, C. M., G. Zielinski, and M. Germani. 1999. "Mount Mazama eruption: Calendrical age verified . . . ," *Geology* 27: 621–24.

Zielinski, Gregory, P. Mayewski, L. Meeker, S. Whitlow, M. Twickler, M. Morrison, D. Meese, A. Gow, R. Alley. 1994. "Record of Volcanism Since 7000 B.C. from the GISP2 Greenland Ice Core . . . ," *Science* 264: 948–52.

Zipf, George K. 1935. *The Psycho-Biology of Language*. Boston: Houghton Mifflin.

Zuidema, R. T. 1982. "Catachillay," in Aveni and Urton 1982, 203–30.

INDEX

References to specific Myth Principles are in bold print, as are the page references to each principle's location in the Appendix. References to figures are indicated by "f", and references to tables by "t".

Abbott and Costello, 24
Abkhaz myths, 227
Abydos relief, 187f
accounting systems (preliterate), 214–15
Achilles, 119, 166
Acrisius, 109, 111
adamantine, blade of, 87, 110, 207, 212n
adversaries, 38, 49–52, 56, 89–91, 93–94, 147, 237f, 241, 242
Adversary Method, 51, **247**
Adversary Principle, 49–50, **247**
Aegean area, 50, 80, 119, 217n
Aegean myth/culture, 36, 63, 208, 217n
Aegean Sea, 75
Aeschylus, 223, 229
Aesir, 65
Africa, 25, 36, 48, 94, 102
agriculture, 50, 67, 140, 178–79, 212, 214n
Ahriman, 225n
Aigyptos, 126
Ai-laau, 144
Aiolus/Aiolians, 127
Ajax, 119
Akhenaten, 66, 92, 92n
Akkad, 116
Akropolis of Athens, 50, 51f, 86, 145
Akrotiri, Thera, 80, 82f, 83f
Alaska quake, 36
Albania, 68f, 70
Alkmene, 102
All Hallows' Eve, 66

Allen, C., 25
alliteration, 154
alphabet, 82, 150
alternatives, 177, 219–20
Amaltheia, 208
Amarna period, 92
Amaterasu, 44
American culture, 97, 172, 219
Amiran[i], 225n, 226, 228n
Amlodhi/Amlethus/Hamlet, 193
Amnissos, Crete, 80
Amon, 39, 66
Anahita/Anahid 189
Analogy Principle, 3, 34–40, 166, 183, **246**
analogy, 15–16, 33, 54–56, 86, 97, 102, 121, 149, 156, 172, 193, 200, 238; of action/behavior, 35–36, 43, 46, 183–84, 189n, 212; of cause, 42; and emotional baggage, 55–56; of form, 35, 57, 67, 184, 189n, 239, 240n (*see also* **Principle of Attraction**); in language, 35, 127–28, 156; and modeling, 15–16; multiple, 54; in ritual, 67; as sympathetic magic, 102; resulting from viewpoint, 56 (*see also* **Camera-Angle Problem**)
Anatolia, 80, 112
ancestors, 66, 104, 126–27, 237; of languages, 45
Andean culture, 66, 177, 191
Andes, 12, 158–61, 160f, 191, 203
Andromeda, 158, 242
Angkor Thom, Cambodia, 193, 213

animals, 19, 38–39, 54, 67, 100, 107–8, 119, 124–25, 129–37, 148, 174; draft, 140n; extinct, 119, 149; fables of, 160–61; language of, 171; possessed, 174–75; protectress of, 226; sacred, 92; as stars, 153, 158–61, 183, 203

Anouilh, J., 140

Anshar, 210t

Antaios, 87n

Antigone, 139–40

Anu, 210t

anvils, 107, 226–27

Apache, 94, 147–49

Apám Nápāt, 62–63

Aphrodite, 189–90

apocalypse, 204

Apollo, 44, 54, 127, 151, 190, 200, 208, 240, 241

Apollodorus, 109, 110

Apollonius Rhodius, 112, 223

appearance. See blurring of appearance and reality

Apples of the Hesperides, 47, 47f

aprons, 68f, 69, 70n

Apsu, 61, 210t

Aquarius, 183, 184f, 209f, 205

Aracaunians, 98

Aratos, 217n

Arawak (South American) language, 60n

archaeology, 3–4, 64, 80, 88, 94, 116, 119, 143, 180, 227, 237

archetypes, 4

architecture, 119, 143, 145–46, 147f, 155, 193, 198f, 200, 213

Arens, W., 93

Ares, 63, 190

Argo (constellation), 193n

Argonautica, 169, 223

Argonauts, 223

Aries, 183, 184f, 198, 206, 208, 209f, 210t, 211

Aristides the Just, 151

Aristophanes, 90, 151, 175

Aristotle, 151

art: analytic, 99f, 105–6; eidetic, 105–6

Artemidorus, 105, 169

Artemis, 44, 54, 111f

Arthurian legend, 100, 102, 114

Asarhaddon stele, 187f

Ásgarð, 204

ash (volcanic), 6–7, 10, 27, 72–73, 80, 81f, 85, 97, 108, 222; mud from, 73

ash-cloud, 72, 76t, 76, 80, 84–88, 111, 212n, 219, 220f, 225–26, 228n; electricity in, 72–73, 77, 85; fallout from, 7, 27, 72, 76, 83, 87; height of, 76t, 76, 86–87

Asia, 94, 114, 126, 168, 193, 223

Assmann, J., 86n, 89, 91–92

assumptions, 119; of competence, 59; recognition of, 24–25; unstated, 23–25, 31–32

Assyria, 145

astrology, 199, 210

astronomers, 178–79, 205, 217

astronomical alignments (ancient), 159n, 182, 196

astronomical monuments (ancient), 159n, 181–82

astronomy, 2, 49n, 159, 162, 180, 183, 203, 212; computer programs for, 190. See also astrology

Aten, 62, 66, 92n

Atharvavedas, 216n

Athena, 46, 47f, 50–51, 60, 63–65, 86, 104, 109, 112, 145

Athens, 50, 63, 80, 86, 90, 113, 126, 140–41, 150–51, 171f, 190

Atlas, ii, 47f, 47–48

Attica, 82, 111f, 140, 148f, 173f

Attila the Hun, 127

Attraction Principle. See **Principle of Attraction**

attraction: by association, 115, 123, 190n; by name, 113–15, 117, 123, 127, 203, 240, 244; by place, 113–14, 123; by quality, 114; by shape/form, 39–40, 173, 177; by title, 115

Audun, 235–36

aurora borealis, 120

Australia, 9, 75, 94n, 97, 163, 170

Austria, 28, 31, 95

authoritative utterance, 96, 98, 99f. See also Hū

axis. See earth: axis of; pole

Baal, 210t
baboon, 55f
Babylonian culture, 145, 205n, 206, 211, 213
Baby-with-the-Bathwater Reflex, 27, **246**
back-formation, 35, 127
backwards-ness, 169, 171f, 171–72
Bagri Maro, 58
Baldr, 20, 48, 107
Bali, 170n
Balkans, 60, 70, 103, 172
baloma, 24
baptism, 174
barrow. *See* burial mound
Bartlett, Sir F., 28n, 30, 221
Basalt, 87
Basques, 90
Basuto, 244
battle myths, 6–7, 9–10, 43–44, 46, 51, 82–87, 90, 97, 119, 140, 156–57, 207, 213, 219, 226
Battle of Gods and Giants, 46, 82–85, 119
Battle of Kadesh, 90
bears, 19, 126, 134, 181f
Bellerophon, 104
Belloc, H., 154n
Beltir, 168
Beowulf, 2, 128, 154, 232–34, 237, 239
Beowulf's Hill, 234
Berawan, 170
Berossos, 204n, 213
Bhāratī, K. T., 216n
bias, 13, 89–95
Bible, 49, 115, 123–24, 154. *See also* Old Testament
birds, 14–15, 27, 102, 112, 124, 131, 134, 153, 161, 203, 205, 206f, 218–26, 220f; language of, 171, 239, 239f; as spirits, 173, 173f
black (color), 72, 105, 108, 111, 130, 134, 147, 169, 219, 225–27; why Fox's tail is, 160, 203. *See also* darkness
black constellations, 158–59, 160f
Black-Ears (Q'ursha), 226
Black Orpheus (M. Camus), 46, 121

Black Sea, 100, 203, 223, 228n
Blake, William, 231
Blessed Peak (Elbrus), 224
blindspot, 30
bloating, 28, 110n, 130, 133, 244. *See also* carcasses; corpses
blood, 28–29, 97, 112, 133, 142, 188, 206f, 219, 224–27, 239, 244
Bloomfield, L., 99
blurring of appearance and reality, 96–108, 242
Blust, R., 45n, 241
boats, celestial, 21, 99f, 125, 179, 191, 193n, 194, 203, 209–10
Bogatikov, O. A., 227–28
Bonaparte, 117
bones, 119, 125, 146, 149n, 233–34. *See also* fossils
Borneo, 170
borrowing, 45, 63–65, 128, 143, 171, 214n, 227
bracelets, in ritual, 67, 68f
Brahmans, 98
brain (human): analytic/sequential reasoning in, 14; cognitive chatter in, 27, 102; data-crunching function of, 14, 37, 127 (*see also* compression); design of, 2–3, 138, 152; and dreaming, 102, 166; experience preferred over logic by, 37–38; explanation-orientation of, 14–15, 102; filling in information by, 27, 30, 33; hemispheres of, 14–15, 102, 106; integrative function of, 14, 102, 157; language-orientation of, 4, 15; language-processing (analytic) sector of, 11, 13–14, 27, 106; and logic (*see* logic); neural networks in, 27; and novelty, 155–57; multiple systems within, 11, 14; pattern-matching in, 33, 35, 37, 123, 158; timing mechanisms in, 154n. *See also* split-brain patients
Bransford, J., and J. Franks, 30
breakage (superstitious), 168–69, 172, 173n
Brer Rabbit, 48
Briareos, 84
bribes, 36–37, 46

brides, 67, 69–70, 125–26, 145, 165, 242. *See also* marriage
Bridge of the Gods, 8n
bridges, celestial, 191n, 209
Britain, 102, 182, 239n
Bronze Age, 10, 69–70, 79, 94–95, 100, 141–42, 145, 150, 216n, 227
Buddhism, 174, 193f
Bulgaria, 67, 173
bull(s), 50, 108, 158, 183, 205, 206f; from the sea, 36, 50. *See also* Taurus
Bumping Upstairs, 145, 177, **250**
burial mound(s), 182, 232–39, 235f, 244
Burma-Shave, 155
Bury, J. B., 151
Byblos, 40, 57

Caesar, 115, 145
Calbuco, Chile, 85
caldera, 81f, 108, 109f, 110n
calendar, 66–67, 161, 167n, 178–82, 181f, 188, 194, 196, 197f, 198, 212, 214; errors in, 178–79, 212n, 214; lunar, 212n, 214
calendrical bowl, 197f
California, 22, 60n, 75, 88, 120, 167, 192f, 222
Caltech, 120, 216n
Camera Angle Problem, 56–59, 63, 80, 90–91, 94–95, 177, 190, 208n, 214, 217, 238, 240, 242, 244, **247**
Campbell, Jeremy, 12, 27, 30, 33
Campbell, Joseph, 4, 151–52
Cancer, 183, 184f, 198–99, 204n, 209f, 210t, 211
cannibals, 93
Canopus, 192n
Capella, 208n
Capricorn, 183, 184f, 204n, 208n, 209f
caps. *See* hats
carcasses, 120, 132–34, 136–37, 163. *See also* corpses
cardinal directions, 55, 194, 196–97
Caribbean magic, 102
carnassial teeth, 132–35
Carolus Magnus. *See* Charlemagne
Cassiopeia, 158, 192f

Castor, 141, 172n
catastrophists, 119
Caucasian languages, 214n
Caucasian myth and saga, 102, 223–25, 228n, 240n
Caucasus Mountains, 112, 180, 181f, 219, 223, 228
cauldrons, 110, 111f
cause and effect, 13, 15, 36, 38, 54, 121, 123, 149
Cautes, 197f, 206f
Cautopates, 206f
Ceci, S., 120
celestial events (unusual), 144, 228n
Celts, 94–95, 147, 167n
Centaur Syndrome, 146, **251**
centaurs, 12, 147, 148f
Centaurus, 159, 160f
Central America, 66, 88, 182
Central Europe, 32f, 64–65, 94–95, 102
Chalybians, 100
champion. *See* hero
change: in culture, 22, 65, 67, 128, 139, 141–42; of environment/technology, 22, 65, 142, 144–45; in language, 19, 35, 45, 64–65, 142, 128, 227 (*see also* renaming); in location (*see* migration); in pattern, 35, 139–53; in speech sounds, 64, 128
changed later forms, 45, 227–28
Changer (Pacific Northwest myth), 44
chanting, 155, 168
Chaos, 207, 209f, 210t
Charachidzé, G., 226–7
Charlemagne/Carolus Magnus, 90, 115, 145
Chela, 183, 184f
Cheops, 116
chests as boats, 40, 109
Chief Lalek, 22
Chief of the Above World, 6–7, 43
Chief of the Below World, 6–7, 10, 15, 29, 36, 49, 137
child language acquisition, 45, 57, 127–28
childbearing/birth, 65, 67, 68f, 69–70, 102, 109, 141, 169, 207–8, 211,

226–27; goddess of, 102; magic concerning, 102, 169

Children of Israel, 20–21, 91

Chiloe, 98

Chimaira, 114

China, 93–94, 114, 182, 203, 211, 237

Chinese (Han) culture, 94, 190, 212n, 237, 240

chin-rests (observational), 180, 182, 198, 212

Christ, 209f, 242

Christianity, 49, 62–63, 70, 92, 106, 167n, 205, 211

Christians, 20, 65–67, 90, 93, 106, 147, 211, 242

Chrysaor, 110, 111, 114–15n

churn (cosmic), 193, 193f, 200, 212

Circassian myths, 227

circular belt of stars, 184, 186f, 190, 192, 201. See also river of stars

Circumpolar Dropout, 19

Clark, E., 222

Class-Action Corollary, 126, **250**

clay tokens, 214–15

coffin-birth, 31–33

cognitive process/structure, 3–4, 10, 13, 27, 106, 138, 154, 163, 227, 240n; concerning numbers, 214–15, 216n; demanding coherence, 14–15, 102, 220–22

cognitive science, 10, 13, 37, 106, 120

Colarusso, J., 240n

color, 69, 81f, 97, 106, 219; classifications of, 59–60, 166

comets, 12, 177

common response to common stimulus, 4, 45n, 163, 167, 227

common source, 45, 125, 227

communal spirit, 90, 151

communication theory, 10, 155

comparative reconstruction, 61, 63, 144

complexity, 127–28, 136

compression, 2–3, 54, 113–28, 154, 177, 240–42, 244, **248**

conceptual drawing, 105–6

conflagration myths, 177, 201f, 204n, 212n

conflation, 86, 92n, 114, 117–18, 135, 166, **248**; of characters, 124–25. See also **Distillation Factor**; time: conflation/foreshortening of

Congo, 112

conjunctions of planets, 188, 190, 191f, 210

connectionism. See brain: neural networks in

consciousness/nonconsciousness, 12, 14, 27

Constantine, 242

constellations, 12–13, 121, 158–61, 160f, 183, 185, 192f; origins of, 217n; as system of markers, 182–83, 192, 196–97, 203, 217n. See also names of individual constellations

Container Corollary, 38–40, **247**

contracts. See covenants

conventionalization, 91

convergence, 45n

coordinates. See Earth; space

Copernicus, 207

Corinthians, 127, 148f

corpses, 123, 134, 164, 168, 236–38, 237f, 244; activities of, 28–29, 31–33, 32f, 110n, 238n. See also carcasses

correlation, 123

cosmic cracks, 167n

counting: of celestial cycles, 178–80, 188, 216n; god of, 178, 216n; notation for, 178, 215; with tallies, 178; with tokens, 214–15

couvade, 169

covenants, 37, 46

Cowgill, W., 63n

cow-goddess (Egyptian), 21, 21f, 53, 55

Coyote, 38–39, 48, 48n

Crab (constellation), 158, 183; Nebula, 107. See also Cancer

crafts, deities of, 50, 64, 98, 228

Crater Lake, 7–10, 8f, 27, 29, 43, 76t, 142, 156, 244

craters, 7–8, 8f, 80, 81f, 107–8, 123, 142

creation/creator myths, 39, 44, 57, 98, 167n

cremation, 28, 191

Cretaceous era, 88

Crete, 62–63, 79–80, 115, 197f, 202f
Cross (constellation), 158, 160f
cross(es): 195f, 197f; as calendrical mark-
    ers, 197f; of ecliptic and equator, 195f;
    equinoctial, 197f, 198f, 200, 201f,
    206f; solsticial, 196, 196f, 197f, 200,
    202f
crowding multitudes, 203, 210t
crystal ball (for fortune-telling), 172
crystal sphere of heavens, 184
Cucuteni/Tripolye culture, 68f
Cumaean song, 211
cuneiform, 10, 150, 187f, 213–15
Curse of Fire, 6–7, 10, 36, 43
curses, 50, 94, 99–100, 171, 171f, 238–39
cutting tool, 87. *See also* adamantine,
    blade of; sickle
Cuzco, 200
Cycladic Islands, 200
Cyclical Phenomenon, 121, **249**
Cyclopean masonry, 146, 147f
Cyclopean walls, 146, 147f
Cyclops, 108, 147f, 219

Dali (goddess), 226, 228n
The Dalles (Bridge of the Gods), 8n
Danaë, 1, 109, 110
Danaids, 127
dance, 121, 122f, 156, 168–69, 212
Danish *wederskin*, 171
Dante, 211
darkness ("Egyptian"), 72, 74, 77, 85–86,
    219, 224–25
data. *See* information
dates, setting of, 178, 180
dating, 8–9, 75, 88, 100, 199, 227–28. *See
    also* ice-dating; radiocarbon dating
Davidson, H., 51, 57, 65, 239n
dead, feeding the, 66, 103; festivals/
    rituals of the, 66, 168–69; land of the,
    2, 58, 164, 168, 175, 179, 190–91 (*see
    also* Underworld; reversal); lord of the,
    40, 167n; pathways for the, 191n, 206,
    209–10; return of the, 66, 103, 166,
    169, 236; souls of the, 57, 103, 164,
    175, 206
death, 56, 72, 76t, 77, 105, 118, 130,

    170n, 191; cause of, 130–31, 133, 135,
        164, 167, 174; and resurrection, 179,
        183, 226 (*see also* dying god; Earth)
decapitation, 28, 109–11, 118, 126, 236,
    237f, 239f, 242
decomposition, 28, 32, 136, 174
degree (as system of measurement), 182,
    205, 216
Deino, 110
Deïphontes, 141
Delilah Effect, 124, 177, **249**
Delilah, 123–24, 152
Deloria, V., Jr., 8n
Delos, 200
Delphi, 125, 200, 208, 208n
Demeter, 207
demons, 69, 93–94, 143, 146, 226; tug-
    ging against gods, 193f, 213
Deneb, 199f
details: as clue-carriers, 240–41; obscur-
    ing of, 240–42, 244; reduction of,
    240–42
Deukalion, 125, 127, 208
Devil, 147. *See also* demons
Día de los Muertos, 66
Diachronic Power Principle, 144–45,
    205, **250**
dialogue as embellishment, 156–57
Diana, 44
difference, absolute, 118, 120, 146, 149
diffusion, 45n, 208n, 211
dimensionality, 216n
dinosaurs, 88, 117, 149
Dionysus, 151
Dippers (Big and Little), 12, 192f, 240;
    names for (Bear, Spoon,
    Wain/Wagon), 192
distanciation, 91n, 117n
Distillation Factor, 125, 127, **250**
divination of future, 104, 165, 167, 172
Dneipr River, 65
dog: many-headed, 114; winged, 226
domain of deity, 51, 66
Dorus/Dorians, 127
double axe (Minoan), 197f, 200, 202f
double belief, 62–63, 65. *See also*
    syncretism

doubles, 164, 166–68, 172, 174–75
Doublet Clue, 65, **248**
doublets (in vocabulary), 64–65, 126,
    200. *See also* syncretism
Draco, 198f, 199f, 208n, 240. *See also*
    dragons; Pytho[n]
dragons, 2, 198–99f, 231–44, 239f; bene-
    ficent, 240; bones of, 233–34; cosmic,
    240, 244 (*see also* Draco; Pytho[n]);
    dispossessed, 198–99f, 240; early de-
    pictions of, 239f, 239n; fiery, 232–35;
    generic, 240, 244; as guarding treasure,
    232–35, 244; having bad smell, 232–
    33, 236, 238; poisonous, 233, 238;
    rainbow, 240–41, 244; unknowable
    shape of, 234, 239f, 240; vanishing of,
    233–34; word for, as attractor, 240
dramatists, 90, 140–41, 151–52, 175,
    223, 229
Draupnir, 100
Dravidian, 94
dreams, 24, 102–5, 164–67, 169,
    172–74. *See also* Artemidorus
dress (ritual), 169
Durendal, 100
Dutch *weerschijn,* 170
dwarf-holes, 95
dwarves, 94–95, 228
dying god, 40, 121, 179, 183, 190

Ea, 87, 87n.1, 210t
Eagle Rock (California), 222
eagles, ii, 2, 33, 64, 134, 218–19, 220f,
    222–26
Earth, 84, 87; as coordinate system, 201,
    201f, 204; as Mother, 87n, 125, 207–8,
    210t, 212n; periodically destroyed,
    121, 122f, 177, 201, 201f, 203–4, 212;
    periodically regenerated, 201, 201f,
    203–4
earth (planet): axis of, 181f, 193–94,
    195f, 198–99f, 198–200; center of,
    125, 193f; as center of world, 66, 186f,
    207; shape of, 62, 201, 201f; tipping
    of, 181f, 182, 194, 195f, 199; underside
    of, 179, 184 (*see also* Underworld); as
    wobbly top, 198–99. *See also* Earth

earthquakes, 6–7, 20, 36, 41, 50, 63, 75n,
    79–80, 82f, 82–84, 87–88, 107, 142,
    144, 224–26, 229. *See also* giants
Earth-Shaker (Poseidon), 50, 87n, 145
East Europe, 67, 68f, 69. *See also* Eastern
    Orthodox Church; Slavs
Easter eggs, 158
Eastern Orthodox Church, 70n, 125, 242
Ebbinghaus, H., 12, 157
ebb-tide, 106
Echidna, 114, 114–15n
echo, 166
eclipses, 182; total solar, 185, 186f, 188
ecliptic, 182–83, 184f, 195f, 196, 198f,
    201f; angle of, 184, 186f (*see also* earth:
    tipping of); axis/pole of, 192n, 198f;
    plane of, 181f, 195f, 200–201, 201f
Edda (Sturluson), 20
Egypt, 20, 39–40, 55, 62, 77, 85–87,
    91–94, 115, 126, 143, 169, 182, 237f
Egyptian astronomy, 178–79, 183, 193n,
    196, 198–99f, 199, 212, 214
Egyptian hieroglyphics, 150
Egyptian myth/religion, 2, 20–21, 22f,
    39–40, 55, 57–58, 62, 66, 92, 98, 143,
    169, 174, 178–79, 183, 193n, 237f;
    cow-goddess, 21, 21f, 53, 55; sun-
    worship, 2, 21–22, 40, 54, 55f, 66, 179,
    186f, 187f
Egyptians: 51, 53, 90–94, 116, 126, 163,
    173, 236, 237f; approach to art of, 99f,
    105–6; language of, 94
Eileithyia, 102
El, 187f, 210t
Elbrus (Elbruz), 220f, 223–24, 226–29
electrical charge, 72, 85, 225. *See also*
    lightning
Elephant and Castle, 142–43
Eleusis, 111f
elevator etiquette, 18
Eliade, M., 168, 175
Elijah (*Ilja*), 67
Elizabeth I, 116, 146
Elwin, V., 58
emasculation, 207, 210t
embalming, 40, 183
embellishment of stories, 11, 33, 156

empirical collection of principles, 3, 16, 130
end of the world, 201, 211. *See also* Earth: periodically destroyed
enemies. *See* adversaries
English (language): American, 61, 128; color words in, 59; double vocabulary in, 64, 128; French borrowings in, 64, 128; homonyms in, 128; Middle, 128; misunderstood, 23; vocabulary: *apron*, 142; *bad*, 45; *bear/bruin*, 19; *caldera/cauldron*, 110n; *frappe*, 23; *have*, 45; *hocus pocus*, 135n; *Jehovah*, 19; *mama*, 45; *milkshake*, 23; *new*, 45; *pea(se)*, 35; *porridge*, 61, 100; *sandwich*, 45; *stood*, 45; *widdershins/withershins*, 170; *wit*, *wisdom*, 55n. *See also* Old English
English lore, 102, 114, 117, 126, 172, 232, 242
Enki, 61, 185, 210t
Enkidu, 104
Enlil, 61, 145, 210t
Enoch, 117–18
Environmental Clue, 142, **250**. *See also* change; **Restructuring Principle**
Enyo, 110
Eon (years in), 213
Eos, 54
Epic of Gilgamesh, 104, 125, 154, 187f. *See also* Gilgamesh
Epimetheus, 151
epithets, 50, 155–56
Eponymous Hero Syndrome, 126–27, **250**
equator: of earth, 170, 181f, 194, 195f, 196f; celestial, 194, 195f, 198f, 201f; plane of, 194, 195f
equinoxes, 159n, 181f, 184f, 194, 196–97, 198f, 199–201, 201f, 205, 206f, 209f; fall, 197f, 210; spring, 197f, 205n, 208–9, 210t, 211
Erebos, 207
error, magnification of, 178–79, 205, 213
eruption(s), of volcanos, 7–8, 13, 23, 27, 29, 43–44, 50, 72–88, 90, 109f, 123, 142, 177, 219–30, 220f; aspect of by day *vs.* by night, 86; death toll from,

76t, 77; explosive, 8, 13, 43, 73–85, 81–83f, 87, 114; hot ejecta from, 6–7, 73–74, 76t, 78, 83–85, 87; idiosyncratic pattern of, 84–85, 88; metaphors for, 107–12, 144; noise from, 73, 75, 82–87, 97, 107–8, 110, 114; Pelean, 75; phreatomagmatic, 80, 85; at rift, 144; sequential analysis of, 84–85, 228n; size of, 8, 76t. *See also* ash; ash-cloud; lava; volcano
Essay on the Original Genius of Homer (Wood), vii
Ether, 207
Ethiopia, 36
ethnography, 63, 67, 69–70, 180. *See also* folklore
Etna, 7, 13, 64, 85, 108n, 112, 227
Etruscans, 23
Etzel, 127n
Eucharist, 135n
Eudoxos, 217n
Euhemeros, 157, 177
euphemisms, 19
Eurasia, 61, 94, 147, 171, 200, 211
Euripides, 141, 151
Europe, 56, 63, 92, 134, 167n, 182, 240n. *See also* Central Europe; Scandinavia; *and individual countries*
European culture, 31n, 68f, 92, 182
Euryale, 110
Eusebius, 242
evening star, 188
Evenki, 9
evidence, 2, 22, 31, 54, 66, 90–91, 119–20, 123, 130–32, 136–38, 140n, 149–50, 244
Excalibur, 100. *See also* Arthurian legend; Sword in the Stone
exhumation, 31–32
Exodus (Book of), 20, 85, 86, 91, 219
Explanation Corollary, 15, **245**
explanation, 36, 42, 53, 56, 58, 119, 142, 164, 177, 221, 234; *vs.* observation, 8, 13, 15, 26–29, 31–32, 42, 50, 135–36, 229, 234, 236, 244; scientific, 36, 38, 42, 45, 56, 119–20, 149, 151, 241; "truth" in, 27

extension (analogical), 35
eye(s), 59, 109–10; all-seeing, 54, 54–55n; celestial, 54, 55f, 55n, 159, 160f;* as light-giver, 54–55, 107–8
eyewitnesses, 7, 33, 88, 112

factoring, 215–16; as linchpin of early math, 216n
Fafnir, 238–40, 239f
Fair Maiden, 44
Fairest-of-them-All Effect, 89–95, 127, **248**
Fallacy of Affirming the Consequent, 37–38, 40, 163, 173n, **246**
false beliefs, 120
feedback, 18
ferries, celestial, 191n
fertility, 36, 50, 56, 57, 65, 67, 69, 121, 126, 197f; figurines for, 68f; motifs for, 68f, 197f
festivals, dates for, 66–67, 178, 180, 197f
figurines, 68f, 69–70, 171f
Finnic myths, 211–12
fire, 111, 145, 167, 177, 191, 222, 232–38; acquisition of by mortals, 38–39, 64, 218–19, 224–25, 228; aspect by day *vs.* by night, 86, 219; breathing of, 114, 232–34; celestial, 191, 204; destruction of world periodically by, 201f, 204; domestic *vs.* wild, 229; pillar of, 80, 83–84, 86, 219; residences for, 38–39, 225; river of: *see* lava flows. *See also* eruption(s), of volcanos; lava; metalworking; volcano
firebird, 120, 149
fire-drill (cosmic), 193f, 200, 212
fire-pit graves, 237
FitzGerald, E., 195
flint, 38, 43, 207
Flintstone, Fred, 117
Flood (universal), 46, 124–25, 127, 176–77, 190n, 193n, 201, 201f, 203–4, 212n, 213
flooding, 56–57, 73, 177, 203; of Nile, 57, 121
FOAFs, 93
Fogging Effect, 107, 138, 142, 226, 229, **248**

folklore, 3, 44, 114, 119, 124, 158, 166, 170, 222, 240
Fontenrose, J., 240–42
foreign devils, 94
forensic science, 32, 120, 134
foreshortening, 116
forgetting, 12, 19. *See also* **Lethe Effect**
forging metals, 64, 95. *See also* metal-working; smithy
form. *See* images
formulaic expressions, 155–56, 241
fossils, 119, 146, 149n, 228n, 240n
fountains, 107, 167
Fox Spirit, 19
Fox (Andean), 153, 159–61, 160f, 183, 203
Fox, D., 242
fractions, 58, 214–15, 216n
France, 64, 68f, 90, 93
Francisco de Avila, 158
Frankenstein (Shelley), 230
Frankfort, H. and H. A., 42, 46, 56
frappe *vs.* milkshake, 23
Frazer, Sir J., 97–98
French (language): loans to English, 64; vocabulary: *sandwich*, 45
Freud, S., 152, 169
Freyja/ Frigg, 65
fringes, 68f, 69, 70n
Frodhi's Grotte, 193
frogs, 38–39, 67, 68f. *See also* Aristophanes
Frost Giants, 56, 143–44
Frost, Robert, 60–61
funerary supplies, 40, 57

Gaia, 209f, 210t, 212n. *See also* Earth
galaxy, 192
Galileo, 66
Gazzaniga, M., 14–15
Gemini, 182–83, 184f, 192, 199, 201f, 208, 209, 209f, 210t, 211
generalization (linguistic), 35
Genesis (Book of), 98, 117–18, 124, 162, 177, 203, 212n.17
geological reconstruction/verification, 7–8, 23, 29, 84, 227–28

geology, 2, 13, 75–76, 84–85, 88, 107, 112, 119, 144, 177, 203, 207, 219–20

Georgian myth, 226

German (vocabulary): *hab-*, 45; *Kaiser*, 115, 145; *Schatten*, 166; *Wiederschein*, 170

Germanic languages, 45, 64–65, 166; proto-Germanic, 64; *Ymir*, 167n

Germanic literature, 154–55, 232

Germanic myth, 4, 48, 62, 94–95, 100, 144, 172, 212, 232, 238, 244. *See also* Norse myth

Germanic tribes, 143–44, 211

Geryon, 114, 114–15n

giants, 46, 51, 82–84, 87–88, 97, 104, 106, 110, 114n, 118–19, 142, 146, 226–27, 236; bleeding, 142 (*see also* blood); bones of, 119, 146, 149n; as chained down, ii, 56, 63, 84, 144, 219–20, 224–26, 229; clawing, 36; *vs.* gods, 48, 56, 64, 82, 144, 227, 229; as inherently evil, 48, 56, 64, 82, 142, 144; one-eyed, 108–9, 219; as throwing rocks, 84, 108, 142, 144, 147f, 219–21; writhing, 20, 107, 142, 144, 229. *See also* Frost Giants

Gilbert, W. S., 96, 162

Gilgamesh, 90n, 104, 177. See also *Epic of Gilgamesh*

Ginnungagap, 210t

Giza, 116, 183

Gleipnir, 100

goat, 207

God, 49, 65, 98, 118, 124, 145, 219, 224, 226–27; challenges to, 49, 226–27, 230

gods: departure of, 92; as inherently good, 48, 55–56, 64, 82, 144

gold, 21, 48, 94–95, 107, 109–11, 125, 226, 232–34, 236, 238, 239f

Golden Age (classical), 209–10, 209f

Golden Age Phenomenon, 118–20, 145–47, 149n, **249**

Golden Calf, 17, 20–21

Golden Race, 211

Goldilocks Principle, 61, 100, **247**

Gonds (in India), 58

Gorgons, 1–2, 109–10, 111f, 112

Götterdämmerung (Wagner), 204

government agents, 130, 135–36

grafting of deities, 63–65

Graiai, 110, 112

grain goddess, 48

Gravettian era, 70

Great Spirit, 43, 222

Greco-Roman tradition, 4, 44, 171f, 172

Greece, 23, 47f, 48, 67, 76t, 80, 104–5, 11f, 112, 115, 119, 143–46, 147f, 171f, 191f, 192f, 203, 240

Greek alphabet, 82n, 150, 171

Greek art, ii, 47f, 70, 111f, 145, 148f, 173f

Greek (language): 64, 94, 105n; color words, 59–60, 166; vocabulary: *adamant-*, 110n, 207; *áristos*, 63; *árktos*, 19; *bárbaroi*, 94; *eídō*, 55n; *eídolon*, 166; *ekklēsía*, 242; *elephair-*, 105; *elephant-*, 105; *galakt-*, 192; *kéras*, 105; *klé(w)os*, 237n; *krain-*, 105; *lēthē*, 19n; *mŷthos*, 149; *né(w)os*, 45; *oîda*, 55n; *phoîbos*, 54; *skiá*, 166; *statós*, 45; *tékhnē*, 50; *trop-*, 194, 195f; *Zeû páter*, 62n

Greek myth, 2, 4, 19, 54, 62, 64, 104, 114, 140–45, 151, 156, 171, 185, 190–91, 212n, 219, 223, 228, 242

Greeks, 2, 23, 56, 59–60, 63–65, 70, 83, 115–16, 140–44, 193n, 205, 212, 223, 242; early science/philosophy of, 13, 149–51, 205, 212, 217

Greene, M., 58–59, 84–85, 108n, 228n

Greenland ice sheets, 76, 228n

Grettir, 235–37

Grice, P., 9n

Grimm Brothers, 95, 98n

Grimnismal, 213

Gudea, 104

Güterbock, H., 87n

Gyges (Ring of), 84

Gylfaginning (Sturluson), 176, 204

Hades, 175, 207

hair, 22–23, 123–24, 147, 163, 219; golden, 48, 226, 228; red, 22, 97, 107, 109, 219. *See also* snaky locks

Halley's Comet, 144

Halloween, 66, 167n
Hallstatt culture, 95
hallucination/hallucinogens, 165–66, 168, 171
Hamlet, 193, 200
Hamlet's Mill (Santillana and Dechend). *See* Santillana and Dechend
Harappans, 212
harmony, theory of, 216n
Harrison, J., 177
Harva, U., 165, 167–68, 175
hats/caps, 94–95, 100, 101f, 110, 206f, 226
Hawaii, 7, 48, 79, 108, 109f, 144
Hawaiian language: *pele*, 144; *wai/kai/moana*, 61
Hawaiian myth/culture, 9, 48, 55n, 61, 88, 144, 204, 217
head of prodigy, 1, 2, 22, 58, 63, 100, 107, 109–12, 111f, 114, 123, 126, 239f. *See also* decapitation
headland, 232, 234–35
heart, 224–25, 239, 239f
Hebrew (language/writing), 19; *YHWH/Yahweh*, 19, 21
Hebrew culture, 19–21, 91
Hedging Your Bets, 62, 66–67, 179, 191, 234, **247**
Heel Stone, 182
Helen (of Troy), 140–41, 189
heliacal rising, 178, 182–83, 184f, 185, 197
heliacal setting, 182–83
Helios, 54, 126, 190
Hellen/Hellenes, 127
Hellenistic culture, 19n, 70
hemispheres (of earth), 3, 160f, 170, 177, 181f, 192, 194, 203
Hent-Taui papyrus, 55f
Hephaistos, 64, 190, 219, 227
Hera, 119, 126, 207
Heraclitus, 213
Herakles, 2, 47f, 47–49, 87n, 102, 114–15, 141, 175
Heraklidai, 127
Herculaneum, 76t, 80
Hercules, 2, 199f. *See also* Herakles

Heretic Syndrome, 66, **248**
heretics, 65–66, 92
Hermes, 48, 109, 190
Hermione, 141
Herodotus, 126
heroes, 93n, 118–19, 157, 241; size of, 119
heroines (in Greek tragedy), 140
Hesiod, 82–95, 107–8, 118, 154, 207–8, 218–19, 221, 223, 225
Hestia, 207
Hilo, Hawaii, 79
hindsight bias, 13, 221n
Hindu mythology, 193f
Hipparchos, 205–7, 213
Hippolytos, 50
historical relatedness, 45, 227
Hittites, 80, 86–87, 90, 100, 101f, 111, 210t, 211
The Hobbit, 232
hocus pocus, 135n
Hoddmímir's Wood, 204
Hoffmann, E.T.A., 173n
Hoffner, H., 87n
Hollywood, 103, 131, 175
Homer, vii, 50, 60n, 70, 90n, 105, 136, 140n, 154–57, 166, 190, 237; puns in, 105n
homonyms, 128
Hopi, 94
hops, 67, 68f, 69
horizon, 180, 181f, 193n, 196f, 203, 216; distinctive, 180, 181f, 182
Horn of Plenty, 208
horn(s), 43, 100, 105–6, 147, 208
Horner, J., 240n
horses, 50, 58, 147, 148f, 169, 228, 238, 239f, 243; eight-legged, 57–58, 57f; winged, 12, 110–11, 225
horticulture, 140
Hū, 96, 98, 99f
Huarochirí, 153, 158–59, 183
Hulst, C., 242
human hide, 148–49
Humane Society of Utah, 129–30
humanoids, humongous, 142, 146, 149n
Humbaba, 104

humor, 25, 105n, 120, 136, 158, 190, 221, 236. *See also* trickery
Hurrians, 150
hybrid creatures, 144, 146–47, 148f. *See also* centaurs; dog: winged; horses: winged
Hydra, 115
Hyginus, 109
Hyksos, 91–93
Hynes, W., 25
Hyperboreans, 112
Hyperion, 54
Hyrnetho, 141

I/Thou principle, 42–43, 88. *See also* **Willfulness Principle**
ice/snow, 22–23, 132, 143–44, 222, 228n
ice-dating, 8, 76, 228n
Iceland, 20, 106, 111, 144
Icelandic myth, 106, 235, 236n
iconoclasm, 174
icons: of the Mother of God, 67; of the Savior, 67
Idavöll, 204
Iliad, 237n. *See also* Homer
Ilmarinen, 188
images, 39–40, 67, 102, 166, 168, 183, 220, 242. *See also* icons; Rorschach images
Inca, 67, 212n
independent invention, 45n, 227
India, 58, 60n, 94, 121, 164, 203, 211, 216n
Indic language, 94, 171. *See also* Sanskrit
Indic myth/culture, 62, 94, 121, 171, 212–13, 216
Indo-European language(s), 45, 54–55n, 63–64, 214n, 226, 237n; vocabulary (PIE): *$^*h_2rktos$*, 19; *$^*yem$*-, 167n
Indo-European myth, 4, 61, 143–45, 227–28, 237n
Indo-Europeans, 58, 61, 63, 65, 237; break-up of, 65, 227–28
Indonesia, 76t, 203
Indra, 62
Infanta of Castille, 143
information: biased selection of, 89–95;

in brain, 14 (*see also* brain: memory); compression of (*see* compression); critical mass of, 3, 13, 45, 65, 102, 113, 149, 179; dreams as source of, 103–5 (*see also* dreams); encoding of, 2–3, 9, 11, 13, 57, 69, 104, 144, 155, 158, 160, 177, 179–80, 205; loss of, 10, 12, 19–22, 112, 136; new *vs.* old, 11–12, 18, 97, 155–57; outside, 20; reconstruction of, 163; stockpiling of, 3, 15, 149–51; storage of, 2 (*see also* memory; writing); survival of, 7–9, 70, 155, 205, 213; transmission of, 2–3, 9–11, 29, 97, 154, 178, 205, 213, 217; winnowing of, vii, 3, 5, 154 (*see also* **Distillation Factor**). *See also* oral transmission; myth: longevity of; stability
inheritance: from common ancestor, 45, 227; systems, 63, 140–41
Inman, 120–21
Innana, 189
inside out. *See* inversion
instrumentalization, 91
insubstantialness, 166
integers, 215–16
Interpretation of Dreams (Artemidorus), 105, 169
interstellar dust-clouds, 159, 160f
Inuit, 94
inversion, 168–69, 171–72. *See also* reversal; Underworld
invisibility, 42, 110, 167, 172
Io, 126
Ion/Ionians, 127
Iran, 126, 211, 214n
Iranian (language): *Aryā-*, 63
Iranians, 65, 126, 211, 225n. *See also* Persians
Ireland, 94, 147, 182, 191n
Irish myth, 62, 156, 167n
Iron Age, 70, 94–95, 237
iron, 94, 100, 238; smelting of, 100
Isaiah (Book of), 49
Ishtar, 187f, 189
Isis, 40, 57, 62, 183, 193n, 203
isolation of people, 93. *See also* **Zone-of-Convenient-Remove Syndrome**

Italy, 76t, 80
Ivan Kupala, 67

Jack and Jill, 99
Jacobsen, T., 40n, 42n, 43, 51
Jalé, 60n
Jamison, S., 61
Japan, 44, 112
Jehovah/Yahweh, 19n
Jelling, Denmark, 235f
Jewish people, 92–93
Jocasta, 152
John (Gospel of), 98
John the Baptist, 67
Johnny Appleseed, 114
Jokul's Gift, 236
Jones, D., 240, 241n
Jove. *See* Jupiter
Judges (Book of), 123
Jung, C. G., 4, 151, 152n
Jupiter, 40, 62, 109, 143, 185, 188, 189f,
    190, 191f, 194, 196n, 210, 213; sidereal
    period of, 185
Justus, C., 214n
Jutland, Denmark, 235f

Kallirhoe, 114–15n
Kamapua'a, 144
Kamchatka, 112
Kamehameha I, 9
Kane, P., 220f
Kar the Old, 235–36
Kassite boundary stone, 187f
Katsina cult, 185n
Katz, J., 61, 111n, 135n
kennings, 155
Kephalonia, Greece, 171f
Kepler, Johannes, 189f
Kerameikos cemetery, 171f
Kerberos, 114–15
Keto, 110
Khufu, 183
Kiev, 67
Kilauea, 13, 88, 108, 144
King of Iruath, 156
King of the May, 126
King of Ulster, 156

king-lists, 117, 213
Kingship in Heaven (change of), 86,
    190, 207–8, 210t, 211
Kinship Principle, 44, 115n, 227, **247**;
    among deities, 22, 43–45, 63, 109–10
Kishar, 210t
Klamath myth/culture, 6–8, 11, 22, 29,
    123, 142
Klee, Paul, 105
knots, 102
Koreans, 93
Korinthos, 127
Kottos, 84
Krakatoa, 13, 75–79, 76t
Kreon, 139–40
Kronos, 118, 185, 207–8, 209f, 210t, 211
Krupp, E. C., 180
Kullervo, 188
Kumarbi, 86, 210t
Kumulipo, 204

La Tène Celts, 95
Laertes, 141
Lake Tritonis, 112
language(s), 3, 14, 59–61, 94, 99, 143,
    150, 155; change in, 19, 35, 45, 64–65,
    128, 142, 227 (*see also* renaming); as
    complex system, 127–28; design prop-
    erties of, 2, 10, 59, 121, 127–28; for-
    mulaic, 61, 100, 241; marking in, 155;
    misdivision in, 142–43; as parallel to
    myth, 3–4, 11, 35, 64, 93, 127–28, 142;
    reconstruction of, 19, 61, 214n; rever-
    sals in, 171f, 171–72; syntax in, 61,
    127–28, 146. *See also* borrowing; child
    language acquisition; linguistics; name
    magic; *and individual languages*
lapis lazuli, 61, 97, 106
Lappish culture, 165
Lares and Penates, 66
Larson, Gary, 232
Latin (language), 115, 194; vocabulary:
    Jupiter/Jove, 62n; *novus,* 45; *status,* 45;
    ursus, 19; *video,* 55n
lava, 6–7, 10–11, 43, 75, 81f, 107–12,
    109f, 142, 241; by day *vs.* by night, 86,
    219; colors of, 81f; lava bombs, 7, 10,

lava (*cont.*)
  27, 78, 80, 83f; lava flows, 6–7, 9–10,
    23, 27, 29, 43, 87, 108, 111, 115, 144,
    163, 226–27, 228n; lava fountains,
    107, 111; lava lakes, 108, 109f, 226–27,
    228n; lava mud, 79; metaphors for,
    107–12; temperature of, 108. *See also*
    eruption(s), of volcanos; magma
laws, 63, 92–93; legal documents, 150
Le Chanson de Roland, 90
Leda, 141
left (direction), 14, 167–70; as
    negative/wrong, 169–70
Leo, 183, 184f, 197, 205, 209f, 210t, 211
lepers, 92–93
Lepesovka, 197f
Lernaian Hydra, 114
Lespugue, France, 68f
Lethe Effect, 19, 22, **245**. *See also* loss;
    River of Forgetfulness
Lethe River, 19n
Levant, 20, 40, 91, 179n, 217n
Lévi-Strauss, C., 50n
Libra, 183, 184f, 209f, 210t
Libya, 112
Libye/Libyans, 94, 126
life span, 117–18
lightning, 40, 56, 62–63, 72–74, 77, 83–
    85, 111, 143, 219, 221, 224–25, 238
linguistic process, 3, 11, 45, 93, 97,
    127–28, 142–43, 146
linguistics, 3, 11, 19–20, 30, 59, 61, 64,
    94, 99, 111, 127–18, 155, 166, 228; of
    counting, 214–15
lions, 12, 37, 107–8, 114–15, 132, 134,
    183, 197, 205. *See also* Leo
literacy, 2–3, 27, 80, 90n, 106, 124,
    149–52, 205; personal, 150–51
Little Black (flying horse), 225
Littleton C. S., 75n, 102n, 207
live burial, 31–32
liver, ii, 96, 218–19, 221, 223, 225
Llama (celestial "black cloud"), 159, 160f
llamas, 12, 158–59, 160f, 201, 203
Logi, 229
Logic Cross-check, 29, 167, 225, **246**
logic, 29, 36, 120, 123, 139, 142, 151–52,

168; fallacies of, 37–38, 123. *See also*
    Fallacy of Affirming the Consequent
Loki, 20, 33, 48–49, 64, 107, 144,
    228–29. *See also* Útgarð-Loki
longevity. *See* myth: longevity of;
    stability
Lord, A., 156
Lord's Prayer, 172
loss, 19, 21–22; of key ideas, 207; of
    visible referent, 107. *See also* **Fogging
    Effect**; **Lethe Effect**; River of
    Forgetfulness
lozenge motifs, 68f, 69, 70n
Lucifer, 49
luck, 169–70, 172
Lucretius, 211
Luvian Hittite storm god, 111
Lyell, Sir C., 119

macaw, 171
Macrobius, 180
Maelstrom, 200
Magi, 210
magic, 67, 69, 95, 96, 102; sympathetic,
    102. *See also* name magic
magma: chamber, 8, 85; composition
    of, 13, 107; molten, 108, 109f. *See
    also* lava
Mahābhārata, 193f, 213
Maikop, 181f
Makalii, 204. *See also* Pleiades
Malay death charm, 96
Malcor, L., 102n
Malinowski, B., 24–25
Mallia, Crete, 197f, 202f
Man who Survived the Flood, 187f
Manetho, 92
Mann, Thomas, 11
maps (ethnocentric), 94
Marduk, 145, 188
marriage, 67, 69, 105, 125–26, 140–41,
    152, 157; foreseeing, 165–67; sacred,
    36. *See also* brides
Mars, 188, 190, 191f, 194, 196n
Marshack, A., 178
Martinique, 76t, 85
Masse, W. B., 9, 49n

Masters, A., 31–33
mathematics (ancient), 58; notation for, 149, 178, 215; refined approximations in, 213. *See also* number(s)
matrilineal system, 63, 140–41
Matthew effect, 124n
Maui, 48
Mauna Ulu, 108, 109f
Mawangdui, 237
May Day, 126, 167n
Mayan myth, 49n, 279
Mayon, Philippines, 112
Mayor, A., 2, 8n, 119, 149n, 240n
meaning: clouding of, 9; construction of, 30
Medea, 126, 140
Medes, 126
Mediterranean Sea, 40, 217; cultures around, 54, 64, 106, 108, 217, 242; floor of, 80; volcanic zone across, 84–85, 88
Medos, 126
Medusa, 109, 110, 111f, 112, 114–15n, 126; sisters of, 111f, 112
megalithic structures, 119, 146, 181–82
megaron, 145
Meli-Shipak II boundary stone, 187f
Melos, 112
memorability, 3, 10–13, 93n, 100, 150, 154–55, 158, 179. *See also* mnemonic devices; vividness
Memory Crunch Principle, 3, 5–16, 114, **245**
memory, vii, 11–13, 33, 90, 116, 117n, 124, 154–55, 244; biases in, 13, 89–95; cultural, 90–91; distortion of, 91–92, 221; limitations on, 3, 9, 13, 114, 154, 244; mapping onto, 158; reconstruction of, 90, 221; selection in, 91; simplification of, 91, 124; stable state of, 2 21n, 225–26; tests/experiments concerning, 12–13, 30, 221
Memphite Theology, 39, 98
Menelaos, 141
mental search image, 240n
Mercury, 188, 190, 191f, 194, 196n
Merton, R., 124n

Mesopotamia, 104, 145, 187f, 214n, 217, 240
Mesopotamians, 51–52, 61, 116, 150, 186f, 187f, 214, 216n, 240
metalworking, 64, 95, 100, 107, 145, 228–29
Metaphoric Reality Principle, 96–112, 114, 242, 244, **248**
metathesis, 171, 225n
meteor(ite), 49, 88, 100, 208n
meter (poetic), 154, 156
methane (marsh) gas, 237–39, 241
Methuselah Effect, 118, **249**
Methuselah, 2, 117–18
Middle (medieval) Ages, 90, 92, 102, 145, 147, 149, 154
Middle High German, 166
migrations, 9, 22, 90, 95, 107, 112, 126–27, 137, 142–44, 154, 182
Milky Way, 158, 184f, 191–92, 209; ferry/bridge to, 208–10; guarded, 187f
mill-wheel (cosmic), 192–93, 200; unseating of, 200, 212
Milton, John, 90n
Minerva, 50. *See also* Athena
mines/mining, 94–95
Minoans, 23, 63, 79–80, 82f, 83f, 106, 114, 197f, 200, 202
Minos, 115
Minotaur, 114
Mirdite, Albania, 68f
mirror-image, 165–68, 170
mirrors, 165–69, 172
Mismatch Effect, 71–75, 146, 156, **248**
mismatch (cultural/linguistic), 59–62
Mithraic cult, 197f, 205–6, 206f
Mithras, 205, 206f, 209f, 217
Mjöllnir, 100, 204
mnemonic devices, 12, 150, 153–60, 225–26, 234, 237n, 244
Moby-Dick (Melville), 133
Modoc myth, 22
monotheism, 65–66, 92
monsters. *See* giants
months, 178, 183

moon, 12, 21f, 185, 187f, 194, 196n, 240;
    apparent size of, 205; as god, 44, 55f,
    178; as goddess, 44, 54, 206f; path of,
    182, 184f; phases/cycles of, 55f, 178,
    185, 188, 189n, 190, 214
Mordvins, 70
morning star, 188–89
Moses, 20, 86
Moslems, 172, 174
motifs, 240–42
mound. *See* burial mound
Mount Adams, 43, 222
Mount Baker, 43
Mount Hood, 13, 43, 222
Mount Lassen, 13
Mount Mazama, 7, 8f, 13, 29, 43, 75, 76t
Mount Pelée, Martinique, 76t
Mount Pinatubo, 7, 13, 76t
Mount Rainier, 43, 87
Mount Shasta, 6, 7, 8, 13, 22–23, 43
Mount St. Helens, 7, 8, 13, 72, 75, 76t,
    87, 220f
Mount Vilcacoto (Huillcacoto), 201–2
mountain: binding of god to, 2, 20, 33,
    48, 64, 219; as celestial pole/axis, 193,
    193f, 208, 213; as home of deity, 6–7,
    15, 22, 35, 46, 82, 104, 137; as kin, 43–
    44; summit of, 107–9, 111, 219, 222–
    26, 228n
Movie Construct Principle, 28n, 31–33,
    49, 64, 82, 135, 203, 221n, 222, 229,
    246
Müller, M., 143, 177
multiple aspects, 39–40, 53–70, 72, 179,
    192; as good/evil, 56; as positive/
    negative, 56; as wild/tame, 50, 50n, 229
Multiple-Aspects Principle, 53–70, 166,
    183, **247**
multitudes (crowding), 203
mummification, 163, 169, 174
mutilation of animals, 129–37, 149
Mutnovsky, 112
Mycenae, 80, 146, 147f
Mycenaean Greeks, 58, 80, 141, 145
Myers-Briggs tests, 152n
myth(s): of catastrophe, 9, 82, 88, 154,
    177; as fiction, 2, 154, 244; garbling of,
    23; as history, 2–4, 9, 157, 177; of indi-
    viduals, 93n, 125–27, 157, 177, 244; as
    natural history, 2, 157, 177–78, 190,
    217, 244; longevity of, 7–9, 160–61,
    172, 177, 190, 205, 213, 217, 223, 244;
    theories of, 177; verifiability of, 3, 217
mythic thinking, contemporary, 130, 138,
    152

Nagling, 233
name magic, 92, 94, 97–100, 102
names, as attractors (*see* attraction);
    frozen, 184f; of individuals, 115, 145,
    177. *See also* renaming; titles
Narmer, 237f
narrative: creation of, 157; as memory-
    aid, 12, 157–58, 183; reduction of, 240
narrativization, 91
Narrinyeri tribe, 164
Narts, 224–25. *See also* Caucasian myth
    and saga
Nasran, 224–25
natural laws, 45. *See also* explanation:
    scientific
Nausicaa, 140n
Navajo, 94
navel of the world, 200, 208, 240
navigation, 13, 161, 197–98, 200, 204,
    217n, 240
Near East, 36, 104n, 178–79, 203, 206,
    211–14
Neblett, W., 38n, 123
Necessity, 212
Nechtan, 62
Nemean lion, 114, 115
Neolithic era, 65, 67–70, 68f, 179n, 182,
    212, 216n, 227, 237
Neptune, 62–63, 145
Neugebauer, O., 216n
neural network. *See* brain
New Guinea, 44, 60n
New Year (Egyptian), 178
Newgrange, 182, 191n
Newman, P., 240
newsreel *vs.* snapshot, 31–32, 53, 95, 135,
    234, 238. *See also* **Camera Angle
    Problem**

Nias natives, 98
Nichoria, 119
Niebelungenlied, 127n
Niger-Congo languages, 60n
Night, 207
Nile: delta of, 76t, 86; flooding of, 36–37, 46, 49, 62, 57, 121, 178–79; source of, 36
Ninurta, 43
Nippur, 145
Noah, 124–25
Nofert, 62
nomads, 126, 147, 200, 237
non-Indo-European relics, 63, 70
nonliteracy, vii, 2–4, 23, 45, 90n, 102, 106, 114–15, 117, 150–51, 154–56, 179, 205, 216n, 237, 244. *See also* oral transmission
Norman Conquest, 64, 128
Norse myth/culture, 44, 51, 55–56, 65, 104, 191, 193, 204, 212n
North America, 13, 94, 130, 182
North Star, 192, 195f, 198–99f; lack of, 198–99f. *See also* Polaris; pole star
north, 19, 49, 56, 112, 180, 192, 194, 195f; finding, 196
Northshift, 198–99f, 198–200, 201f, 203, 205, 208, 240; path of, 198–99f. *See also* precession
number(s), 58, 69; abstract notion of, 58, 214–15, 216n, 217; cubic, 215; as divine and permanent, 217; factoring of, 215–16; fractional, 215, 216f; invention of, 214n, 215; prime, 215, 216n; properties of, 214–17; as sequencers, 214n; square, 215, 216n; system bases for, 214–16
numbers (special): *6,* 214–17; *7,* 194, 215, 216n; *12,* 183, 184f, 185, 188, 194, 199, 213–16; *30,* 185, 199, 205, 213–14, 216; *60,* 188, 214, 216; *72,* 205, 213–14; *360,* 199, 213–14, 216; *540,* 213–14; *800,* 188, 213; *2160,* 199, 205–6, 213–14; *4320,* 206; *10,888,* 213–14; *432,000,* 213–14
numerical tables (ancient), 215, 216n
Nun, 62

nursery rhymes, 12, 35, 161
Nut, 179
Nyiragongo, 112

Object Permanence, 175
obligations (ritual), 37, 46
observations. *See* explanations
obsidian, 212n
ocean, 50, 61–62, 86–87, 106, 108–9, 145, 190n, 200, 204; celestial. *See also* Ocean; river of stars
Ocean, 83, 110, 185, 190n, 200, 212n
Ocean of Milk, 193, 193f, 212
Od/Oðr, 65
Odin, 55n, 57, 57f, 65, 100, 204, 210t
Odysseus, 50, 108, 140n, 141, 147f
Odyssey, 105, 140n, 157, 190. *See also* Homer
Oedipus, 152, 157
Ohio, 114, 166–67, 169
Okeanos, 185. *See also* Ocean
Old Christmas, 165
Old Church Slavic *sláva,* 237n
Old English (language), 128; vocabulary: *worm,* 238
Old English epic, 232
Old Testament, 19, 91, 125. *See also* Bible; Exodus (Book of); Genesis (Book of); Isaiah (Book of); Judges (Book of)
Oliphant, 100
olive, 50, 140n
Olympia, Greece, 47f
Olympus, 56, 82–84
Omar Khayyám, 185
omission, 18–19, 22. *See also* loss
omphalos-stone, 208n
opposites. *See* adversaries
oracles, 54, 111, 152
oral composition, 154–56
oral transmission, 5, 7, 31, 82, 90n, 100, 115, 123–25, 150–52, 155, 158, 160–61, 177, 179, 182. *See also* nonliteracy
orange, 14–15, 27, 59–60, 102, 108, 221
Oregon, 7–10, 8f, 72–73, 76t. *See also* Klamath

Orion, 158, 183
Orpheus, 217
Orthros (Geryon's dog), 114
Osiris, 40, 57, 179, 193n, 183, 203
Ossetians, 180–81
ostracism, 151
Ouranos, 207–8, 209f, 210t, 211, 212n
Ovenden, M., 217n
Ovid, 102, 218

Pacific Northwest, 4, 8n, 23, 38–39, 44,
    72–74, 88, 218, 222. *See also* Klamath;
    Oregon; Washington
pagans, 90
Pahto, 222
Palaeolithic era, 68f, 70, 145, 178
Paqua, 224–25
Paria Caca, 153
Parnassos, 125, 200, 208, 240
Parry, M., 156
Parthenon, 151
Pataraz, 224–25
patriliny/patriarchy, 141
Patroklos, 166, 237n
patron saint/deity, 63, 66, 145
pattern analysis/extraction, 27, 35, 123,
    127–28, 158. *See also* analogy;
    explanation
Pegasus, 104, 110–12
Pele (Hawaiian goddess), 9, 144
Pemphredo, 110
Penelope, 105, 141
péplos, 46
Perses, 126
Perseus, 1–2, 109–12, 126, 158, 242
Persian *bad*, 45
Persian Gulf, 217n
Persians, 126, 210. *See also* Iranians
Perspective Principle, 91n, 93n, 117,
    127, 146, **249**
perspective: loss of, 116–17; temporal,
    116–17 (*see also* time); visual, 116
Perun, 62, 67, 143
petrification, 1, 2, 109–10, 112, 126
pharaoh, 66, 90, 92, 98, 113, 115, 183,
    191
Philippines, 76t, 112, 143

Phoenicians, 150, 211
phoenix, 204
Phoibos Apollo, 54
Phorkys, 110
Phrygian cap, 206f
Picasso, Pablo, 105
Pihassassi, 111
pillar(s)/posts, ii, 53, 55, 220, 226; Mi-
    noan (cult), 200, 202f; destruction of,
    55, 121, 200, 201f, 202f; of fire/smoke/
    cloud, 73–74, 80, 86; reestablishment
    of cosmic, 200, 201f; as steep moun-
    tain (cosmic), 193, 193f, 208, 213, 220;
    of world/sky, 55, 121, 193, 200, 201f,
    202f
Pindar, 1–2, 62, 104, 110, 112, 157
Pirua/Manco Capac, 188
Pisces, 183, 184f, 210f, 206, 209f, 210,
    211
planetarium, 190; replicated by software,
    185n, 190
planets, 40, 97, 184–85, 188–91; align-
    ment of, 196n, 204n; cycles ("speed")
    of, 185, 190; massing of, 190, 191f;
    path of, 184f, 192; rising/setting of,
    182; as willful deities, 185, 190. *See
    also*: conjunctions; retrograde motion;
    and names of planets
Plato, 54, 151, 212, 217
playing-cards, 147–49
playwrights. *See* dramatists
Pleiades, 158, 190, 204
Pliny, 116, 172
Plutarch, 150
Poetic Diction (Sturluson), 238
poetry, 151, 154; memorability of, 150;
    structure of, 60, 154–56
poison conspiracy, 92–93
Polaris, 12, 192, 192f, 195f, 198f, 199f,
    210, 240. *See also* North Star; pole star
pole star, 192f, 199; as immobile, 192,
    192f; lack of, 199. *See also* North Star;
    Polaris
pole: celestial, 192f, 192–94, 195f, 196,
    197f, 198–99f, 200, 212n, 240; of the
    ecliptic, 192n
Pollux, 172n. *See also* Polydeukes

Polydektes, 109–10
Polydeukes, 141
Polyneikes, 140
Polynesia(ns), 144, 177, 182, 204
Polyphemus, 108
Pomo (California) language, 60n
Pompeii, 76t, 80
porridge, 35, 61, 100
Poseidon, 50, 51f, 62, 63, 86, 87n.2, 110, 145, 190, 207
Post Hoc, Ergo Propter Hoc, 121, 123, 135, 207, **249**
Power Principle, 143–45, 205, 227, **250**
precession (of equinoxes), 121, 159–60, 198–99f, 198–213, 201f, 217n; ancient predictions of, 206, 212n; calculation of, 205–7, 213; dates of, 206, 208, 209f, 210–12; direction of, 160, 198–99f, 199–200; rate of, 159–60, 198f, 199, 205, 212–13; recognition of existence of, 160, 198f, 205–7, 212–13. *See also* Northshift
predators, 120, 130–34, 137, 241n
predictability, 42
pre-Hellenic culture/tradition, 80, 140, 200, 208n
prestige, 145–46
primeval mound of mud, 57, 98
Prince Philip of England, 141
Principle of Attraction, 93n, 113–18, 120–21, 123–27, 135–36, 190n, 244, **248–49**
Principle of Uniformitarianism, 119
Procrustes, 114
Prokris, 173f
Prometheus, ii, 33, 49, 63–64, 125, 151, 152n, 208, 218–20, 220f, 222–23, 225–30
prone *vs.* supine burial, 169
Prope hoc, ergo propter hoc, 123
prophecy, 109, 152, 157, 172–73, 204, 212n. *See also* oracle
Propp, V., 240
protection measures, 50, 67, 69
proto-Indo-European (PIE) language. *See* Indo-European
protoliterate period, 214–17

proximity (as explanation), 123
Ptah, 57, 98–99, 185
Puckett, N., 166n
punishment myths, 20, 43, 48, 56, 64, 84, 219, 223, 229
Pushme-Pullyou, 14
Puzur-Amurri, 125
pyramids (Egyptian), 57, 116, 183, 196, 198f, 199
Pyriphlegethon, 204
Pyrrha, 125, 127, 208
Pythagoras, 149, 194, 216n, 217
Pythagoreans, 207, 210, 212
Pytho[n], 208, 240–41. *See also* Draco

quakes. *See* earthquakes
Quechua, 158, 171; vocabulary: *akwa*, 171
Queen (in *Snow White*), 89
Queen of the May, 126
Q'ursha, 226

Ra, 66, 179
Rabaul, New Guinea, 44
Race of Iron, 211
radiocarbon dating, 9
Raglan, Lord, 93n, 114, 117, 145–46, 156–57, 177, 244
Ragnarök, 177, 204, 213
rain, 36, 56, 62, 79, 143, 240–41; of fire, 204
Rainbow Corollary, 61, 165–66, 175, **247**
rainbow, 59–60, 241, 244
Ramāyāna, 193f, 213
Ramsund, Sweden, 239f, 239
randomness, 9, 12, 158
Rationalization Syndrome, 26, 28n, 229, **246**
rationalization, 13, 26–33, 31, 221
reanalysis (linguistic) 142–43
recall. *See* memory
reciprocating motion, 212
reconstructability, 8, 10, 112, 137–38, 163. *See also* stability
red, 22, 59–60, 69, 81, 97, 107–9, 114, 142, 188, 219, 221–22, 226–27

reduction: of details, 24–41 (*see also* compression); of pantheon, 65
Redundancy Strategy, 11, **245**
redundancy, 10–11, 155
reflections, 110, 165–75. *See also* mirrors; spirits; water
regeneration/repopulation of Earth. *See* Earth
Regin, 238–9, 239f
reinterpretation, 110n, 127–28, 139, 151, 172, 184, 184f, 186f, 219, 222, 228n, 242. *See also* restructuring
Relevance Corollary, 9, **245**
Remus, 167n
Renaissance, 194
renaming, 66–67, 204–5
renown, 237
resemblance. *See* analogy
reservoir, celestial, 201. *See also* Ocean; river of stars
residency, 38–40. *See also* **Container Corollary**
Restructuring Principle, 3, 139–52, 211, 244, **250**
restructuring, 127, 149n, 172–73, 177, 215, 224, 229–30, 242. *See also* re-analysis (linguistic); reinterpretation
retrograde motion, 185
reversal, 104–5, 162, 164–65, 168–72; in day/night of the dead, 162, 168, 170, 175; in dress, 169; efficacious, 172
Rhea, 207–8
rhyme and rhythm, 154–55
Rig Veda, 213
right (direction), as correct, 170. *See also* left (direction)
rising/setting as birth/dying, 21, 179, 183, 190
ritual(s), 67, 155, 157, 169, 226; viewed as source of all myth, 177. *See also* sacrifices
River of Forgetfulness, 19, 91, 142. *See also* **Lethe Effect**
river(s): of fire (*see* lava flows); as flowing backwards, 168; importance of, 61–62, 145; shift of, 2, 114, 118; of stars, 178, 184–85, 186f, 194, 201, 203

Robin Hood lore, 114
rock drawings, 239–40, 239f
rocks hurled/thrown, 74, 84, 108, 110, 125, 127, 219–21. *See also* lava bombs
Rodriguez Island, 75
Roland, 90, 100
Roman myth, 4, 50, 62, 65
Roman numerals, 215
Romania, 68f, 69–70, 214n, 244
Romans, 23, 62, 65–66, 93, 205, 242
Romantics, 230
Rorschach images, 12, 158–59, 183
Rose, H. J., 114–15, 126–27, 141
rotation: of earth, 181f, 195f ; of heavens, 180, 188, 192f, 192, 199–200, 204, 212; of mill, 188, 200; of world, 159
"ruler" as world coordinate-system, 201f. *See also* Kingship in Heaven; Saturn
rules. *See* pattern analysis
Rumpelstiltskin, 98
Rusalii festivals, 67, 197f
Russian (language): *dvoeverie*, 63; *Ilja*, 67; *korol'*, 115; *medved'*, 19; *novyj*, 45; *sanvich*, 45; *stal*, 45; *tsar'*, 115
Russian myth/culture, 62–63, 67, 68f, 120, 143, 228n

Sacks, O., 216n
Sacred Mount, 193f
sacrifices, 7, 29, 36–37, 46, 167n
Sagittarius, 147, 183, 184f, 192, 201f, 209, 209f
Saint Elmo's fire, 77, 85
Saint George, 2, 117, 242, 243f
Saint Onouphrios/Onofre, 62
Sakurajima, 112
salt water, 50, 61, 193
Samos, 119
Sampo (Finnic), 193
Samson, 123–24, 200
Sanskrit (language), 121; vocabulary: *nâvah*, 45; *srâva-*, 237n; *stitáh*, 45; *Yama*, 167n
Santillana and Dechend, 185n, 190, 200, 203–4, 212
Saracens, 90, 92–93

Sardinia, 119, 146
Sargon the Great, 116
Saronic Gulf, 50, 51f
Saturn, 185, 188, 189f, 190n, 191f, 194, 200, 210–11, 213; as measurer of time, 185, 188, 200; sidereal period of, 185
Saturnalia, 180
savant syndrome, 216n
Scandinavia, 57f, 144, 235–39, 235f, 239f. *See also* Norse myth/culture
scarabs, 40
scavengers, 130–34, 136–37
Schacter, D., 27, 33, 117n, 221n
Schank, R., 11n, 240
Schmandt-Besserat, D., 214–15
Schudson, M., 91, 117n, 124n
scientific laws/rules, 45, 54, 119–20. *See also* explanation: scientific
Scorpio, 12, 158–59, 160f, 183, 184f, 187f, 192, 205, 209f
Scorpion Man, 187f
scorpion(s), 158, 183, 205, 206f
scribes, 150, 215
scripts. *See* writing
Scyldings, 127
Scythians, 223
seasons, 158, 179–80, 181f, 182, 194
security in religion, 65–66, 147
seeing as knowing, 54–55n
selection of information. *See* memory: selection of
self-glorification, 89–95
Semites, 150
Sentinel Island, 44
September 11 attacks, 75n
sequencers, invention of, 214n, 215
sequential analysis, 9, 84, 85n, 228n
Seriphos, 109–10, 112
serpent. *See* Draco; dragon; Pytho[n]; snake; World Serpent
Seth, 40
Seti I, 21f, 99f, 187f
Seven Macaw, 49n
Seven Sisters, 158. *See also* Pleiades
severance of earth from sky, 87, 207, 210t, 212n
shadows, 165–69, 172–73

shamans, 9, 62, 165, 167–68, 174, 193
Shamash, 187f
Shannon, C., 10
shape-home. *See* image
shared resemblance, 45–46. *See also* analogy
Sheol, 49
ship(s), 50, 77–78, 108, 124–25, 191, 200n, 223; as constellation, 193n. *See also* boats
Shiva the Destroyer, 121, 122f, 212
shower of gold, 107, 109
Sia, 98, 99f
Siberia, 62
sickle, 87, 110, 207, 212n
sickness demons, 69, 167
sidereal period, 185
Siegfried, 2. *See also* Sigurd
Sif, 48–49, 228
signs (of Zodiac), 184f, 199. *See also* Zodiac
Sigurd, 238–40, 239f
Sigyn, 20
Silence Principle, 3, 11, 16–27, 28n, 29, 32, 36, 142, 154, 221, 228, 244, **245**
Simargl, 65, 68f
similarity, accidental, 45, 227
similes, 156. *See also* analogy; metaphors
Simonides, 157
sin (Christian), 242
Sin (Moon), 187f
Sirius, 178, 183; 70-day cycle of, 183
skookums, 38–39, 48, 218
Sky Spirit, 22, 43, 46, 107
sky, 120, 158–61, 176–217, 240; colors of, 97, 106; goddess of, 21, 21f, 53, 144, 179; moving coordinates of, 201f, 205, 212; support for, 2, 21f, 47f, 47–48, 53, 118, 200–1. *See also* sphere
Slavs, 4, 62–63, 65–70, 102–4, 156, 197f. *See also* Russian myth/culture
sleep, 24, 103–4, 118, 123, 164, 166, 174, 178; talking in, 24. *See also* dreams
Sleeping Beauty Mountain, 43
Sleipnir, 57, 57f, 58
slippage of system, 197–98, 212; in Chinese calendar, 212n

small-channel problem, 3–4, 154
smith(y), 107–8, 188, 219, 226–28, 238
Smith, G. E., 163
smoke, 22, 35, 44, 46, 64, 84, 108, 228n;
    pillar of, 73–74, 80, 86, 219
snakes, 51, 111f, 114, 153, 205, 206f,
    226, 238; cosmic, 193, 193f, 198–99f,
    208, 240; hissing of, 107–8, 110; poi-
    sonous, 20, 33, 37, 112 (*see also* drag-
    ons: poisonous); as Christian symbol,
    242, 243f; writhing, 107, 110
snaky locks, 1, 2, 97, 107–9, 111f, 219
snapshots/tableaus, 31, 95, 135. *See also*
    newsreel
Snegurochka (Snow Maiden), 143
Snow White, 89
snow. *See* Frost Giants; ice/snow
Snowball Effect, 146, 242, **251**
snowball story, 145–49, 242
Socialization Antidote, 25, **246**
socialization of children, 18, 22, 25
Socrates, 65, 217
Solon, 116, 150
solstices, 55, 67, 159n, 180, 181f, 184f,
    191, 194, 196–97, 198f, 199–201,
    201f, 205, 209f; summer, 67, 182, 197,
    204n, 210–11, 210t; winter, 66,
    159–60, 182, 191n, 195f
The Song of Roland, 90
Sophocles, 139–41, 151
sorcerers, 174
Sothis, 178, 183
soul-bird, 173f
souls. *See* dead; spirits
South America, 60n, 66, 182. *See also*
    Andes
South Slavic poetry, 156
Southern Cross, 160f
sown field motif, 68f, 69
space aliens, 120, 129–30, 135, 137,
    149. *See also* **UFO Corollary**
space: as marked by shift of coordinates,
    121, 198, 201, 201f, 204–5, 211; or-
    ganization of, 192–93, 196–98, 216
Spain, 66, 93
Sparta, 90, 141
speech, mechanisms of, 2, 29

Spence, K., 199
sphere: celestial, 194, 195f, 207; crys-
    talline, 194
Sphinx, 229
Spieden Island, 44
spindle (cosmic), 193, 200, 212
spirit world, 103, 162–75, 193. *See also*
    Underworld
spirits, 19, 22, 24, 27, 29, 38–39, 42, 46,
    65, 69, 103–4, 115, 126, 143, 149, 158,
    162–75, 197f, 236; day/night for, 162,
    168, 170, 175; distinguished recently
    from souls, 172–73; possession by, 175;
    recycled, 115, 174; as servomech-
    anisms, 174–75
split-brain patients, 14–15
Spokane Lake, 8n
square-dance calling, 156
stability (of reference/story), 9, 22, 88,
    106, 137–38, 163, 217, 223, 244
stars, 6, 12, 42, 97, 158–61, 160f, 163,
    176–217, 241; brightest, 183, 192n;
    deathless (non-setting), 192; fate/
    destiny in, 185, 191, 206; ground out
    by mill, 193; mantle of, 193, 206f; as
    markers, 182; position(s) of, 158–61,
    183; as souls/spirits, 191. *See also*
    comets; constellations; planets; river of
    stars; supernovas; *and names of stars*
Staryj Rjazan', 68f
statues. *See* images
steppes, 63, 143, 145, 147, 222
Stheno, 110
Stockpile Effect, 149–52, **251**
Stone Age. *See* Neolithic; Palaeolithic
stone: as missile (*see* rocks
    hurled/thrown); as substitute (*see* Zeus:
    birth of); turned to (*see* petrification)
Stonehenge, 182, 197
storms, 22, 40, 56, 61–62, 67, 72, 97,
    143–44, 219, 221, 226, 228n
storm god, 86–87, 97, 111, 143
storytellers, 7, 9–11, 114, 142, 156, 212,
    234
Strabo, 169
strength (prodigious), 114, 118, 226
string skirt, 68f, 69–70

Stripping Procedure, 28n, 29, 136, 234, 236, **246**
Stromboli, 85
Sturluson, Snorri, 20, 107, 111, 176, 204, 229, 238
Sufi elephant story, 72
Sullivan, W., 66, 153, 159, 160n, 171, 185n, 190–91
Sumatra, 75, 79
Sumerian (language): AN, 187f; DINGIR, 187f; MUL, 205n
Sumerians, 94, 97, 117, 125, 187f, 205n, 244
sun, 49n, 77, 86, 97, 111, 143, 176–214; as ball, 40; birth of, 21, 55, 179; as center of solar system, 66, 207; as circling earth, 66, 175, 179, 190–91, 207; cycles of, 180, 185; daughter of, 176, 189, 204; as disk, 20, 54, 66, 185; as eye, 54, 55f; as god, 2, 20, 21f, 40, 44, 54, 97, 99f, 143, 177, 179, 179, 190, 206f; as goddess, 44, 176, 204; path of, 170, 175, 179, 181f, 182, 184f, 190, 207; shadow of (as marker), 180, 196; in Underworld (*see* spirits: day/night for; Underworld); as winged disk, 20, 186f, 187f; worship of, 20–21, 55f. *See also* eclipses; precession; seasons
Sunda Straits, 77
sunrise, 54–55, 66, 145, 159, 180–82, 189–90, 194, 196, 199, 209f; as banishing spirits, 166
sunset, 55, 170, 180, 182, 194, 196
supermen, 118, 188
super-natural events, 120, 149
supernova, 49n, 107
Surt, 111, 204
The Survivors, 120–21
Sūrya/Sūryā, 189
Sus scrofa, 134
Suslov, I. M., 88n
sutras: mathematical algorithms in, 216n
Svan myths, 227
swallowing of gods, 208, 210t
sword god, 100, 101f
Sword in the Stone, 100, 101f, 102n

swords, 100–2, 101f, 107, 110–11, 233, 236, 238, 239f, 240
Sylmar quake, 75n
syncretism, 65, 200; guerrilla, 66–67
synodic period, 188–89
Syria, 90, 187f, 214n

taboos, 9, 19, 21, 25
Taliban, 174
Tambora, 76t
tangling of information, 13, 27, 29, 33, 50
Tarim River, 114
Tartarus, 83, 207
Taurus, 183, 184f, 192, 197, 205n, 205–6, 208, 209t, 210t, 211
technology: change of, 22, 65; goddess of, 50; modern, 88
telegraphic speech, 10
Temenos, 141
temperament types, 151–52
Temple of Artemis, Corfu, 111f
Temple of Hera, Samos, 119
Temple of Zeus, Olympia, 47f
Tentpole (as world axis), 200
tephra, 80, 81f. *See also* ash
Teshub, 86, 210t
Texas City firestorm, 75n
textiles, 50, 64–65, 67, 68f, 69–70, 95, 143, 145, 155, 169, 237
Thales of Miletus, 149–50
Theban Sphinx/Phix, 114
Thebes, Egypt, 21f, 99f
Themistocles, 116
Theogony (Hesiod), 82–84, 107–8, 207–8, 218
theories, adequacy of, 13, 29
Thera, 13, 50, 51f, 75–76, 76t, 79–80, 81f, 82f, 83f, 84, 86–87, 112
Theseus, 50, 114, 126
Thiassi, 56
Thompson, S., 240
Thor, 51, 56, 62, 65, 100, 106, 143, 144, 204, 229; in Icelandic names, 144
Thorfinn, 235–36
Thoth, 55f, 178
Thuban, 198f, 199, 199f

Thunderbird, 219
thunderbolt, carrier of, 111. *See also*
    lightning
Thurston, H., 205n
Ti'amat, 61, 210t
tidal wave. *See* tsunami
Tiddy, R.J.E., 117n
time: 93n, 107, 116–23, 125, 154n, 176–
    217; astronomical, 107, 159n, 161; be-
    ginning of, 87, 212n; conflation/
    foreshortening of, 86, 92n, 116–18,
    120–21, 244; cyclical, 121, 122f; linear,
    121; measures of, 161, 180, 185, 216;
    perspective on, 86, 116–18; reversed,
    162, 168, 170, 175; significance of,
    179; succession in, 121–22; telling/
    keeping, 13, 178, 183, 193, 196–97,
    213. *See also* calendar; **Diachronic
    Power Principle**; **Perspective Principle**
Tinamou (partridge constellation), 153,
    158–61, 160f, 183
Tiryns, 80, 146
Titans, 82–5, 228
titles, 115, 145
Toda (India) language, 60n
tombe di gigantic, 119
Tomlin, Lily, 120–21
torch (equinoctial), 197f, 206f, 205, 206f
tortoise, 193f
Toutle River valley, 72
tracks/tracking, 130–32, 137
tragedians. *See* dramatists
translation, difficulties of, 60–61
treasure, 94–95, 228, 232–38
tree(s), 239f; and deities, 40, 57, 103,
    172; flattened by blast, 73, 88; resins
    from, 40; rings in, 76; World, 193
trickery, 25, 46–48, 94, 228
tricksters, 25, 48
Trigon (Great), 188, 189f, 213
Trinity (Christian), 65
Tripolye culture, 68f, 69
Trobriand Islanders, 24, 25
Trojan War, 156, 190
Tropic circles (naming of), 184f, 194,
    195f, 204
Troy, 119, 141

Tsukiyomi, 44
tsunamis, 36, 50, 51f, 63, 75, 77–80, 86–
    88, 107, 143, 154; causing displace-
    ments, 80; height of, 77–79; noise of,
    36, 79
Tungus area, 9, 88
Turkey, 76t, 80, 87, 100, 101f
turquoise, 61, 97, 106
Tver', 68f
twins, 44, 54, 109, 167n, 172, 183,
    216n. *See also* doubles
Tylor, E., 164–5, 167
Typhoeus, 85, 107
Typhon, 114

Ubelluri, 86, 87, 87n
UFO Corollary, 120, 135, 149, 175, **249**
Ugarit, 150, 187f
Ugaritic script, 150
Ukraine, 67–69, 68f
Ulansey, D., 205–6
Ulawun, 44
Ullikummi, 86–87, 110n, 212n
under-side of world, 175, 190–91, 207
Underworld, 114, 165, 168, 171f, 175,
    190–93, 211
uniformitarianism, 119
universality, 4, 11, 12, 42, 119, 155, 163–
    64, 170, 177, 203, 241n, 244
un-understandability, 12, 21, 72, 106–7,
    120, 128, 136–37, 139, 142, 149, 161,
    163, 220. *See also* restructuring
upsidedown-ness. *See* inversion
Ur, 187f
urban legends, 93, 152, 156
Útgarð-Loki, 106, 229

Valhalla, 213
Váli, 204
vampires, 28–29, 31n, 56, 103, 123, 244
Vanir, 65
Vasuki, 193f
Vega, 198f, 199f
Venus, 179, 187f, 188, 191f, 194, 196n; as
    brightest planet, 188; crescentic phases
    of, 188, 189n; cycles of, 188–89; as
    female planet, 189–90

Venus figures, 68f, 70
Vergil, 90n, 116, 210–11
Vesuvius, 13, 76t, 80, 85
Viðar, 204
viewpoint. *See* **Camera Angle Problem**
Vikings, 204, 237, 239f
Virgin and Child, 211
virgin, 183, 211, 242, 243f
Virgo, 183, 184f, 201f, 209f, 210, 210t, 211
visibility as anchor. *See* stability
vision, nature of, 54, 59, 108, 166
visions, 164–67
Vitagliano, D., 8n
Vividness Principle, 158, **251**
vividness, 10–11, 93, 156–58, 160, 183, 188, 230
Vlachs, 70
Vlakke Hoek, 77
volcano: 6–8, 8f, 72–88, 104, 107–12, 114, 115n, 137, 142, 163, 212n, 219–30; collapse of, 7–8, 29, 75, 80, 85; deity of, 9, 144; having eyes, 107–8, 219; heat from, 7, 83–85, 108; on island, 75, 80, 85n, 144; as kin, 43–44, 114; noise from, 73, 75, 107–8, 112, 114, 219, 221, 223. *See also* ash-cloud; eruption(s), of volcanos
Volsunga Saga, 232, 238, 239
Volsungs, 127

waka/huaca, 171
Wang Ch'ung, 237
war deities, 50, 63, 188
Washington (state), 8n, 72–74, 76t, 77, 87
Washington, George, 146, 237n
water: encircling, 62, 186f, 190n, 203 (*see also* river of stars); gods of, 62–63, 126, 145, 190n; primordial, 57, 62, 98, 162; as spirit-catcher, 67, 165–67, 173–75; types of, 61, 210t. *See also* reflection
Waters, P., 156n
Watkins, C., 155, 240–41
Waugh, Evelyn, 10
Waw an Namus, 112
weapons, naming of, 100

weaving. *See* textiles
weeping, 102, 107, 224
Weld-Blum tablet #62, 213
werewolves/were-animals, 174–75
west, as abode of dead, 190–91; due, 194, 196–97
Western tradition, 124, 159, 194, 240n
whirlpool, 200
Who's On First, 24
Wiedemann, A., 164
Wiglaf, 233–34, 240n
wildness, 50, 143. *See also* **Multiple-Aspects Principle**
Wile, I., 169, 170
Wilk, S., 110n
willers, 54, 62, 69, 94, 111, 143, 154, 161, 174, 177, 185, 191, 200, 229, 234, 240; naming of, 49, 98, 100; as not necessarily "people", 49, 229
Willfulness Principle, 41–52, 82, 97, 100, 120, 143, 157, 164, 166, 185, 220, 227, 229, 234, 238, **247**
Wilson, J., 39, 42n
wind, 22, 41, 44, 67, 73, 76, 80, 84–85, 108, 110, 177
wine-dark sea, 60, 166
wings, 110–11, 186f, 218–19, 223–27; and weather/storms, 219, 224. *See also* dog: winged; horses: winged
Wiraqocha, 185
wisdom: deity of, 50, 55n, 87
wishing wells, 167
witches, 92, 174
women in society, 139–41; as heroines, 140
wood as fire-container, 38–39, 225
Wood, R., vii
word-power. *See* curses; name magic; willers: naming of
Works and Days (Hesiod), 118
World Ages, 122f, 201, 209–11, 209f, 212n
World Serpent, 51
worm. *See* dragon; Old English *worm*
writing: backwards, 171, 171f; invention of, 2, 4, 149–50, 178–79, 215; structure of, 19, 149–50

written *vs.* oral text, 90n, 124–25. *See also* literacy; nonliteracy; oral transmission
Wyeast, 222

Xinjiang, 174
Xuthus, 127

Yacana, 158–9
Yakima, WA, 72, 77
Yangtze, 237
yawning void, 84, 210t
Yazılıkaya, Turkey, 100, 101f, 102n
Yellow River, 114
Yeti, 146
Yggdrasill, 193

YHWH, 19, 21
Ymir, 167n, 210t
Yucatan, 88

Zeus, 40, 47f, 62–63, 83–85, 109, 111, 125–27, 143, 175, 188, 190, 193, 207–8, 209f, 210t, 211, 219, 221, 225, 230; birth of, 208
Zodiac, 121, 183, 188, 192, 198f, 199, 201, 205, 212–14; wheel of, 184f, 209f
zonal analysis, 72–75, 80, 82, 85, 88, 90, 97
Zone-of-Convenient-Remove Syndrome, 93–95, 149, **248**
Zuidema, R., 12, 159